Endorsements

"This memoir is a must read for anyone who loves Hawaii, its people, and its culture. Beautifully written and illustrated, it takes readers on a fascinating, personal journey that also includes how Native Hawaiians, along with the early immigrants from Asia and Europe, shared their history. Their culture, language, cuisine, beliefs and family values create the wonderful melting pot of diverse cultures and peoples found only in Hawaii. A wonderful read!"
~ Maile Apau Jachowski, MD
Native Hawaiian Pediatrician

"Treat yourself to a new adventure. Open your heart and sensibilities to a unique perspective about Hawaiian and Filipino life on the culturally rich island of Molokai. The author's precision in word usage captures the nuances of meaning in social interactions in a setting of historical significance to Hawai'i. Her unabashed love and deep respect for the family, the people and the island is captivating. This is an inviting read for anyone who appreciates beauty in nature and art, anyone who enjoys diversity in cultures, and most of all, anyone who has known the wonders of being wildly, passionately in love with the love of your life. Give yourself a treat today."
~ Elizabeth Ayson, PhD

"Christine and Philip are an unlikely couple. They have shown that two very different cultures can come together and create an amazing love, which has already spanned over half a century.

"On its surface, this book is their love story. But beyond that, it is an amazing tale of the customs, cultures, and beliefs of the Hawaiian and Filipino people of Hawaii, which few outsiders ever see.

"This book will enlighten and delight readers no matter what your interest. Love story, history, vanishing cultures, metaphysical or spiritual beliefs and magic—it is all here for you to discover and enjoy."
~ Bill Hibbett

MY PULE O'O

*In this writing through my pule (prayer)
I have wrapped and bound every word.*

A love story and cultural journey on Molokai, Hawaii

The Essence of Time
PULE O'O

Christine Sabado

The Essence of Time: PULE O'O

Copyright © 2024 by Christine Sabado

All rights reserved. No part of this book may be reproduced by any mechanical, photographic, or electronic process, or in the form of a phonographic recording; nor may it be stored in a retrieval system, transmitted, or otherwise be copied for public or private use—other than for "fair use" as brief quotations embodied in articles and reviews—without prior written permission of the publisher and author.

DISCLAIMER: Please note the stories and experiences in this book are those of the author. She, Christine Sabado, does not represent the Hawaiian or Filipino people.

To protect the privacy of certain individuals some names and identifying details have been changed.

ISBN: 979-8-9868130-7-3
Library of Congress Control Number: 2023919656

Artwork by Philip Sabado
www.SabadoArtHawaii.com
Photos by Paul Donegan and Philip Sabado

Sacred Life Publishers™

SacredLife.com

Printed in the United States of America

*Mama and Me,
a Dedication, 1970,
Honolulu, Hawai'i.*
Photo by Paul Donegan

Dedication
Severina Georgia Blen Sabado
"Mama"

From our first moments in that dimly lit hallway in Molokai,
you saw that I was the one your son chose for life.
Yet he would be my prize.
Now I return the tribute with this dedication.
As I stood by your deathbed,
you told me stories for the future.
After your passing, you came every night in my dreams,
reminding me which stories to tell;
now the world will know them as well.
Mahalo.

Contents

Endorsements i
MY PULE O'O iii
Dedication vii
Kamalalawalu xi
'Ike xii
Introduction xiv
Prologue xv
1 – Molokai 1
2 – Travels 8
3 – Dolores, Abra 15
4 – Meeting Mama 25
5 – "Das How" 35
6 – My Glendale Hometown 45
7 – Honolulu and Love 64
8 – Wedding Preparations 76
9 – Wedding Day 89
10 – Newlywed Adjustments 106
11 – Mom 130
12 – About Babies 136
13 – And Then There Was Fishing 151
14 – Mama Told Me 171
15 – Herbs, Circumcision, and Coconuts 183
16 – A Passing 193
17 – Ancient Understandings 203
18 – Mad Dogs, Spanish Camp and Selling Frogs 208
19 – For the Love of Molokai 217

20 – Kalaupapa	224
Acknowledgments	268
About the Author	269
Upcoming Books by the Author	271
Preview Book 2	272

Kamalalawalu

In ancient Japan, time was measured with sticks of incense known to be units of time. In my difficult years, I would follow the custom of lighting incense. As it burned, I would see my story untangle in a stream of smoke. In this writing through my pule (prayer)I have wrapped and bound every word. In a parallel universe amid a great battle between Maui and Molokai, kahunas (elders) sat in a circle before a stone bowl of embers where a curling ribbon of smoke wafted before them. The silver stream carried their fervent prayers up to the heavens for Molokai for all time by deflecting the warriors of Maui. Their pule for the island and people of Molokai became known from that time forward as The Island of Pule O'o, the island of the Powerful Prayer. The kahuna protected and governed Molokai in this way. In ancient times we lived in an oral tradition, then we progressed to a two-dimensional world. Art became the visual image of the oral world. These spheres are trying to communicate with ours.

Ulumaika ~ Flat but Round

'Ike

The word "'ike" (pronounced: ee kay) is ripe with meaning. In the recent past, I was reminded that I now possess 'ike. As a kupuna (elder) said this, she pointed to the center of her forehead so I would understand. I nodded and said, "Mahalo," to my friend, Peaches, a Molokai woman of 'ike. Like all protocols in 'olelo Hawai'i, the spoken Hawaiian language, it was not my place to question or correct her or to deny the compliment. Thus, I would need to consult a dictionary for the translation, or my husband, Philip, the most asked question in our years together, "Explain this one to me, please." He would think a moment and explain the meaning. In our first years on Molokai after our marriage, my questions would keep him awake as I reviewed the day's conversations and ask the meaning of so many words and innuendos. We often spoke in whispers under the bed sheets. It was impolite to ask, even innocently in public, "What does that word mean?" You are in their home, their islands; "go learn," was the unspoken message.

Philip taught and tutored me in the Molokai way. I was a sun-dried sponge that soaked up every word. Blessed with a keen memory, I can and did learn. Plus, my mom knew it all before I did. As a newly married woman, still a girl at nineteen, I would write long letters home about my new life. I'd married a man the color of dark chocolate in the middle of a ripening pineapple plantation on the far west end of Molokai. I was one of five Caucasians out of five thousand on the island (the other four were teachers or nurses). Mom would answer her letters this way: "This is a book, you do not know it yet, but I will keep all your letters for the future." After she passed some years ago, I found them in a bureau bound with a silk ribbon.

As time passed and more information made it to my pages, most of my experiences and gained knowledge were so powerful, I felt humbled and overwhelmed. It took me years to accept this task. After completing three books and still fussing about the responsibility of holding the secrets, and a "why me" scenario, I unloaded all my angst on a kupuna on Molokai. She listened and then asked a potent question. "Are you pau? Can I talk now?

Are you ready to hear what I am going to tell you?" I placed my arms to my sides and nodded yes, terrified.

The next question stumped me, but after I gulped, I answered. The question was asked in a calm, direct way, "How many years have you enjoyed your husband's body?" (This still makes me smile.) My husband's body? I answered truthfully, like it was a quiz.

"Ah…forty-three years?"

She smiled and inhaled deeply. "Well, then, who else can do this!"

What a metaphor! Up to that moment, all I cared about was what others thought about my writing or if they approved. I am on my own and always have been. Why should I care what others think?

I have sent out countless copies of selected chapters and stories to interested friends, hoping someone would understand it, or more so, approve. When I never heard from them, I would chastise the negative child within me, "See, it is no good. They don't know how to tell you." And I would slink away. A new day, a new deal, like it or leave it, these stories are 100 percent true, according to my perception. My kuleana (destiny) has been to tell these stories and write these books. As often as I tried to put them away and ignore this task, they would not stay on the shelf. These stories are about the fabric of time.

My son Ian, at eight years old, told me as we sat under the tall ironwood trees in Kula, "Mom, the world is waiting to know what you will write." And now you will know as well. Enjoy the read.

'Ike: the ability to see.
I can now accept this task.

Introduction

An immigrant family was placed by chance on an island that held an unknown, yet powerful place in history. Molokai, partially torn with tragedy, was rewarded with love, tradition, and filial duty. This sacred island became home to this Filipino family. They flourished according to the preset mandated by the family's matriarch affectionately known as 'Apo Baket.'

I was a young girl, blonde and blue-eyed from California, who walked off the plane on Molokai some fifty-odd years ago. When my foot first touched the island, I instinctively knew I would experience magic. I had no idea what awaited me in the tiny pineapple village on the far west side of Molokai, yet my anticipation was a magnet, like a salmon swimming through cascading waters, pulling me closer to my life's destiny.

While beginning art college in Honolulu in 1968, the dark-skinned fellow in the third row made me look his way. I clearly remember his laugh enticed and pulled me like a tickle on the back of my neck. I turned to look behind. His laugh was infectious, one of a kind. His first offer was lunch, and another time he offered me a ride home. Time moved quickly and soon we would be one.

In 1969, I married into his traditional family of farmers, known as 'sakadas.' They arrived by ship in four phases. They were held in the bows, as were many of those of that time, little more than human cargo in search of a better life. This family came from the Philippines with the second wave of immigrants in the late '30s. They had been recruited by scouts who canvassed the Northern provinces for able-bodied workers to harvest sugarcane and pineapple. Faith, as well as superstitions, anchored and guided these people to a Molokai village. Culture and a tribal unity became the marrow that nourished them. This story, written in truth, speaks of gratitude and love for Philip, my marriage, and his people.

Prologue

In 1990, on a chilly night in Wailuku, we were invited to a friend's house for a small gathering. With visitors and other locals present, there was always laughter and music. Later, we sat around casually sipping coffee and having small cakes with our host, a young Hawaiian man, who would later become a world-renowned singer. I monopolized our host's attention, pulling out story after story. I had captured him in my web, weaving a silken thread around him while regaling him with tales of Hilo and the small Japanese woman who had become our friend. My stories tumbled about like frothy waves at high tide. In all these stories were secrets I had kept silently for years, yet I trusted this young man, and out they poured.

I believed my tales held magic and intrigue. My heart quickened, my eyes widened, and I felt a sense of urgency and excitement. It was as if what I had to say was the most important thing that evening. I even broke my most rigid rule: I told stories about my son who was born in the shadow of a volcano.

As we left, I shrugged my shoulders in the dark starlit night, wanting to shake off the strangeness that seemed to close around me, as if there was something stuck to me, I could not dislodge. As I walked to the car, I berated myself. Why do I talk so much? *It was late when we reached home. The oddity clung like a heavy cloak sticking to my skin. Even after I knelt at my altar and chanted the three prayers of the evening, the heaviness persisted.*

Curling into my bed, I sought the warmth of my husband's smooth skin against mine, which seemed cold and removed. Somehow, I hoped the intimacy of lovemaking would create a diversion and shake this strangeness from me.

Our closest moments always transported me to another place where I could be free to enjoy the mingling of our bodies and spirits. He lay still in a deep satisfied sleep, the only movement being his chest rising in rhythm with a deep rumbling as he snored.

Now at peace, I closed my eyes and within moments, startled awake sensing a presence in the room. I felt distinct movement on the bed, a release of weight that shifted on my side. In the flicker of a heartbeat, the corner of the mattress lifted. It was as if someone or something had sat on the edge of the bed and then stood and moved away as the bedsprings bounced back and naturally eased into their usual position.

My mind flashed a warning. My heart froze in place and then accelerated into a panic. My eyes flew open seeking a tangible form in the darkness. I turned toward the door, my body rigid. The door remained closed and latched; it always was when we made love. How could someone be in the room? Who or what was with us? Had something or someone been watching? Still watching? My heart pounded, speeding gallons of blood through my arteries and attacking my panicked brain.

No doubt the bed had moved, yet neither Philip nor I had moved; his leg lay motionless on mine, his breathing remained slow and steady. I had felt the movement and subsequent spark igniting my senses. Something was there. My eyes popped wide, searching the darkness. I was fully awake.

In the next second, without prompting, my mind began the rapid-fire chanting of the same Buddhist prayer I had intoned earlier, this time to suppress my fear. As a child, I had been taught to say my Hail Mary's in quick succession. It always worked. When my dad's old car stalled, my mom would turn to my sister and me and command us to "start the rosary." On cue, we would recite Hail Mary's and the engine would sputter and start. Three Hail Mary's was the charm. Now I chanted. What was the difference? Faith is faith.

With my entire being, I focused on the moment. I could see nothing and then I felt a presence alarmingly close, like a pressing heat that felt heavy in the room. As my eyes darted to the four corners from ceiling to floor, my heartbeat and breathing accelerated and a gagging anxiety crept into my throat. The air was charged. I remained frozen in place and resistant to awaken my sleeping husband. I could not get my brain to signal my arm or fingers to move. It, whatever it was, was at my side. Magically, as if a switch had been flicked, I felt a wave of calm, much like a refreshing breeze tingles the skin on a hot day, followed by a voice within my mind. The voice spoke to every cell within my being, and said, *Write the stories; don't talk the stories.*

Absorbing those words lifted the oppressive pressure, and the strange feelings passed. My heart slowed. I felt calm return, and the stillness of the night reverted to the lightness of a soft pillow. I felt grounded, returned to the room I knew. I exhaled a long breath and inched closer to my husband, seeking his warmth, strength, and smooth skin. He slept on, oblivious to the thunder that had beaten in my chest and disturbed my rest.

As we lay motionless on the bed, my eyes continued to dart, anxiously searching the room for the invisible intruder. My breath and my heaving chest slowed. Only the curtains swayed in folds as the night breeze furled through. Amid the whirling winds of my mind, I pondered. *The message had been meant for me.*

Unable to sleep, I took a deep breath and exhaled, which came with renewed calmness. I would begin the work and tell the stories; the time was now. I decided to begin with his people's arrival from another island chain across the vast Pacific.

1 – Molokai

Molokai Nui a Hina
Kaunakakai, Molokai
Commissioned by the Hawaii State Foundation on Culture and the Arts
Artwork by Philip Sabado

1

*In the middle of the Hawaiian chain is an isolated island we refer to as the piko, like the bellybutton, because it is the center of Hawai'i. This is Molokai, the axis, where it all begins. This is the island where my husband was raised and where we were married. My stories begin here. In my marriage, I would have six children: four sons and two daughters. As I began this work, I realized I could only be myself. I learned to listen and more—to show respect for what I could not understand or question.*

Many of these stories have never been told, and to this day, Molokai remains an island of seclusion and mystery. Once a Hawaiian woman spoke to my husband on an evening filled with crimson and gold light. She whispered as she leaned into his ear. "Brother, when you go Molokai, you must remember...walk softly and talk softly." She disappeared, dissolved into the crowd; no one knew her or saw her again. She was 'Uhane, a spirit with a message. In these stories, I aim to walk and talk softly, especially with the words I compose honoring Molokai. With respect and love to this island and to our family, I will strive to do my best to honor both with aloha.

Molokai, in the center of the Hawaiian Island chain, remained seemingly unaffected by progress and development. Remote Maunaloa to the far west stood alone and stubbornly remained untouched by the fast-paced modern world.

In the sacred myths, the island of Molokai was known as Pule O'o, the place of the effective prayer. A master teacher of the dance, a kumu hula from Molokai, explained the true meaning of this name. "To pule is to pray," and although the word O'o has several meanings, the one that applied refers to the time of maturity. He used a brilliant example. Imagine a mango that hangs heavily on a tree. To illustrate this concept, he held his hands above his head. To enjoy the best flavor, he explained, one needed to allow the fruit to ripen completely. A fruit that was not ripe was still green, not ready, and one that was too ripe would tumble to the ground—poho (no good). The perfect fruit would literally fall into your hands.

He continued to explain that in ancient times, the kahuna, the priests of Molokai, would pray until their prayer reached fruition—that is, when it was literally answered or manifested. They chanted for purity to do this work. Their combined energy could transcend all fields. Their prayers emanated a large energy field healing to all of Molokai. This was why their effective prayer was so powerful. Pule O'o manifested only when the time and conditions were correct, like our perfect mango, and until that point was reached, the wise ones would continue their prayers.

In the twelfth century, a great battle took place between the armies of Kaikololani, Chief of Maui, and the people of Molokai. Both men and women from the surrounding Ahupua'a (the lands from the mountain to the sea) assembled to defend their 'aina (land). The armies landed on the eastern end where a great battle was fought, and many lives were lost. During the battle, a runner was sent to Mahana on the western side to ask for spiritual intervention. At the site of the impending battle, the kahuna formed a circle, lit a fire in a stone bowl, and began their prayers. After a long lull in the battle, Kaikololani gave the order to attack. Before his eyes, when his troops touched the shores of Molokai, they fell dead. Only Kaikololani was spared so he could return to Maui to advise them of the battle and the powerful prayers of the kahunas of Molokai.

The people of Maui would look to Molokai in a mixture of fear and wonderment and say, "Molokai, Pule O'o." The population of the island was small and the *Ali'i* (chiefs) of Molokai could not match the larger islands in war. They depended on the prayers of their kahuna to keep their island safe. Since Molokai was a gathering place for the most skilled among the kahuna, those prayers were extremely powerful. Even Kamehameha the Great could not conquer the island; he won the people over with diplomacy and friendship.

To understand Molokai, you only need to read the Hawaiian story of creation found within the Kumulipo (sacred chants). It was here the ancient ones charted their existence from the stars. To comprehend the chants was vital and complex. It was originally an oral tradition created for the Ali'i from the time of Lonoikamakahiki of Waipio from before recorded time.

A gifted Molokai man known as Kumu John, (referenced earlier in the mango example), was the respected authority, kumu (teacher), and instrumental in the creation of a mural painted on canvas that communicated nine hundred years of Molokai's creation and history. Phil worked on this mural, which was commissioned by the Hawai'i State Foundation of Culture and the Arts. Measuring forty feet in length and six feet high, the mural entitled Molokai Nui a Hina (Great Mother of Molokai) hangs in the Kaunakakai Elementary School auditorium on Molokai.

These two talented men met and unleashed the afore-mentioned chants by way of the artist's hand to the children of Molokai, as well as the world. Periodically, Phil brought his layout for approval and confirmation. I was privileged to be present at one meeting. I was brimming with questions as we drove above 'Aiea on O'ahu. Kumu John lived with his parents then. It was expensive to fly inter-island, and this was our third attempt—the last two times he'd taken ill and been hospitalized. A robust, large man, he tipped the scales at over three hundred pounds and his health suffered. We feared he could pass before the project was completed.

Phil forgot where to find the house. As he drove along a steep hill in Makakilo, I kept pressing the redial button on my cell phone, but the line was busy. We drove on, befuddled. Suddenly, I remembered that I had not done my prayers that morning. I saw a spot to the side of the road with a bench under a shade tree and told Phil to pull over. As I walked there to chant for a successful day, my mind spoke, bartering a deal: Be silent and all will be well. Upon sitting down, my shoulders sagged with resignation like a scolded child.

I spoke aloud to the universe in the breeze and to a small fly that circled me. "Damn!" I kicked the dirt and a stone skidded away. "Okay, I promise to be quiet if he can find the house and complete the meeting." I looked at the car and Phil was giving me the thumbs-up sign. Kumu had answered his phone, and we would be on our way. I smiled and waved, again confirming to no one present, "Okay, okay, I will be quiet." A deal was a deal, especially one made in prayer. I finished my chanting in lightning speed and ran to the car. Once in Kumu's house, I pretended to watch television yet listened to every word the men spoke. On that sunny Hawaiian afternoon, every question I would have asked and more, was answered to a degree I could not have imagined.

As we readied to leave, I walked to Kumu and said, "Mahalo, Kumu, this afternoon you have answered questions I did not know how to ask."

1 – Molokai

The knowing man was quick to answer. He looked into my eyes as the air stilled around us. I imagined the wind outside the house paused and listened as well.

"Sista, you already know what pule is. Now you need to go find the o'o!"

I nodded, bowed low, and repeated my thanks, "Mahalo, Mahalo," like a child completing a lesson. It was not his job to explain further, but my obligation to find the correct dictionaries and discover the complex meaning of this word, and how it would shape our future. In time, I would learn that O'o is "the essence of time."

In mythology, it has been written in the chants that Molokai was born from a union between Hina, known as Earth Mother, and Wakea, Sky Father. The full name for Molokai is Molokai Nui a Hina, meaning Molokai, child of Goddess Hina. Molokai is known as the birthplace of the hula and a center for culture. Historically, Molokai was a place of great wealth due to the vast amounts of fish that could be caught by hand. Hundreds of fishponds formed a virtual necklace around the eastern and western shorelines.

According to mo'olelo (oral story), La'ila'i introduced the hula around AD 900. La'ila'i was not part of the western migration. She had come from the east where the sun rose and was related to those who migrated a thousand years before. It has been written that she was fair-skinned with 'ehu (reddish) hair.

After La'ila'i's arrival, the hula was only taught to her 'ohana in Ka'ana in the westernmost part of Molokai. Visitors came from all the neighboring islands to watch the dance we know as hula. Those who came by sea, beached their canoes to travel to the sacred place to witness the descendants of La'ila'i's 'ohana. Five generations later, a granddaughter, Kapo'ulakina'u, agreed to teach the hula to outsiders only if they agreed to learn by her strict kapu (set of sacred rules). These classes were given with respect and humility, and a commitment by the dancer to commit fourteen years of living and training in Ka'ana.

Laka, Kapo'ulakina'u's youngest sister, became the most gifted dancer and teacher. When she learned the basic ninety-eight steps of hula, she used them for life and preservation. Ultimately, she would travel throughout the islands with her twin, a male named 'Olohe. He used the steps of hula for defense and taught lua, a traditional martial art. The two shared their knowledge of hula with the mission to preserve their ancestral stories and traditions.

The Essence of Time: PULE O'O

At a pristine moment when the sea and sky met as one band of tangerine color, the dancers came from every island to dance on one of seven natural terraces at the school of Ka'ana. Each island danced on their chosen level.

Just as Harvard, Yale, and Cambridge are celebrated centers of learning in the Western world, Hawaiians had Ke'ie'ie, the school of the elite kahuna, located on the western slope of Molokai in Mahana near where Maunaloa is today. All the kahuna's who went there to hone their skills to become the highest practitioners would travel to Molokai to be instructed in Pule O'o, (powerful prayer).

Philip's storytelling of the entrance exam always made me stop and listen because his eyes would widen, and the respect and love for his culture permeated every word. The entrance exam was challenging and the one on Molokai in this ancient time was even more so. During the exam, ka pua'a moe, the "sleeping pig," potential students needed to possess the ability of life or death. To enter this esteemed place of Ke'ie'ie, the place of learning, the applicant was to pray a black pig dead.

A live pig was set before them, and once the pig rolled over dead from the product of their thoughts alone, the first part of the exam was complete. The next portion was to bring the creature back to life by praying. Bear in mind this was only the first entrance exam; it intensified as it continued. Afterward they were allowed to participate and heighten their learning. On Molokai it was child's play to move clouds and arrange the sky. Large boulders located on the western slopes would be found in the eastern valleys. Those students and residents willed them to move across the terrain—they could do these amazing feats. Molokai is the most sacred island! All the while, the kahuna held the island in pule. This class of priests were masters in their disciplines: architecture, astronomy, botany, agriculture, medicine, voyaging, and religious ceremonies.

You could pause here and ask, "Is this pure myth? Is this true?" Yes, it is true, but to be validated or to receive validation you need to come where these mysteries occurred, immerse yourself in the spiritual reality of these places, and then sincerely ask to be shown. Molokai history has been hidden. I never doubted because these stories resonated as an unquestionable truth. Philip coined a phrase many years ago: "What others consider mythology; I consider history." Because this 'aina was now my home, I, too, could never question.

1 – Molokai

I chose to see Molokai and the camp as an intricate bird's nest. All the leaves, twigs, and other material had been gathered to assure this nest was pono (balance) and ultimately Hawaiian. Whatever was placed into this warm, protected nesting space would inevitably be pono as well. All who lived and passed through this island and village would be affected, whether they chose to be or not. Lifelong residents of Molokai agree that Maunaloa, the small pineapple plantation camp on the top of the hill, was special. The Filipinos, Japanese, Portuguese, Puerto Ricans, and Chinese people living in the camp all became Hawaiians in their hearts. For whatever reason, it worked out this way.

From my first night, I remembered the star-filled skies in the camp. From the western slopes of Maunaloa Mountain where the small camp perched, I could see Diamond Head rising from the island of O'ahu. Far in the distance across the inky sea, a dome of light created a misty halo over Waikiki and Honolulu. I could see the etched black silhouette of Diamond Head. A block of filmy light crested and reached the stratosphere where it mimicked the curve of the planet. At nightfall, the Molokai Channel, also known as the Ka'iwi Channel, appeared as black as India ink touched with tufts of white foam like whipped cream on rich cocoa.

Honolulu from Maunaloa was not only separated by an ocean, but light-years in time. As a new arrival, I was like an infant in my understanding; all was new to me. The simplest tasks took root in this sacred small sliver of an island. Across the road from Coconut Grove, was a row of churches as far as the eye could see. This was written up in *Ripley's Believe It or Not*. Buildings of different faiths are lined up like a string of precious pearls. Spirituality abides in all on Molokai. The council of kahuna holds court over the welfare of the island. Molokai's place was manifested by a vote of no changes to the island by county government, the consensus being to "Keep Molokai, Molokai." This has not been easy. Many parents cry out, "Yah, but what about our keiki (children)? How can they stay here if there is no work?"

Molokai must evolve in the changing world, even though "Keeping it Molokai" proves harder and harder. Things change as the people of the island require. Community presence in the form of a county council representative on Maui means a lot and is their only voice to offset any drastic change.

2 - Travels

Kalia, the Gateway to Waikiki.
Artwork by Philip Sabado

2

A phenomenon occurred when I was a young teen on vacation at a Waikiki beach with my parents and sister, a near encounter with my future. Mom always planned at least one big vacation a year. We were a typical tourist family with wide-eyed kids full of innocence and wonderment. Mom always planned one special night with dinner and a show. The entertainment she'd chosen, Pearl of the Orient, sounded enticing—a Filipino dance ensemble featuring the magic, culture, and music of the seven thousand islands and provinces of the Philippines. As a child sitting in the third row from the sparkling stage, it proved to be exotic and unforgettable. Distinct experiences can crystallize for a lifetime, and I can still envision myself in that seat. As fate would have it, Philip, my future husband, was one of the main dancers spinning and performing that starlit night. We never met, but later we did the math. That was the year after his service when he lived in Honolulu and danced in Waikiki.

On another trip, this one to Puerto Rico, we were in Old San Juan at the same time, and hotel as a young GI on leave. The possibility of us passing each other on a pathway could have happened.

The third time was the charm. We met in 1969 when I had just turned eighteen. I had left my comfortable upper-middle-class home in Glendale, a suburb of Los Angeles, the day after my high school graduation. I planned to attend school in Honolulu and make my life in the islands. My mother grudging approved if I agreed to continue my education, so I chose art school. Plus, I'd earned every penny to finance my future. In hindsight, I recognize a push forward, my destiny.

I had spent most of my teenage years fussing about my derriere. Apparently, this was an attraction for Phil. He loved following me from class, watching me walk to the bus stop. In later years, he would grin and point to someone and say, "See her, she walks like you, so sexy." I would laugh and blush. I still smile, thankful for my good fortune.

The first ride with Phil was on a clear Honolulu day. He took me to the Kuhio Park Terrace where I lived in Honolulu's infamous public housing with my Filipina girlfriend's family, admittedly a rough neighborhood. Her mom was divorced with three grown children. Life in any big city could be challenging and in costly Honolulu many ethnic groups survived hand-to-mouth.

At first, Philip and I were friends, traveling companions, and schoolmates. That changed in an unforgettable moment, a kiss that could only be compared to a jolt of electricity.

My memory is a mix of sweet and sour. As a toddler, I had found a safety pin and inserted the point into an electric socket in my room. I felt a jolt that shot me skidding back on my cloth diaper across the room. My back hit the opposite wall with a *thump*. My mother came running. I was crying and terrified! The words "electric shock" brings this memory to mind. Phil's kiss had that same jolt of electricity except it shocked me in a good way! The first time we made love, we spent the entire day in bed in his family's house in 'Aiea.

In a short time, we fell in love. In mere months, we boarded a small plane destined for Molokai to visit his island home. As the silver-green propeller-driven Piper made its final approach, I pressed my cheek to the cold glass. A cigar-shaped sliver of land lay beneath us with patches of ash-green pineapple tops growing in perfect rectangular plots as far as I could see. We slowly descended, cutting through the clouds, and as we drew closer, I could make out the pineapple plants snuggled within a soil the color of burnt sienna. Flatland and mountains rose to the east and west. Molokai is around two hundred sixty square miles in area. It stretches thirty-eight miles long and is ten miles at its widest point.

From the air, the small airstrip looked like a shiny stripe of black tape on a fluffy green carpet. I felt the inevitable bump as the wheels and earth met. A puff of blue smoke rose and faded as we taxied to the small terminal building. The airport crew ran toward our plane with large chunks of wood to place behind the tires. When the door opened, beams of yellow and orange morning sunlight filled the cabin. There was no standing room. We waited as the pilot disembarked and lowered the stairs that were attached to the plane with two thick ropes. The moment my foot stepped onto the black tarmac my mind spoke words I would always remember; *this will be magic!*

The breeze shifted as I inhaled its sweetness; all those pineapples ripening, I mused. These were the winter months and although the heat still caused a wavy blur to arise from the tarmac, the air felt cool and pleasant. I smiled and said a silent prayer for good fortune on this important day. My purpose here was to meet the parents and family of the man I would marry. If all worked out, our wedding would likely be about seven months later in June.

We sought his family's approval and permission to marry. According to their custom, there was not to be a parade of prospective brides. A son was allowed to bring one, and only one girl home to meet the parents. The unspoken message was clear, make up your mind and choose someone. There would be no second chances. (I cannot claim this for all Filipino families, but this custom did apply to his family.)

This attitude was new and felt strange, especially after having spent my teenaged years in California. I was modern and considered myself liberated. I had many beaus from the time I started dating in my mid-teens. Deep within my heart, I had already made a sacred pact with the gods of destiny to make this work. I agreed to abide by these intriguing customs, willing to step into this world of pineapple, garlic, and superstition. I loved Philip beyond measure. Centered and with an open mind, I stepped onto Molokai ready to enter his home and become one with it all.

I had dressed casually for the trip; I wanted to look nice, but not overdone. I had no idea what to expect. As I made my exit from the small plane, a great gust of wind blew my long blonde hair in every direction. I stood transfixed on the last step as my eyes took in the horizon, the mountains, and valleys on both sides. Nestled in a valley to the east, I saw misty bands of color—a rainbow held captive in the crescent of green hills. The clouds and light shifted the bands of color, which directed my gaze to another valley with a half rainbow, the other half dissolving in the sunlight. The color-filled rays seemed to point where I should go, beckoning me from a distance, like a siren calling—come and see.

My eyes lingered on the rainbows, and I made a mental note to go there one day. I learned this was the entrance to the Kalaupapa Lookout. Kalaupapa Settlement was the infamous leper colony. My fascination with the rainbow and the valley was interrupted with a stirring about my legs as the mischievous wind whirled at my feet and under my slip. I must have looked like Marilyn Monroe over the subway grate in the famous film clip from *The Seven Year Itch*. I thrust my hands down to stop my skirt from flying over my head. Again, the naughty wind whipped around for another try.

Philip nudged my side and turned me in the direction of a red dust cloud coming from the west. I saw a truck approaching with gleeful children in the truck bed. I turned my focus to the man I hoped would become my husband. His smile beamed with warmth at the sight of his family coming from the camp to meet us.

His emotions pooled in his eyes, he was from this place, and he was home. Others not only looked like him, but even walked and spoke with the same slow, easy Hawaiian style. This was the Molokai way. I, with my long ash-blonde hair and blue eyes was the exotic one. Philip's eyes glinted in the light, brimming with tears of happiness. I returned my gaze back to the engaging vista so as not to embarrass him.

Once within the terminal at the Ho'olehua Airport gate, we were greeted by a Hawaiian man, Mitchell Pauole. This welcoming person embodied what I think of as the aloha spirit. Because of his kind heart, Molokai will forever be known as the Friendly Isle. This older gentleman went to the airport almost every day, wearing a woven straw hat with a colorful feather haku (woven crown) above the brim and a bright aloha shirt. His warm smile and gentle manner welcomed all the passengers to his island. In his way he was not just spreading aloha, he was aloha. For him and most born to this island, it was the natural thing to do.

As the old pickup truck rumbled toward us, I could see how his family stared at me; their only experience with Caucasians had been seeing them on television. Their laughter grew louder as the truck neared. Shyly, they cupped their hands over their beautiful smiles as their black hair flew in the wind. Their skin was as dark as toasted coconuts, as was Philip's. The women's jet-black hair went to their waists and was adorned with yellow and pink plumeria blossoms pinned behind either the right or left ear. In the Hawaiian culture, wearing a flower behind your left ear means you are married or unavailable. Wearing a flower on the right signifies you are looking for love.

I could tell Philip's heart was full as he watched his family waving from the moving truck. His physicality changed at that moment, as if everything that may have seemed important just melted away. He became happier and more relaxed than I'd ever seen him. I could see that being home was his bliss.

As they rounded the last corner, a cloud of red dust rose with the wind and followed like a stray dog. The encrusted truck rattled and shook and came to a halt a few paces from the curb. They had made a lei of beautiful white plumeria blossoms with perfect yellow centers to give to their brother and his visitor.

His sister, Rosita, drove with an assembly of kids sitting in the back. As they pulled to the curve, their beautiful dark hair swooshed as the children jumped and ran to their uncle in one surge. His sister moved slowly around the front of the truck. "Howzit, brother?" she said with true aloha, a smile, and a tinge of humor.

"Hey, sis. Howzit? You look great!"

She was shorter and much darker than her brother, having worked in the pineapple fields since age thirteen, way before statehood and child labor laws. She had pulled her long hair into a tightly twisted bun, a chignon, at the back of her head with numerous black bobby pins holding stray hairs in place. Her only indulgence seemed to be her golden earrings. I'd seen these hoops on other Filipino women. She may have worn them night and day, so heavy in a rich yellow Spanish gold that her earlobes had stretched longer from the weight. She stubbed out her cigarette and moved to the driver's seat, ready to drive home.

After a flurry of introductions and shy hugs, I sat in the back of the pickup with Philip and the children. I tried to be modest and tucked my skirt under my knees and placed my satchel on my lap. The wind whipped at everything in the back bed as we drove. We were like a human sandwich pinned against the rear window. Philip, at my side, could not have been more comfortable, his blissful smile constant.

At the main Maunaloa Highway, we turned right and rumbled along the road to their home in the pineapple plantation camp at the far west end of the island. For about twenty to thirty minutes, every bump and pothole elicited screams and shrieks of laughter. Billowing red clouds engulfed us and dust trailing behind lingered as a filmy mist suspended over the twisting highway. In the distance, the red cloud with its iron-rich particles drifted onto the miles and miles of pineapple fields that we sped past. Each bump interrupted the light conversation between Philip and the children and produced giggles. They would peek at me and then slide away into more giggles.

In this exquisite setting, the sun seemed brighter than anywhere I had ever been. Everything shone with blinding brilliance. As we approached our destination, I was becoming nervous. Soon I would meet Mama, the matriarch of this 'ohana (family). I recorded every moment, the beginning of my destiny, my life's journey here and now.

Philip told me before our arrival that Mama was frail and thin as many illnesses had robbed her of strength. I would come to understand that she was a woman who had earned great respect in the village. In their culture, she was known as an anting-anting, *a wise woman with power and an understanding of pono (balance), and truth. In the kahuna tradition, both Hawaiians and Filipinos had shown her respect.*

Maunaloa was set high on a plateau at over four thousand five hundred feet. I had lost sight of the teasing rainbows, but noticed the air was even sweeter in this place. This pristine village enjoyed a constant cool breeze and was clear and free of pollution. Honolulu, some thirty miles northwest across the Ka'iwi Channel, had experienced the sad effects of pollution. A dull haze had formed a dirty halo over the city and would intensify in the coming years. Maui was in the opposite direction with Haleakala rising above the clouds. Maui fought to hold on to the simpler life. There were signs this island would be next to succumb to the Western way and ultimately be lost to the development craze.

3 - Dolores, Abra

Mama,
Adorned in Native Attire.
Artwork by Philip Sabado

3

 The largest group of immigrants from the Philippines to the Hawaiian shores hailed from the Northwestern section of Luzon, a geographic area known as Ilocos Norte. Adjacent to the Ilocos region is the Cordillera Mountains, which comprise the provinces of Abra, Apayao, Benguet, Ifugao, Kalinga, and Mountain Province. Here, the people known as the Igorot, the collective name of several Austronesian ethnic groups in the Philippines, lived in Banaue, a region of secluded, clouded-terraced mountains. The Ilocano were hearty, strong-spirited, and deeply superstitious, as well as spiritual people.

There was a secret here in these mountain terrace villages and caves that drew the Spanish galleons in the 1400s. The Spaniards were like bees on the wing, gathering pollen to feed their insatiable queen with honey—gold! Records showed more gold in these misty mountains than in the Lower Nile of Egypt.

The Spanish stayed for over four hundred years and though they tried, they failed to access the treasures of the North. The gold remains, and the peoples of this place were fierce and wielded deadly bolo knives. It has been written that the sheer shirts we are familiar with as formal Filipino attire, *barong* Tagalog, served a dual purpose. In addition to being comfortable clothing, it allowed the early Spaniards to see through to the long knife they carried.

A siren of opportunity beckoned from a distant set of islands in the Pacific. In the early nineteenth century the sugar and pineapple fields were managed and planted by the descendants of New England missionaries. These fields required laborers, and the recruiters were sent to these distant shores offering work to those in the provinces, as well as a way to help the families they left behind. All the while, the Hawaiian population dwindled rapidly because of the diseases brought by the whaling ships that followed Captain Cook. In 1853, measles and smallpox eradicated over 100,000

Hawaiians. Having never been exposed to these diseases, the natives wilted like grapes on the vine and died in the ocean water from first contact.

A new infusion of workers was required and arrived in the deep hull of ships crossing the Pacific. Chinese folk came first, then the Japanese, some Mexicans and Puerto Ricans, followed by the Portuguese. Those accustomed to the heat and long hours under the relentless Hawaiian sun worked best. They invited immigrant Filipino's for one dollar a month (seemingly paltry, but a fortune in the 1920s). Those from Ilocos Norte stayed in the fields until hotels provided a seductive alternative. The Chinese lasted a month in the fields. Always an industrious people, they created huis (societies), which enabled them to buy out their contracts and establish businesses in all the islands, opening restaurants and other establishments.

Filipino recruits were often young single men. Couples had to be married. These brave ambitious men and women were willing to change their fate to begin a life in a new world. The *Sakadas*, the first recruits, are celebrated and appreciated to this day as true pioneers.

In the early 1900s, a fever made its way around the globe. People from Europe and Asia unwittingly chose a mysterious and unknown future over the predictable world of their forefathers. Many causes heralded these changes: famine, bigotry, and autocrats to name a few. Imagine during that time with scant communication skills, leaving villages knowing there was a possibility of never returning. The islands were far away, yet seductive for a new, better life.

My husband-to-be's parents were among those sailing forward but had yet to meet. A strange twist of fate would seal their union. On her voyage to these eastern islands, the fourteen-year-old Severina never looked back and feigned being a spouse to an older uncle so she could make the trip to Hawai'i.

Mama's home was in Dolores in the province of Abra, a landlocked mountain village hidden deep within the mountains that spanned a mere eighteen square miles in the early nineteen hundreds. She was from the Ifugao, derived from Ipugao (earth people), known for their spiritual prowess. Some believed the town was a place of mystery, a village reputedly populated with sorcerers and those who could wield powers; that is, they possessed *anting-anting*. The word itself often invoked fear. A harbinger known to command spirits and dispelled curses could occupy a place in the village as one who challenged fate. Often this practice involved the use of objects, amulets or talismans, anything from crocodile teeth to black diamonds to a religious scapular. All objects were believed to be a conduit of their powers.

A friend shared a story about her father who always kept a small pouch tucked in a pocket. Their children knew that on washday, they had to check Papa's pockets carefully. Once the satchel was located, it was placed on a shelf. One time my friend said she was rushed and simply forgot. Her father was furious! He thought his powers were gone, clearly washed away. She never saw the contents of the pouch but knew to him, this was where his powers emanated from. In using the amulet, there was the extension of a visual aspect, whereas the person was the real carrier of the powers.

Everyone born within these islands has heard this story about the village of witches and sorcerers. When others passed through the village, they were strictly advised to be cautious. Not one piece of clothing was left behind, or if a strand of hair fell from one's head, a curse would befall them. Thus, hair was twisted and bound tightly in buns. Many years later, my brother-in-law returned after a cultural exploration to this province to discover this was in fact Mama's village. There are two forms of *anting-anting*. As in all life's duplicity, one was used for love, and the other to cause revenge and havoc. Mama's way was always love.

The Lagben River was the seventh largest in Benguet Province, and at a quarter of a mile across, separated Dolores from the sister village of La Paz. In the early 1900s, rafts fashioned from bamboo were woven watertight to accomplish river crossings. There were no bridges and strong men used a pulley system set up on both sides of the river to pull the rafts across. The area was heavily forested with tall pines, mahogany, and mangrove swamps. The islands were home to thousands of species of flowering plants and ferns, including hundreds of orchids, some extremely rare. Tall, coarse grasses canvased much of the area.

The Ifugao and Kalinga had adapted to working long hours. They were short people with muscular calves from long walks in the mountainous regions through miles of thick bamboo forests. Tall trees bent to breezes that had been funneled through distant valleys and over snowy mountaintops. Most born to this village in the early 1900s would only know this place their entire life; there were few visitors. Old records indicated that two hundred to four hundred inhabitants populated these remote regions. Farmers would rise early in the darkness before the sun crested the horizon. After the monsoon, the sun would bring sweltering heat by eight a.m., and wavy ribbons of heat would rise from the growing crops. Their *carabaos* (water buffaloes) were considered the finest. Both could withstand the summer months and mountainous terrain to harvest the crops.

Despite its remoteness, some still found their way to remote villages. A sister-in-law shared that Mama's father was a musician from Shanghai, China. From old photos, I could see Mama was a striking beauty as a young woman. Her skin was fair and her eyes dark and penetrating; there was no mistaking her charisma and silent power. Her name at birth was Estepania Severina Georgia Blen, but her friends and family coined the nickname "Paning," which was spoken with a playful lilt.

Agricultural terracing was their principal means of livelihood along with traditional farming. Their social status was measured by the number of rice field granaries, family heirlooms, gold earrings, and *carabaos* they owned, as well as prestige conferred through time and tradition. The more affluent, known as *kadangyan,* were usually generous by nature, giving rice to poor neighbors in times of food shortages or hardships. Their culture was known for their advanced legal system, using one of the world's most extensive oral legal traditions that specified the offense depending on the use of custom law: trial by elders (influenced in part by public opinion) or trial by ordeal. The wealthy were subjected to greater fines than the poor.

Untouched by the influences of Spanish colonialism, the Ifugao valued kinship, family ties, and religious and cultural beliefs. They were unique among all ethnic groups in the mountain province for their narrative literature such as the *Hudhud*, an epic dealing with hero ancestors sung in a poetic manner, and their wood carving art, most notably the *bului* (carved granary guardians) and the prestigious ceremonial bench of the upper class, the *hagabi*. Their textiles are renowned for their beauty in colorful loom-woven blankets and clothing. Square houses were well-built with wooden floors, windowless walls, and pyramidal thatched roofs. Elevated from the ground by four sturdy tree trunks, they featured removable staircases that were hoisted up at night to prevent entry by enemies or wild animals. Lastly, the traditional attire for male Ifugao, the *wanno* (G-string), included six types, which were used depending on the occasion or the man's social status.

Ifugao women, on the contrary, wore *tapis*, a wraparound skirt.

All things considered, the early 1900s proved to be a volatile time in Philippine history. A vicious warring group of mountain people known as the Pulajans cut a wave of terror from the mountain villages to the seaside communities. Their battle cry was tad tad (chop chop). *These red-garbed mountaineers with white flowing capes descended on villages with their crescent blades in a frenzied wave of sheer terror. They were as feared as the Moro native, the peoples to the south. They left a trail of broken bodies and bloodstained earth.*

Concurrently, a prediction was made by a two-headed snake hidden in the tall grasses that spurred the young Severina to leave her homeland. She must have endured a painful choice to either opt for life in a distant land or stay and face survival in the mountain village with warring tribes.

There was a story about Ferdinand Marcos before the war. He was an attorney and a brilliant negotiator. Many Ilocano workers owe their livelihood to his being the key element that brought the recruiters of the sugar and pineapple fields to the north. The largest and sturdiest workers came from this region to the fields in the Hawaiian Islands.

Marcos was keenly aware of the powers reputed to be in this area. As a precaution, he had a sliver of wood placed in his back from one of the village's trees in hopes that the power would transfer to him, not understanding one must be born to this. (It did not work.)

These beliefs persist into modern times. My daughter Severina, named after her Apo Baket (Phil's mother), once worked in a department store in Honolulu. As Seve was helping an older Filipina, the woman commented on her beauty and asked about her nationality. Seve smiled and answered with pride, "I am Filipina, Chinese, and my mother is Irish."

The woman then asked from which village in the Philippines her father's family heralded. When Seve gave the answer, the woman's eyes darted from side to side, she dropped the scarf she was holding and slid it back across the glass counter. "You will excuse me. Your father's people come from a place of power. I would prefer to shop on another day." Posthaste, she turned and walked away. Seve stood bemused, shook her head, and laughed to herself as the woman wove through the crowds.

3 – Dolores, Abra

Severina, our third child, was born almost a year to the day after Mama's death and was Philip's first choice for a name. Older family members told me that our daughter was born with "Mama's ways." They noted how she walked with the same gait, ease, and posture as her Apo Baket.

I sat with Philip's oldest brother, Santiago, one day as he remembered his mother. As we spoke on the lanai, he kept looking at Seve who stood across the room. The warm breezes wrapped a sunset glow around us with the ocean scent close, sweet, and tangy. The pounding waves of the ocean were less than a mile down the road. Before Santiago had left the islands as a young man, he recalled a conversation where Mama had said that all her daughters were not strong women and would need to marry strong, capable men. His gaze remained on Seve as he spoke. "There is only one person in this room who is my mother, she is there, your daughter." He did not look at me but held a steady gaze on her. In the short years I'd been married into this family, I continued learning how these traditions and superstitions would weave and color the texture of my life. I shook with a chill because I understood this was a responsibility Seve had been born to fulfill.

Being born into a village of mountain people had distinct advantages for young Severina. Bathing was done with great modesty. They would sit in the cold mountain waters immersed to their necks. Sunset was the most common time for bathing. With work in the home and fields done, people were readying themselves for a relaxing evening.

A cold clear river with an abundance of plump fish ran by the base of the village. The villagers wove large baskets to trap fish in the transparent water. An upside-down basket made a unique trap. The fish swam in and could not escape. Their catch was later served with rice for the evening meal. There was a particular tree in this region, a *tabigi*, that imparted a mild narcotic effect when cut, and when swirled in the water, the fish became momentarily groggy and slowed just long enough to be speared.

The Ifugao, known colloquially as the "inhabitants of the known earth," live primarily in the province of Ifugao in Central Cordillera in the far reaches of Northern Luzon. Their name was synonymous with the world famous, man-made Banaue Rice Terraces in Northern Luzon, which had once been hailed as the Eighth Wonder of the World, attributed to amazing engineering knowledge and agricultural terracing. Ifugao culture and values were not transformed by the Spaniards who ventured into those lands.

Anthropologists have regarded the Ifugao as possibly the oldest residents of the highlands. Their origin, attributed to Indonesian migration, dates back as early as 800 to 500 BC.

Among the mountain people, it was common knowledge that mermaids swam in these rivers. They were called serena, *an enchanting name that called up visions of sirens who would lure unsuspecting victims into underwater kingdoms from which there was no escape. Naturally, their beauty was unparalleled!*

One village story tells of a townsman who saw a mermaid deep in the river as he was fishing. He was drawn to this place because rocks slowed the river's flow, and the bigger fish could be seen resting there as if sleeping between the giant stones. As the fisherman prepared to lay his traps, he peered closely into the clear waters to see what appeared to be an opening to a cave he had never seen before. There before him was a serena. *The mermaid with her beauty and enticing ways beguiled and drew him into the water and ultimately into the cave. He did not return home, and the family became concerned. The fisherman's brother fell into a trance and the lost fisherman spoke through his brother, telling the woeful tale of the mermaid who had enticed him. His final message to his family from the underwater world was that he would not ever return to them, he was now part of another kingdom, alas, another world.*

Many stories in the village were about how mysterious sea creatures could transform themselves. Known as shape-changers, these beings could walk among the villagers at will. They were said to have even joined the populace in church. To know whether the one sitting near you was a serena *was a little tricky. As Mama explained, all one needed to do was reveal a needle point and the imposter would disappear,* poof, *just vanish.*

Often a serena would engage a villager in conversation. Invariably, the mermaid would casually ask the villager what he or she had eaten that day. The villagers would never confess to having eaten a fish. They knew that anyone who bragged about eating a fish to a serena *would be dragged to the creature's underwater kingdom and disappear without a trace. Instead, they would say they ate some sort of vegetable, preferably a bitter-tasting one like* padiya *(bitter melon), a local favorite that grew in the cool mountains on a vine.*

When Mama left her village, courageous to do so at age fourteen, she had a plan. Workers had to be able to handle working arduous hours in the

Hawaiian sun. Once they were signed up, the rules were set. On the voyage to Hawai'i in the early 1920s, as mentioned, only married women were allowed to travel from the Philippines. With so many single men on board, a single woman traveling alone would have been too vulnerable with four to seven males to every female. The uncle, her pretend husband, provided a convenient foil. Perhaps her family was more willing to release her, knowing that once she was in the new land, she would have a family member upon whom she could rely.

Despite our differences, Mama and I were alike in spirit. As a young girl from the Philippines, she left her isolated mountain village and boarded a ship to a distant place, eagerly seeking her future in a new land. Her life change was profound. Other than her uncle, family and old friends would not be there to help her endure the hard times. Could she have known the faces in her homeland would fade from memory? Financial fortune would never be hers, and she never booked a return passage.

When I left high school and came to Hawai'i, I was alone as well, and I, too, felt my life began when I stepped onto Hawaiian soil. However, I did not leave poverty and hardship behind. My childhood was comfortable and without any real conflict. Nor did I feel completely cut off from my family and my former life. When I left my home in 1969, five airlines served Hawaii from Los Angeles. I could pick up a phone anywhere and call my mother, and if I needed it, a ticket was a heartbeat away. Our worlds were not the same, but we both had courage.

There would be two increments of Filipino immigrants brought to the Hawaiian fields during the early 1920s through the 1930s. One region, the Visayas, an island group to the south, provided many of the first workers. A total of 928 workers were recruited from the distant Philippine shores. According to the contracts, the plantation was required to furnish housing, fuel, water, and medical care for three years and the monthly pay went up to sixteen dollars. This was a fortune compared to the life of struggle they had left behind. The contract stipulated the laborers were expected to work a ten-hour day, twenty-six days a month for the required three years.

The first ships to arrive in the early 1940s docked in Hilo on the Big Island of Hawai'i, where an organized system of plantation life of housing and jobs awaited. Work was available in either the sugarcane or pineapple fields. Filipinos were held at the bottom of the socioeconomic scale.

Moreover, the possibility of advancement was never realized, rarely did they become the luna (boss). Housing was often less than adequate, and they naturally became a tight community. Subsequently, because of a human rights movement, labor unions evolved and became a vital force within the Filipino culture.

Three distinct groups, those from Ilocos, Visayas, and Luzon, emigrated on those first ships. The Visayans came from the southern islands of Visayas. These people spoke Bisaya or Cebuano. Those who spoke Tagalog, the national language of the Philippines, were the city people of Manila and from the other provinces of Central and Southern Luzon. The people of Ilocos Norte spoke Ilocano, as did those from Ilocos Sur, La Union and Pangasinan. Papa must have been good with language because he spoke both dialects and enough Tagalog to get by.

Although these island groups are separated by the vast Pacific Ocean, some similarities exist. Philip discovered the origin of taro in a book about Philippine tribes. Its first recorded image was on the pyramids in Egypt, then traced to India, across Asia to China, and on to the Philippines. He learned of a remote region where the Lepanto tribe lived. The same large velvety leaves etched upon the pyramids had found their way to the mountain slopes of this remote village. The study observed that this was the only Filipino tribe to grow and eat taro. When the chief was asked about the plant, the answer proved profound. According to their legend handed down for generations, the name Maui was heard in the appreciation chant intoned by the chief of the Lepanto. This tribe planted, harvested, and ate taro. The Lepanto were near Mamas village.

As in the Philippines, crops were planted by hand and harvested in the broiling sun. Nestled deep within the heart of each pineapple plant's needle-sharp spiky leaves was the golden treasure, a fruit with a delicious mix of sweet and tart. Pineapples were harvested by snapping off the mature fruits at the base and placing them in burlap sacks as workers passed along the steely green rows. Harvesting sugarcane was tedious backbreaking work. A sharp machete was used to slash the tall cane from the root. The cut cane was burned to remove insects and excess leaves before it went to the mill.

4 - Meeting Mama

Ku'u Home (my home),
Sister Rosita on porch.
Artwork by Philip Sabado

4

 The sun shone brightly on the neat row of houses as the dusty pickup came to the outskirts of the camp. Tall Norfolk pine trees lined the roads, and the children and dogs were given priority in this place where the cool breeze lived. A sea of galvanized iron roofs painted in pastel colors glistened in the bright sunlight; all the houses were clean and freshly painted. Most yards had a garden and flowering plants on the porch, and orchids hanging from the shaded eaves greeted every arrival. Amazing red anthuriums grew in abundance. Padiya grew on the fences, a dark green, leafy vine that would be used in soups. Everything they grew could be used as food. Tall papaya trees grew in abundance, and the green fruit before they changed to orange could be cut into chunks for *sabau* (soup). Very healthy, that one!

The settlement of tiny Maunaloa unfolded as a cluster of small homes placed amid the surrounding vista of West Molokai. Set among the whispering pine and eucalyptus trees, the plantation houses were a deep forest green with shiny white enamel window trim. Others favored a creamy peach or beige, all with pastel tin roofs. The first emotion I remembered on this auspicious day was a mixture of peace and joyfulness; I suspect the children's happy nature I'd experienced from the bumpy truck ride was truly infectious.

Looking toward the mountains, two white plantation-style homes with verdant manicured yards heralded the Haole Camp where the luna, the plantation supervisors, lived. Next on the road to the right was the loading station. The saccharine smell of the fruit lingered in the air, sweet and strong, like slicing into the ripest fruit. After the pineapple was harvested, the sticky fruit was stacked high onto semi-trailers. The laden trucks lumbered down the mountain to the docks at Kaunakakai Harbor and onto barges. From there, the flat-bottomed boats pulled the cargo across the Molokai Channel

4 – Meeting Mama

to the Libby Cannery in Honolulu. This was the mode of transit for all commercial goods.

A post office shaded by banyan trees and a baseball field provided gathering spots for the camp workers. This relaxing setting at the entrance to the community center greeted every visitor and resident and was representative of the idyllic life on the western slope of Maunaloa. Housing had been assigned early on and families rarely changed residences unless an additional bedroom was required. There was no stated intention to segregate, but everyone understood Haole Camp was at the top of the road and Japanese Camp was across from the school on the main road. The remaining residences housed a mixture of Portuguese and Puerto Rican families. Filipinos comprised the majority of this village, perhaps evolving in this fashion because most family units chose to live on the same lane. At this time, the Libby-McNeill-Libby Pineapple Company maintained the upkeep of both the houses and the roads, including potholes. Plantation households paid no more than thirty dollars a month for these services, rent, and retirement.

Chicken coops lined the Filipino perimeter of the village; in truth, they were probably placed there so the stench from the chickens would be blown out to sea. An old story told of an elder Filipino man who did not trust banks and hid thirty-five thousand dollars—all his retire-ment money—inside the coop. One day, a mysterious fire broke out. Crying hysterically, the old man dashed into the coops to save his chickens and hidden wealth. Alas, all was lost. The coops were rebuilt, and the story lives on today.

Chicken fights, imported by the Filipinos from their homeland, were a cultural event whereby families enjoyed the best food and camaraderie. Women and children would visit with friends and sample the many varieties of kankanen *(sweets). The fights were held every Sunday and had a carnival-like atmosphere; gambling being the major focus of the old men who sat hunched over on their heels. Half-smoked* Toscani *(a type of cigarette) dangled from their lips as they held fistfuls of dollar bills in their wrinkled brown hands.*

From the start, I could not watch the chickens fight. What I saw was too raw and brutal, but I loved to watch the people. The men squatted with their feet firmly on the ground and their bottoms inches from the dirt but never touching. I tried it once. I teetered and fell backward on my behind like a rolling ball. All the men sat in this fashion for what seemed like long periods of time, smoking, laughing, talking, and gambling as the hours whiled away. As per tradition, the day after my husband and I married, the men of the camp dedicated a chicken fight to us. My father caught every moment with his Nikon.

Manong Perfecto, known to all as "Pete."
Artwork by Philip Sabado

Near eleven a.m., the dusty pickup came to a stop in front of a house with a certain lived-in appeal, yet it was not unlike the other homes on the lane. Philip's sister, Manang Rosita, and her husband, Manong Perfecto, lived here for the present. Mama and Papa resided at all of their children's homes from time to time. A large avocado tree Phil had planted as a boy shaded the entrance where a rickety gate swung in the breeze and opened to a pathway of broken cement slabs. The yard held a profusion of island plants and flowers. Along the front porch hung sweet smelling honohono orchids that cascaded in long fragrant chains of purple flowers. I stopped to inhale the fragrance, strong enough to make me dizzy.

As we drove and rattled along in the old pick-up truck, I was distracted

4 – Meeting Mama

about where we were going and why. As my foot touched the russet-colored road my nervousness radiated from my toes to my crown, as if the earth penetrated me in waves. A moment from my arrival ran through my mind. *Remember, you are the exotic one here, listen and learn.* I repeated this mantra to center myself.

As we were about to enter the little plantation house, I felt overwhelmed with nervousness. Clearly, this was the decisive moment for me and Philip, and the flowery perfume in my surroundings held me in an embrace. Absorbed in sensation, I stopped and wrapped my arm around the porch post to steady myself. I paused on a painted step crusted with the russet soil of the fields and looked to the man who would be my husband. Our eyes locked.

I swallowed hard, caught my courage, and spoke in a stuttering whisper, "Th-this is it then. If we don't work out, you cannot bring another girl to meet the family."

Philip gazed into my eyes without saying a word. I released my grasp on the post and reached for his hand. We entered the little house on the lane, together.

I sensed a dramatic shift from the sweet floral landing to that of simmering garlic and bay leaf, which I would discover was a constant enticement of walking into the camp house, his home. Being there was an explosion for all my senses. A meal was always being cooked or set on the stove for "Who never eat yet." Even if you just ate, I heard, "Never mind, go eat again."

No fewer than a dozen coats of paint had been applied to the walls over the years to offset the constant crimson dust that nestled into every crack and crevice. Even the water was a russet shade tinted by the iron-rich red dirt that permeated everything. On later trips, I learned to never wear white on Molokai as the strongest bleach or most powerful detergent was no match for the insistent russet earth. The interior wall colors chosen by the camp administrators were a creamy white or pale sage green, yet all the walls seemed to have warmth painted into them.

The floors were a natural dark wood worn by small bare feet over many years. These floors were kept highly polished with the amber oil of the kukui, a Hawaiian black nut the size of a walnut that was hand-rubbed into the wood by using the husk of a coconut. Philip regaled me with stories of hours spent on his knees polishing these floors each week as a child, a task passed along to the young ones.

Upon entering a house, the greeting was always *"Mangantayon"* (Let's eat). To refuse to eat was an insult to the hosts. You had to eat something, or they would be shamed and offended. Kitchens were often the gathering place, reminiscent of my own Irish customs.

Philip inhaled deeply, savoring the smells of his childhood. His whole body relaxed as he left the outside world at the steps. In this place, his home, he was at peace within his heart and soul. He walked through the living room into the kitchen to greet the rest of his family while I nervously sat on the edge of the couch and looked around.

"Howzit everybody?" Phil said with his singsong happy voice.

Alone in the parlor, I sensed the family's warmth evident in the organized clutter where photographs abounded on small tables and wall shelves. Framed pictures of various shapes and colors were set neatly on crocheted doilies and their weathered cardboard frames were stained with a red hue from the inescapable field dust. Represented in the family pictures were babies, children in caps and gowns, and wedding photos of every relative from the beginning of time. I felt enchanted seeing pictures of his sisters with bright youthful faces in beautiful, flowing satin ball gowns with butterfly sleeves in the Filipino style from the many Terno Balls held in the village. In the stillness of the room, I straightened my back, afraid to relax or get too comfortable. The people in the photos seemed to be looking at me.

From where I sat, I could see the delicate lace curtains in the bedrooms gently folding in the breeze. Colorful quilts handmade from fabric scraps of Hawaiian cloth sewn in various shapes and designs adorned the beds, each handicraft an explosion of color.

Philip appeared at the hallway door. He had been calling me to come eat and was ready to lead me to the kitchen. As I stood, he pointed to a corner of the hallway at a large steamer trunk. "There is Mama's *la casa* (household goods), where all her treasures are kept." His eyes lit up as if he were speaking of Christmas. Later, he would open the large steamer trunk to show me the long, beautiful satin and lace dresses ordered from the Philippines and specially sewn for his sisters to attend the many Terno Balls held in the camp, as I had seen in the photos.

4 – Meeting Mama

After sitting in the sun-drenched living room, I blinked to adjust my eyes in the dim, narrow hallway. I could not see clearly until a bedroom door at the darkened end of the hallway opened, shooting a slice of light into the passageway. The silhouette of a short, delicate Filipina woman emerged from behind the dark wooden door, illuminated from behind in brilliant light. I knew this must be Mama. Stunned, I gasped and caught my breath. She walked to me with her eyes cast down. She was smaller than I'd imagined, old, thin and frail with sparse white hair. Years of hard work had left a map of deep-set wrinkles on her fragile face. She had fair-colored skin, like a rich coffee with heavy cream, not as dark as her children who spent hours toiling in the Hawaiian sun. I sensed that age and illness had not robbed the powers she wielded as the family matriarch. As we stood within inches of each other, she looked up into my eyes, and I felt caught by the energy in hers. At five feet nine inches, I towered over her, yet her small frame was merely a disguise for the strength and energy planted within.

I knew then that I must set my course to win her over. If I succeeded, her favored youngest son would be my prize for life. This realization centered and eased my nervousness. In hindsight, if I could have set these seconds in slow motion, I would say this moment was the axis, the place where our lives were set to begin.

Philip's jitters showed as he stuttered and struggled to make formal introductions. Everyone froze in place as his sister and nieces peered over one another at the kitchen door, all eyes watching to see how this was going to go.

I could see that to them he was their treasured jewel. The youngest of twelve children, he was the *budidik*, the youngest, favored son. The dark space where we stood warmed as pride and love poured to him from his sisters. Winning approval from all these strong Filipino women was not going to be easy, and to be honest, not completely attainable. Finally, under his mother's proud and loving gaze, Philip blurted, "Ma, dis Christine, my friend." He stopped abruptly, seemingly unable to go on while time hung, suspended in air, as we waited for Mama's reply.

She lifted her head to see me, and her dark penetrating eyes saw into mine. Her voice was clear and her first words in broken English would never leave me. "My son is a poor boy...and you are not. Why you like marry him?" She did not pose the question in an arrogant or aggressive tone; it was simply a question.

My answer came without pause and I often reflect on the wisdom I was given on that day. "Yes," I said, "that may be true, but he will not always be a poor boy, will he? Things will change."

Her response was immediate as she cupped her hand to her mouth. A smile creased her frail face as she gave a knowing chuckle.

Why I responded as I did, I will never know. I could have said something typical like I loved him deeply because I did, passionately. That would have been a mistake. She was a Filipina, and as I have noted, from a distinct mountain tribe with a unique power to "see." She was also part Chinese. Her father had been a musician in Shanghai. Most of all, she was Ifugao, a spiritual people who understood so much more than the present moment. She understood destiny and as I would later understand, she could see our future manifested.

She must have realized that I knew this, too, and believed, as she did, that her son had tremendous talent and potential. She could already see it was safe to pass this life torch to me. The still air broke when someone called in singsong fashion from the kitchen. "Mangantayon."

We had our moment and went into the kitchen. I entered the bright room and the aroma of food intensified. An older man stood before a big pot placed in the center of the stove. Papa greeted me with an open heart, and I understood why Philip was such a good person. Here was the other integral half of this family. His father had an infectious way of laughing, not unlike his son's. He grinned when he spoke, his eyes sparkled, and the entire room responded. Papa wore a casual print aloha shirt buttoned second from the top. He turned from the waist as he continued to stir the steaming soup. Having his son home set a fixed expression of joy on his face and it seemed likely that this mid-day meal was special for their returning son. I surmised that I would have no problem with this man; somehow, I could see we had clicked already. Never mind that he'd missed all the drama in the hallway; no doubt his wife would fill him in later.

Philip pointed for me to sit by the window. He stood joking with Papa as I moved to a worn wooden table, painted many times with the current color resembling the gullet of a red rooster. In lieu of chairs, there were two

4 – Meeting Mama

benches. As I slid onto the wooden bench, the afternoon light flickered through the two windows each framed with red checkered curtains. One of the windows would not stay open and was propped with a wooden pole stuck in the frame. I imagined it had been that way for years. The curtains had faded from the bright sunlight and showed more wear on the bottom from the times wet hands would pull them aside to see the garden. Small loose threads dangled as the breeze played with the stray ends. I peered into the garden that overflowed with blooming orchids and the largest red anthurium I'd ever seen. All the plants grew in well-worn green pots set on large, dirt-stained wooden tables. Some thrived in the ground, but most were at waist level where they could be nurtured and transplanted. I thought, *ah, they are very serious about their plants, many a day and afternoon has been spent in this garden.*

I returned my gaze to the room and looked around. The walls had been painted a bright, shiny yellow, and inevitably, the red dirt from the field had settled into every crevice. Even with the curtains slightly soiled, the room imparted a festive quality. Open shelves attached to the walls held stacks of white china plates, bowls, and large mugs for coffee. On the top shelf, I glanced at a hazy glass punch bowl, a colorful ceramic chicken, and a dusty teapot with a design from the forties. *Her treasures, perhaps wedding gifts,* I thought.

In the center of the kitchen table sat a large glass that held spoons and forks. A steaming bowl of soup with vegetables and pork was placed on the table. Rice was served on the sideboard attached to the stove. The vegetables had an unfamiliar consistency for me. They all appeared to be fresh and homegrown, deep in color, with a texture very different from the Irish boiled potatoes, carrots, and other common vegetables I knew from my childhood. The strong smell of garlic, ginger root, and bay leaf filled the room as Papa ladled more soup into the bowl from the steaming pot.

Papa quietly prepared Mama's plate. He placed her rice in the center, a precisely scooped mound. He then ladled the soup from a white ceramic bowl decorated with a golden wheat design that had seen many meals. Philip followed suit and scooped rice onto my plate. Mama sat near the window, across from me. I could not keep my eyes from her face. She glowed, beaming like a proud bird surrounded by her family, all smiling and fussing about. They spoke pidgin English with many Ilocano words mixed in. The lines of age softened on her frail face in the natural glow of the diffused light, as golden as the yellow beams filtering through the curtains. Philip placed my plate before me and ladled the soup and vegetables onto my rice and then prepared his own plate. He sat between his parents, took a moment with eyes closed and intoned a pule (prayer) before the three began eating with gusto. But not everyone dug in. Each person in the room eyed me in silence.

Smiling to all present, I exclaimed, "Oh, it looks and smells wonderful."

None of the others moved to serve him or herself. I glanced at Philip with a questioning expression. He was engrossed, slurping his soup, showing his enjoyment of the meal. He looked up from his now half-empty bowl.

"They won't eat until Mama and Papa, and we have eaten. 'Das how!'"

Plus, Philip was the youngest, the *budidik*, and everyone knew he got away with everything.

5 - "Das How"

La'amaomao, The Wind Goddess,
"Das How,"
The time and condition, we cannot explain.
Artwork by Philip Sabado

5

We seemed to live suspended somewhere between this real world and another of compromise with a spirit world for which we must show respect. For my husband, this was the inevitable "das how," but for me, it felt as though I had entered a place very few go and experience. His mother had taught him these ways, no doubt a continuation from her childhood in the mountainous regions where her village always bartered with the spirit world for a peaceful life.

That catchphrase "das how," meaning "this is the way things are done," would be repeated at least a dozen times a day for any situation under this island sun. Once I became more comfortable with the family, I tried to understand the code of "das how." Most of them had a hard time explaining it. The phrase served as a point of no return. For example, in telling a tale, especially a spooky one, when you hit that unexplainable part, the inevitable "das how" would be the appropriate end. A shrug of the shoulders was a natural addition in any given circumstance.

Only Mama could explain the delicate weave that was the fabric of living in this pristine pineapple plantation camp on the ancient spiritual hill. I was told in a kind, patient way, "You may not believe or understand our ways or customs, but you must respect them." It was never appropriate to ask, "But, why?" The answer inevitably would be a predictable shrug of the shoulders and "das how." Including the shrug was not mandatory, it was a given, an involuntary rise and fall of the shoulders.

For most people, the menehune are the small ceramic figures sold in Waikiki curio shops. Again, myth crossed an invisible line when I overheard Phil's sister, Rosita, casually mention that the menehune would be playing ukulele on one particular moonlit night on Mo'omomi Beach a short distance from the camp. I wanted to go and see! I didn't understand what they told me. "No one sees them, cannot!" Their tone was final as all heads shook in a united movement. I protested and was met with the ubiquitous shoulder shrug and "das how." We had reached an impasse. Philip and his sister stared at each other as the silence floated like an ominous shroud. The meaning was clear. How do we explain this to her? Ah, another lesson, one that brought to mind the feeling of being a fish out of water, a saying that often reminded me of all I would need to learn and understand.

Years later, I would come to appreciate "das how" in a profound way. In its simplicity, it is that space between the words, the connection to what is spirit, to what we have no words for. Living in such a powerful spiritual place, Molokai is not only overwhelming, but humbling. Hawaiians and those from other cultures that followed them in the fields to work got it in a heartbeat. For me, though, it was akin to crying "Uncle!" or a guessing game where I would inevitably say, "I give!" The bigger picture is this: if you can connect to this culture and this land, it will silence you in a similar way as if sitting in the center of the most majestic cathedral.

I am humbled by this land and this family. In conversations with many mainland transplants who have lived here twenty or thirty years, I tell the story of "das how." Interestingly, they also shrug their shoulders, but say, "That's funny, I have never heard that term before." I smile and realize I have access to a semi-private local world. Life has provided me with this experience, and I can share "das how."

Eating lunch was an event that required resting afterward and everyone went to *elade* (relax). From the familiar tropics of the Philippines and the heat of mid-day Hawai'i, they continued to partake in their Spanish-style siesta. I was encouraged to go to one of the bedrooms and go moe moe (lie down to rest) on one of the bright quilts. I felt exhausted that first day and agreed. After all the traveling, the truck ride, and the highly charged emotional experiences, I fell into a deep sleep within moments. I would come to learn the ways Molokai could lull you into a feeling of rest and relaxation. Time does not exist, and the day passes with the gentle sway of the coconut palms as the orchid fragrance wafts through the window.

In between dreams, I became aware of being watched; the small hair on the back of my neck had triggered the response. Then I sensed many eyes surrounding me, though I heard no sounds. I opened my eyes a crack and saw the late afternoon sunlight that poured through the lace curtains. Speckled dots cast shadows across the room like a kaleidoscope. I opened my eyes. Standing before me were the brown-eyed children home from school surrounding my bed and watchiing me sleep.

When they saw I was awake they ran giggling into the next room. Their bare feet on the hardwood floor sounded like a small herd of elves. As my bare feet touched the wooden floor, I could hear their small voices speaking at once. "Uncle Phil, Uncle Phil, she pretty, she pretty...for one haole." I smiled to myself and stood slowly, allowing myself to awaken. The well-worn oiled floor felt cool on my toes. I leaned against the door and peered into the living room to see Philip's adoring nieces and nephews huddled around him like a gaggle of geese. They were too shy to look at me as Phil made introductions. Their silky ebony hair swung as they hid their faces, and their dark brown skin blushed a burnished gold.

Laughing aloud, Philip took control of the moment and said, "Now, you're going call her Auntie Chris." Giggling even harder, they sang in a chorus, "Aloha, Auntie Chris," as they ran outside down the wooden steps to meet and play with their friends on the red dirt road. Their beauty took my breath away. These were not the children from the morning ride, they were the younger ones still in elementary school.

After our short rest, we went to another sister's house. This time we walked. Philip took me on pathways through the hibiscus bushes between the houses. He was excited as if on a treasure hunt in search of his boyhood trails, all shortcuts from one sister's house to the next. An indentation in the russet, hard-baked soil showed where years of footsteps had worn a path. The passageways were still used by the nieces and nephews as well as other camp children, assuring that these traditions and secret pathways were passed down to the next generation.

There was more activity in this next house, and his sister, Eulogia, known as "Sister Lolly," in the camp, was close to Phil. She showed happy signs of being a bit weary in the warm afternoon with so many children running in and out. With each arrival and departure, the screen door clapped with a bang. I liked their house with its constant activity. The children were so simple, pure, and unselfish. Their best friends were each other, as if all you needed was family. These were all new experiences for me. In my childhood, there had only been my sister and me, my parents, Nanny (my mother's mother), and another grandmother. My childhood had no parallel whatsoever to this pineapple village, yet I loved it all.

As the apple of his mother's eye and as the youngest of children, Philip had lived a charmed life. He went anywhere he pleased in the camp while growing up. Each of his older sisters had married young and started their

5 – "Das How"

own families. At first, they all lived in one house, and each had a bedroom with her new husband and baby, which was economically sound and apropos of their culture. Eventually, they all had their own homes on different lanes in the camp. Philip could sleep at any of his sisters' homes whenever he chose—a week here, a couple of days at another sister's house, and so on. There was always a new niece or nephew to visit. More often the decision was based on the choice of what each sister had cooked for dinner.

Eulogia and her husband, Reyhino, an expert fisherman, took young Philip under his wing, teaching him about the ocean and survival in the endless miles of unexplored Molokai beaches and wilderness terrain. As a team, they would also hunt deer, pheasants, quails, and wild turkeys.

Ultimately, Philip would end up at home with Mama and Papa. After all, he was the *budidik*, the last-born son. Mama did not let him go very far; they were always together, and no one could separate them.

As an ongoing source of income to offset their struggling finances, Mama ran the camp laundry from the house. She collected bundles of soiled work clothes from the single men of the camp and returned them washed, pressed, and neatly folded.

As a young boy, Philip was one step behind Mama on the red dirt road. The wind would whip clouds of red dust as they delivered carefully tied bundles of folded shirts and pants wrapped in bleached cotton rice bags. These outings were great adventures. His *tata*s (older men in the camp) would always have extra coins for Phil, and the plantation store had a good stock of candies. Philip, as well as most of the kids in this plantation town, would lose their teeth to the plantation store candy. Dental care was never about repair; the dentist only came to the island once a month and just pulled rotten teeth.

His sisters shared that Mama nursed her youngest, my future husband, until he was four years old. Finally, too embarrassed to continue seeing this boy with his feet dangling to her knees as she held him, all the sisters agreed weaning was past due. They locked the boy in one room and Mama in another and made her promise to stop nursing him. Their physical connection was broken, but spiritually their bond lasted a lifetime.

Philip's given name was Alipio, and only Mama would use it. Many of the children had an English name as well as their Filipino name. Mama would bleach cotton rice bags to make his clothing. The young Alipio was always dressed well. Store-bought clothes only became available much later when the sisters worked in the camp general store. They spoke only the Ilocano language as they went from house to house in the quaint pineapple village. Time stood still in the pau hana (after work hours). Field workers finished at two o'clock in the afternoon having been in the fields since six a.m. They could while away the hours until dusk as their rice cooked for dinner.

Philip slept on futon mats on the floor, known in their language as *ikamen*, which were made of tightly woven abaca grass. As was the custom or economics, they all slept in one room, Mama and Papa on their mat, Philip, and his brother Eugene on another mat. When the sisters married, the newborn babies were rocked in a small hammock known as an *indayon*.

When Philip was chosen to study on Maui at Lahainaluna High School on a full scholarship, Mama adamantly refused to let him go. He was excited about living in the dormitories and participating in team sports. He asked every available person in the family to reason with her, but her answer was final, no, and that was that. Apparently while in the hospital, she'd seen many boys with injuries from sports. She was not to be deterred and would not send away her youngest son.

When he signed up for the Army, Mama was beside herself and stayed in her bedroom for days. Speaking in Ilocano, Papa stood at the locked door and tried to reason with her. All the family tried to convince her it was best for him to leave. When he left, she remained in her room, not able to bear the sight of him walking out the door. Once I understood more, I believed her heightened intuition was astute, fearing he would be injured.

Philip was grown and knew it was his time to experience adventure. Almost all his friends from Molokai High had signed up for the 9th "All-Hawai'i" Company. This was before the Vietnam War. Except for one friend, the other island boys would be called "Pineapple" for the next three years. Toward the end of his enlistment, orders came for Philip to go to Vietnam. He quietly filed the papers away until his hitch was up and happily returned to Mama and Papa.

Going to Vietnam would have involved reenlisting. He was offered a sweetened deal with a generous cash and promotion incentive, but to no avail. He had known many friends who had gone to Vietnam with no return, and perhaps he, too, would not have survived. He had an ally in this, the great Senator Daniel Inouye (Hawai'i), who proposed issuing a halt in recruiting Hawai'i boys, especially the local kids. Not unlike his experience during World War II as a part of the 442nd Infantry Regiment, he had seen unbelievable bravery. Local boys yearned to prove their loyalty as patriotic Americans. They pushed and tried harder, surging to the front, and suffering more losses than other states per capita.

Philip was devoted to his mother. I was keenly aware of his deep love for her, above anyone. I was not about to compete with his devotion at the start of our marriage, nor would I ever be jealous of it. In some ways I envied it. My parents were only children, and their childhoods were affected by poverty and a world war. My parents' world worked best when there were not too many people or distractions to complicate life. My sister and I learned to adjust within these parameters. Within my heart, I understood if my marriage were to succeed in this island paradise, I would need to join forces with Mama.

Phil had another family member whom he'd saved for last for me to meet, his cousin Jackie. Born in the same year as Phil, she'd married a boy from Ho'olehua. He was from a third generation paniolo (cowboy) family, a tradition brought to the islands by the Portuguese and Spaniards. The Hawaiians took to horses and cattle like fish to water. It was a natural connection that allowed them to be free in the land. Jimmy, Jackie's husband, was clearly Hawaiian yet had a distinctive French surname from one of the two large French descendant families on the island.

A story I heard told of a time when a French frigate had run aground on the outer reef of Molokai. It was said that two sailors were so rowdy they were thrown overboard in barrels. They rolled in with the surf and survived, swam ashore to stay, populated, and made Molokai their home. The two families rarely intermarried in those early years, though things changed in time, and thus, both have remained distinctive in appearance. The family our cousin married into was tall and lanky, and the other family was shorter and more robust.

The French frigate continued south to New Zealand where more Frenchmen would settle. From this, my niece told a *Believe It or Not!* story. Our Molokai family traveled to New Zealand on ranching business. As they drove around, they saw a name identical to theirs on a road post. The circumstance could not be ignored, and they decided to investigate. Molokai people are very humble, yet this was too intriguing. They drove up to the house and knocked on the door to say, "We are from the island of Molokai in Hawai'i, and we share the same last name." Here is where the story defies belief: the New Zealanders were the family of the twin that remained on that French frigate!

There was a local story that accompanied the relationship between niece and uncle. Philip's oldest sister, Magdalena "Maggie," had her daughter around the same time as Mama birthed Philip. Subsequently, they were nursed together by Mama. The two kids bonded. They would go to school together as classmates, yet she would have to address him in the culturally correct, respectful term for her uncle, Manong, even though they played together more like siblings. Their love for each other was deep and eternal.

I desperately needed a person besides Mama to help me bridge the enormous gaps in the cultural divide. Jackie was younger than Philip's sisters, who looked at me suspiciously. She proved to be a friend and confidant in the years to come. When I met them and their first-born daughters, they were in their first home on the shoreline to the left of the harbor in a thick kiawe grove. You could literally look out her front door and see sharks swimming inside the shallow waters of the reef where they would give birth.

Jimmy told an endearing story about that time. "You know us Hawaiians of Ho'olehua, we would always tease and taunt those Filipinos...until we saw the girls. They were beautiful!" His eyes shifted and he looked to his wife. She held his gaze, showing off her lovely smile. He spoke of befriending Auntie Rosy as an ally. "If auntie wanted that papaya up so high, I would be the one to climb that tree for her. I was the first to marry and come from the outside into this family, and then came the haole." He meant me. "Then came the Japanese," he said, referring to a cousin's wife.

We are truly Hawaiian, a United Nations bounded by love. This is Hawai'i, but more...this is Molokai!

Once on the mainland while Philip was still my fiancé, we'd gone to visit friends of my parents who had a gracious home. In a private moment, Phil pulled me to the side and asked, "How many people live here?"

"Only two, because their one son is in college."

He looked around wide-eyed in amazement. "Do you know they could have five families living with them? Aren't they lonely in this large house?"

I laughed, but I realized changes would have to be made in small increments. I could not live and adjust to a Filipino lifestyle all at once.

We returned to Honolulu and city life soon after our idyllic weekend. The next time I saw Philip's parents, they came to visit us in Honolulu. Mama shared a story I will always remember. As she spoke her eyes were centered on me and full of spark, laughter, and honesty.

"All my life," she said, "I never see my boy not happy, his whole life, he not sad, never once. When you left Molokai for that first time, he was sad and never smiled. Dat how I know…you the one." She laughed heartily, cupping her hand to her mouth as was her way, enjoying the moment. My initial nervousness was gone after that.

I guessed it was okay to confess that Philip and I were in love, and perhaps everyone could see this. Young love is transparent, marked by shy touches and side glances. Again, this was Mama's way of passing the banner to me. I was his future, and we would both love and have him in our own way. Her statement still amazes me. What other mothers could say she had never seen her child "not happy ever?"

Mama took me into her heart. Intuitively, she must have known this would not be easy. There was much for me to learn in a short time. She spoke slowly as her eyes communicated to her son the seriousness of her message. "You have to teach her our ways." She paused to let her words gain importance. "It is not her fault she does not know or understand. Teach her our ways."

Shyly, he looked down and said, "Yes, Ma."

This was not spoken in English, this was in their language, and piece by piece I was learning. The other half of this equation was this: I was willing and eager to learn, first their native tongue, then the cultural nuances.

The contrast to my suburban life could be measured in polarities. There was love in my Irish Catholic home, but different than the Molokai families, which proved deep and unconditional. In time, I would learn about babies, where to walk, and more important, how to understand the delicate balance of spirit and magic. I was discovering *mana* (one's own inherent spiritual power), through the love of this man and his family, as well as the world of

Filipinos and Hawaiians from the perspective of ritual and spirit—and I was learning the Molokai way.

Mama reminded Philip many times that it was his job to teach me. Then she would turn and scold him in their Ilocano language. The "das how" was enough of a lesson to walk this unpredictable path with him. Mama knew best and was keen to watch for the moment to help me in this different land.

An old Chinese woman who lived on Molokai once taught me a lesson. She leaned in close as if she were whispering a great secret. "When you go to Molokai, be stupid, let them teach you. Even if you know, allow yourself to be taught their special ways. This is the place to learn to listen, nuff." Her example was convincing. "Say this: 'Auntie, how you grow that one, so 'ono in soup? What is your secret?' Then they will give you their all." The ticket was so simple—just be humble.

Molokai people grow impatient with those who come to teach them their outside ways. This was made clear during the hula festival held on Molokai each year in May known as Hula Piko. Many outsiders came to experience Molokai during the festival. I commented to my sisters-in-law that this was a good thing because many people would come and add to the prosperity of the island. After all, everyone struggled financially, and tourists brought money.

She was silent a moment and then spoke in her quiet way, "Yeah, but, what...they going come back?" After a pause she added, "Here on Molokai, we are 'ohana, we are family, more bettah we stay like that."

They meant Molokai was a good place to visit for a day or so, after which they would prefer you leave. I understood in a heartbeat, as if I had been sitting with Mama and she wanted me to understand their way of seeing. This was their place and things "going change if others start coming in with ears that cannot hear or listen."

After Philip and I had our initial visit on Molokai, we would return to Honolulu and prepare for our visit to the mainland to meet my parents. When it was time to say goodbye, Mama gave me an endearing compliment. She stood at the door that opened to the red dirt road and our future, and with a chuckle in her voice she said, "Good you stay a little bit big." I'd always fussed about my weight, yet she was sincere. "Bumbye your parents goin' tink we no feed you." I smiled at the irony and waved my goodbyes to my new family.

6 - My Glendale Hometown

Dad on the porch of their home.
Artwork by Philip Sabado

6

 I grew up in Glendale and consider it my hometown. My family lived comfortably in what was then a small community over the hills from infamous Hollywood, a ten-minute drive north of smoggy bustling Los Angeles. Griffith Park and Silver Lake created a buffer between these communities. I remember the visage of driving over the Los Feliz hills and descending into a cloud of smog that was visible from above the Los Angeles Basin.

My mom's pastime was looking for houses for the family. They never purchased one until we left home. On one occasion, I commented that I liked a particular house, and she said, "Oh no, that is way too expensive for us, that house is thirteen thousand dollars!" Those numbers stuck with me, funny.

Rarely in my youth did the smog enter the communities in the outlying urban sprawl of what was commonly known as the Valley. We were not in the Valley but clung to the pristine hillside. As a child in the fifties our town was quiet, in my estimation near picture-perfect, and predominantly Caucasian. The only people of color were either Mexican or Black, and at that time, the hired help. They would arrive daily on the city buses as the sun broke over the mountains. I had heard about a so-called "sundowner law" that stated all Colored people were to be out of town by six p.m. Coincidentally, that was when the last bus left for Los Angeles. My father once called the police because a Black person was walking on our street. His question to the officer was a point of fact. "No Black people live here, so what was he doing in our neighborhood?" I asked my father about the phone call. He seemed to think that was the natural thing to do. Within minutes, a squad car arrived and after a brief chat, the man was whisked away.

In the early 1950s, the trolley cars were referred to as electric cars. Clunky wires were strung above the traffic lights and crisscrossed the main street of Brand Boulevard. The trolley had a long cable that attached from the center of the car to the bigger cables that conducted electricity. As they rumbled down the street, sparks would fly as the cables connected and were energized. All the while you could hear the zzzt! of the electric current connecting. At night, bursts of light flew out like mini fragments of Fourth of July fireworks.

The city hung swags of Christmas lights from one side of the street to the other. Large, decorative stars and twisted silver trim glittered above our heads. Giant lights, five times the size of regular Christmas tree bulbs had been twisted around the silver foil and lit at dusk.

The Alex Theatre sat in the epicenter of town. In the grand Hollywood era, the theatre had a long walkway and may have had a premier or two. An iconic towering candlestick at the front of the theatre acted as a beacon and dwarfed nearby buildings. The theatre is still there and showing some age, but for new generations to enjoy.

As a child while waiting with Nanny for the trolley, I noticed a swastika design forged in the metal around the base of the lampposts along the city streets. I commented that it did not seem right. She said the lampposts had been put in way before the war and the design did not mean the same thing. I shook my head; it sure looked the same to me. (The lampposts were installed between 1924 and 1926.)

I'd heard from my Grandmother Donegan that in the early forties the American Nazi Party and the Ku Klux Klan both had headquarters in Glendale. My father told us about the time the clan burned a cross on my Uncle Charlie's lawn on Maple Street because they were Irish Catholics.

The first Black person I ever saw, besides the housekeepers waiting for their buses, was at a Sears loading dock where we bought our first Philco television. As we returned from a day of shopping with Nanny and our bus climbed the hills to the north side of town, I used to stare out the window while another bus carrying the Colored help was rolling out of town. Women stood at the bus and trolley stops dressed in their starched white uniforms trimmed with lace collars, and often wore a pointed hat of some sort. California developed a liberal reputation, but at another time, things were quite different in secluded communities. When the Watts riots ignited the city to the south, the next destination reported to burn would be Glendale—a little known fact. Police officers responded to the threat and were stationed at every corner in Glendale. Happily, when I was a teenager, Glendale would change with the times—in part because of my mother.

My sister Kathy was about a year and a half younger than I, and we were very different. She had dark curly hair and deep brown eyes. Mine are blue, and I am a tall blonde. Upon reflection, we were always separate in our ways while we lived under one roof. In school we had different friends and activities. As adults, our relationship ran from cool to tepid. Happily, as we have grown older, we bonded and are close as only sisters can and should be.

It is funny how memory can stick like a gooey gumdrop left in the sun. I remember the phone number from the house where I grew up: Citrus 1273. I remember walking down the street coming from Mass with my dad and sister early on Easter Sunday morning; I may have been four. On that day, I wore a red checkered dress, and a straw hat with a red grosgrain ribbon and a big rose in the brim. I held a snow globe, and my father who stood tall above me, told me not to break it, yet it slipped from my grasp at that very second. The glass shards flew and they all looked at me in disbelief.

I grew up in a yellow house in a middle-income neighborhood just off the corner of Glenwood. Three large camellia bushes bloomed by our large bay window. There was red, pink, white, and my favorite, a lovely mix called candy cane. I'd heard Nanny brag about the poinsettias on the side of the house that had red foliage the size of a dinner plate. We kept the lawn neat with a manual push mower and edge trimmer. A hidden bee at the base of a weathered faucet by the front steps stung me and I was persuaded to never walk in the wet grass or sloppy mud with bare feet ever again.

The bay windows with white Venetian blinds were cleaned monthly. At holidays, we rolled them up to show our neighbors the large, hand-picked pine that was our pride and joy. Not many visitors came to this house where we lived for over twenty years. My parents didn't have siblings and preferred being just us, our small nuclear family, Nanny included.

We walked a straight and narrow path—it was the fifties, after all. I went to Catholic school and my parents both worked. Nanny took up the slack at home with cooking and cleaning. Both of my parents were native to the East Coast, so we had no other family nearby. My parents had each other and a handful of business friends who came for an occasional dinner party. My memories are vivid scenes. We had pale beige Naugahyde furniture and chintz fabrics, nothing too extravagant or flashy. In hindsight, I had a traditional childhood considering my background, but curiously, I always felt out of place, like a picture slightly out of focus. No one's fault, per se, I just knew this lifestyle would be temporary.

I was loved and respected as a child. No one abused me or tortured me. This pristine time was defined by that new box—television. Ours sat near the center of the wall beneath the bay windows. One of my first memories—before I could even walk or talk—was sitting under our large wooden dining room table. I had crawled there. It was dark and cool, and smelled of oiled wood. Nanny saw me and gave me an oil cloth. She said in an East Coast accent, "Aw, good, now you can clean and work! Dust the table legs. This will be your first job." And so it was. There were always chores and jobs to do. I carry that lesson to this day, as do my children—a strong New England work ethic.

Once I overslept and rushed uphill two blocks to catch the bus. I heard my name and saw my father waving to me from the corner. I ran back to see what he wanted. Out of breath, I approached him thinking there was an emergency of some sort. "You did not make your bed." I protested that I would miss the bus and be late. Without blinking he said, "Another bus will follow, finish your room." I followed him home, pulled my bed together properly, returned to the bus stop without a note for class and waited until the next bus huffed to a stop on Kenneth Road. I have no memory of ever being driven to school. My sister and I took the bus or walked the two and half miles each way all twelve years. Was that mean or strict? I never thought about it. In my day, we called it character building. I never received a car for graduation as many of my friends did. I smile when I see kids driven to school these days. My kids walked, too, but not always. Phil was a softy and drove when they would be late or if it rained. No complaints: I have always been a hard worker, ask anyone who knows me. I earned every penny and dime to fulfill my dream of moving to Hawai'i. I attribute this to my youth and that oil cloth under the table.

Years later I watched Archie Bunker on the TV sitcom All in the Family. *Everyone laughed at his ignorance and arrogant comments. I remember telling Phil between segments, "He is just like my dad." Edith, to some degree, was Mom, complacent and compliant. I was Michael, the rebel, always up for a debate. No wonder I'd saved every nickel and dime to leave the day after graduation. My father coined an oft repeated saying: "Christine, you would argue with God."*

My parents rented during my childhood years. My sister and I never understood why buying a house was never an option. The landlords, a Mormon family, lived a block and a half up the road. As Catholics, we were clearly different, and Mom was on guard as she delivered the check, leery they were out to convert us.

We had a large National Geographic map pinned to the wall in our breakfast room with red thumbtacks securing the four corners. It folded out from the magazine to take up almost the entire wall. Dinners were never boring at our house. Looking at the world map, we talked long after the dishes were cleared about the news and travel. As a preteen, I looked for the small dots in the ocean and saw tiny Hawai'i, a hopeful dream. Ahhh, destiny!

In the late fifties, the draw of Hawai'i was akin to the pull and instinct that impels salmon to swim upstream. Hula-Hoops and skateboards were the rage. At fifteen, with a work permit in hand to finance my life after high school, I took an across town bus from school to the employment office in Glendale to check on job openings. I did this daily until I got a part-time job after school as a dinner cook at an old folk's home in Burbank. I wanted the job so badly; I lied and told them I cooked at home. I got the job, but Nanny, who was the real cook, talked me through the recipes. I made $1.60 an hour and saved all the money like a church mouse piling crumbs in a dark corner. I never bought a Beatles album or even a blouse. As a young woman of seventeen, having saved for four years, my nickels and dimes totaled $725.00. I felt like I was the wealthiest person alive. I stashed away money from odd jobs and babysitting for fifty cents an hour since I was thirteen. My mother gave me a hundred dollars for my high school graduation. It came with a note that said: "I would never send you away. This money will bring you home." Nanny was in my corner as her journey had been vast, bringing her as a single mother from Austria to America. She understood my drive and the journey I would begin.

My new job was a couple of miles from my high school. One experience at work would stay with me for life and I still quiver at the memory. As I prepared the trays for the dinner service, a small transistor radio in the old-fashioned box style, sat on a window that looked out onto an alley. The Beatles broke the stillness of the dinner hour.

We had a Black janitor, a cordial, middle-aged gentleman. All the other workers were women in white starched uniforms and peaked caps, and it seemed most of them had a Southern accent. They would tease this man in a sexually demeaning way by saying things like: "Hey, Joe, what are you gonna clean that pipe with? Is it long enough?" He would laugh, but the comments were obviously derogatory. This was the late sixties, but what could he have done? I'm sure he needed the job.

On this day the Beatles' music was interrupted when an announcer broke in with the news that Dr. Martin Luther King had been shot. I was stunned. My mom had been a devout believer and follower of the Civil Rights Movement and marched with him in the South. I turned up the radio, clinging to every word, and then I moved from the kitchen to the hallway, vacant of patients or staff. I saw Joe slumped against the wall, heaving in great sobs. His head rested on his arm as his body convulsed in grief. My hand went to my heart, feeling his pain and anguish. My other hand covered my mouth and hushed my gasp.

I heard laughter and the pop of a cork from the opposite end of the hall. The nurses were celebrating the event with bubbly. "Well, that bastard is gone for good now," they cheered. Joe had heard as well but could do nothing. I shrank back into the darkened kitchen, perplexed by the two worlds I had found myself caught between; I, too, needed the stupid job. Little did I know that this dichotomy would affect and influence my life. I was sixteen and needed to mature to find my courage. I had felt paralyzed and shaken to my core. I resolved to move on to a place where such thinking and evil would not exist.

My blue eyes came from my mother whose eyes were a pure sky blue, while mine are more smoky blue, not as remarkable, but nice. My paternal grandmother, my sister and my father all hailed from the black Irish with their dark eyes and dark curly hair. Mom's hair had a tight natural curl, and my sister inherited this trait.

I asked Nanny if their side had any other nationalities since they both had such tight curls. She turned from her cooking at the stove and gave me a look that could have frozen fish. She and my mom were European, which as I mentioned earlier was not elaborated upon. Their Catholic faith was their chosen identity and the secret of their heritage remained.

Nanny was the cook and general keeper in our house. She was always there for my sister and me while Mother worked full time. This was not Nanny's burden. She told us often that we were her joy, and we knew she loved us. We would hear her on the phone telling her church friends what the family was up to. Later, as my sister and I grew, Nanny got to travel and take cruises with her female friends from church. Nanny was born in 1896 and could boast that she had seen the turn of the century. In general, I believe she had a full life.

Many years before I lived in the Islands, my family visited Hawai'i on multiple occasions as tourists. Like millions before us, we stayed in Waikiki and did the predictable tourist things, staying near the International Marketplace. Waikiki in those days was a tropical adventure. Commercially, Waikiki fulfilled all the fantasies one thought Hawai'i to be.

On my arrival as a young preteen, I felt as if I had been struck by a thunderbolt. I was in love with Hawai'i the same as one falls in love with another person. When I returned home to California and entered high school, I wrote "Hawai'i" all over my yellow folders and decorated my book covers with detailed fine-line drawings of Diamond Head and swaying palms.

As a young adult and avid reader, I often chose history books. Upon reflection, I realized that I was born at the end of the war years that had dominated the world. I was born on Christmas Day in 1949 late at night. Mom said she pushed hard because she wanted a Christmas baby. After the insanity of Hitler, Pearl Harbor, and the Korean War, the fifties must have seemed like a bright time. Elvis performed in Hawai'i and made films there. TV sets were being bought and installed in almost every home and would soon be occupying the world stage. Shows such as **Father Knows Best** *and* **Leave It to Beaver** *redefined our American culture. Tract homes and an updated Sears catalog contributed to our American dream. In the early sixties, the Cuban Missile Crisis made us freeze in place and the following year, President Kennedy was killed. I was a happy child, but an undefined agenda pulled me in another direction. For some, life was idyllic. It was a façade, after all, the world was far from ideal or peaceful. Only the TV sitcoms and Westinghouse commercials colored that delusion.*

Years later, when Philip and I and our family visited my parents, we were walking through the new mall in Glendale when Severina, who was four at the time, tugged on my sleeve and asked me why everyone was staring at us. We were so accustomed to our interracial family in the islands that I was surprised anyone took special notice of us. I thought a moment on how to answer and discarded the obvious reason. I said, "Oh, I hadn't noticed. It must be because we are so attractive." She smiled innocently and said, "Okay," and that was that.

In the Catholic high school, I attended one town over in Burbank, there was only one Black student, and she was in my class. I saw her at lunch sitting alone. I was on my feet in a heartbeat and asked her why she sat alone and to join me. I offered to show her some of my artwork. We became best friends for our four years of high school and then lifelong friends.

Every day this girl left school early, and I didn't know why. She explained—some forty years later—that one afternoon while waiting for the bus that would take her to Pacoima, some rednecks pulled up. They asked why she was in their town and threatened her. Their message was simple yet terrifying: Get out of their town. When her father came to address his concern with Mother Superior, she thought he'd come to apply for the janitor position. They decided to allow her to catch an early bus and avoid the racists.

Our parents respected our friendship and agreed to sleepovers at each other's houses. We did this many times over the four years. If the sleepovers were an issue, we were not aware of it. We were best of friends and that was all that mattered.

Years later, I learned we had something in common: both of us had been born in Glendale. By some fluke, the closest hospital to their home was in Glendale. Her father was stopped at the hospital door because no one believed he had a newborn Black child in Glendale Memorial. My friend's mother was fair-skinned and at birth, so was she. Her father was dark and was not allowed to enter the hospital. They had told him it was not possible that a Black man or child could be in this hospital. He stood his ground. He was not arrested or run out of town.

Her family invited me to attend her debutante ball for her sweet sixteen. As a California girl, the idea of a ball of any sort was new to me. I was immersed in the Beach Boys and the Beatles, not traditions from the Old South. It was held at the Santa Monica Civic Auditorium, and I was the only White girl among the hundreds if not thousands of guests and family, quite intimidating for me. While still in the lobby of the large auditorium, I took a step closer to her mother and nervously said, "I am really so honored that you invited me." I did not feel very welcomed at that moment in the auditorium, but her mother warmly assured me that I was their guest.

My mother enrolled me in art classes when I was six. Early on, she and I would pour over art books by lamplight after dinner. This was usually after she purchased a new coffee-table book. She would quiz me on the masters' names and the period they painted. In this game she'd invented, she'd cover the artwork title and artist's name with her hand, and I would guess the artist and title by the style and period.

Books fueled my curiosity. I was not an A student but devoured certain books. The library was at the corner of our street, walking distance, and I went through many library cards—they just wore out. I would watch a movie and say, "I'll bet that is even a better book" and the next day I would order it or check it out.

My favorites in the beginning were driven by my passion for history, books by Michener and Leon Uris. I'd seen QB VII *as a miniseries and knew it would be a great book. Afterward, I read everything he wrote. When I read* Mila 18 *about the Warsaw Ghetto in Poland, I was smitten with good writing and fell in love with the compelling characters. I read it three times before I finished the last page. I knew they would all die and I could not bear it. My eldest son, Paulo, was also a good reader and had a similar experience. On the third try, he finished. History was just good gossip!*

When I was young, Mom chose to send me, and not my sister, to a summer camp that had an exchange program. Camp David was for Jewish children from the Los Angeles and San Fernando Valley area. Why she chose to send me remained a mystery. It took many years to fully understand her intentions. In this place, I learned to dance the hora and was introduced to new foods, all kosher. I thrived because I always felt more comfortable with those who were dramatically different, yet in some ways the same as me.

In the sixties, Mom went outside the city to find experiences for us that did not exist in Glendale. Moving was never an option, and besides, Glendale was a beautiful town.

When I brought my dark-skinned Island boy home for Christmas as my soon-to-be fiancé, I joked that I had to sneak him in at night—even though it was not all a joke. I had never told him about the backward, ignorant side of Glendale.

Today the city has dramatically changed. Armenians, as a group, selected Glendale as their destination from thousands of miles away. Glendale is now known as the Armenian center. A new mall, and many shops and restaurants line the main streets. As I have returned over the years, I'm happy to have seen the face of the city change to one that is multiracial and intercultural.

In my youth most of the churches in Glendale were Protestant and the dominant nationalities were Northern Europeans, Germans, and Swedes. Two Catholic churches and one Jewish synagogue completed the city. I attended the Catholic school in the next town because we were officially in that parish.

In the fifties, Catholic families were required to send their children to Catholic schools. No excuses! I suspect if you could not afford the tuition, arrangements were available. I went to this school for twelve years and had the unique experience of being taught and disciplined by nuns who wore full black habits. I never knew any bullies or was ever bothered. The Catholic schools handled it this way: you paid a yearly tuition and if you were expelled, you were not refunded. Imagine what it was like going home to parents who had to deal with misbehavior and then had to send their child to public school.

Most Sisters came from Ireland, and they were known as BVM's—Sisters of the Blessed Virgin Mary. We would always know them as the Black Veiled Monsters. In the fifth grade, more than once I saw a baseball bat come out of the corner to discipline unruly boys.

For some strange reason our uniforms resembled those worn in World War I. Nanny, who was an excellent seamstress, sewed all the uniforms for my sister and me for those twelve years. She may have been the only one to go to the warehouse in Los Angeles to buy up bolts of fabric.

Old Monsignor Keating had a strange slant on patriotism, a twist on the semblances of Cardinal Bellarmine from the sixteenth century and Thomas Jefferson. He gave the same patriotic speech about these two men from different eras at least a hundred times.

My father's family immigrated to Boston with other countrymen fleeing the Irish Potato Famine. Our name was originally Dunnigan spoken with a roll and brogue. It was changed on the docks by an immigration officer, so the pronunciation was simpler. There were perhaps three or four pages of Donegan's in the Boston and New York City phone books.

My father set the theme for our family by bringing in Old World traditions. His family's claim to fame was his mother had worked for Joe Kennedy when Kennedy held sway on the Boston docks. Not surprisingly, Kennedy hired the Irish, in part because no one else would in those days.

Both my parents were from poor European backgrounds and to them, education was the only way out of the war and postwar era. This was communicated to my sister and me in many ways. As she tucked us in at night, my mother would ask about our goals and plans, wondering, "How did we see ourselves as adults?" I never reflected on how progressive she was until later. This was her way of lighting the torch for our future.

My paternal Irish grandfather was a large man with wavy sandy-blond hair. His people hailed from Donegal in Northern Ireland, but my father was quick to point out we were not Orangemen or Protestants. My father schooled my sister and me in the basics of Irish politics, which were built on religious bias hundreds of years old.

Later in life, I realized how important it was to show my father I was brave and could be strong. Daddy developed a theory with his psychology training that pain existed only in your mind. To illustrate this point, he had endured all his dental work with no painkillers or Novocain. As a child, I went to the dentist and in a moment of bravery wanted to prove I could be like him, but I was stupid! It hurt like hell! From this, I was able to pull on strengths I never realized. I felt the pain but would never let on. I still have a hard time going to the dentist and I make sure they give me double shots. As a child, I think I pulled it off. Impressing my father was my primary goal as was the emotion I felt that went with it.

When I was six or seven, I had an old-fashioned red scooter with four wheels and a wobbly handle to steer. Its redwood footboard was chipped and worn. Grass and weeds grew in the sidewalk cracks and helped me focus as I picked up speed. I would ride down the block where there was a steep ramp that connected the school and the large playground.

One day as dusk was setting in, I decided on one last ride. I skidded on the gravel, was thrown off, and rolled down the steep ramp. I was a bloody mess at the bottom with gravel embedded in my lips, and my face and knees shredded. My two front teeth had broken in half, exposing the nerve. I staggered home and Nanny immediately called my parents.

The Irish are stoic and are known for their few words. As I waited to be taken to the doctor, my father sat next to me. His head and body seemed to sag with the weight of what he was about to say. He stuttered a moment and told me he was really sorry this had happened to me. The moment was so startling, I moved away from my pain to see how much effort it took for him to say the word "sorry." He shook his head to confirm his regret. I only heard him say this once in my life. This moment stood out as an example of the differences I would appreciate later in my new married life. I felt as if I had migrated from a cold distant north into an embracing environment full of color and caring. My parents loved me all they could, I knew that then as I do now, but there were oceans of difference between these cultures and worlds.

My mother and her mother, Nanny, converted to the Catholic faith when my mom was thirteen years old. They were devout Catholics, as most converts are. Nanny worked most of her life at the Holy Family Church as the cook for the priests. She mostly served the boiled Irish foods familiar to the priest and my father from their homeland.

Once I watched intently as she prepared the items for Mass, pouring the wine from the squared-off, dark amber bottles. I noticed the wine was kosher (Manischewitz). I looked to her questioningly. She shrugged and said, "Oh, they like the flavor." I found out she bought the wine. I learned later that in her youth she had been a kosher cook for doctors' families to support herself prior to moving to California in the forties with my mother.

As a child, I asked why we did not have a housekeeper. Other families in town had hired help. Nanny said that when she was a child her family always had a woman that came in or often lived with her family. In the early 1900s, this was usually a Black housekeeper. After a moment of reflection, her comment was matter of fact. "Well, that is what your mother gets by marrying the Irish." Her point was clear: she and my mother were not Irish. Nanny and her family emigrated from Austria to England in the late 1800s, and then to America. Ultimately, they would settle in the Chesapeake Bay area of Baltimore.

I was aware from a young age that my ancestors on Mom's side were

Jewish. In her First Communion photo, at age thirteen, she was older than most communicants. I asked her why she was so big in the picture. Most kids receive communion at six or seven. Nanny's European past was never spoken of, but there were clues my mother would impart to me through my youth. After I read Michener's *The Source*, I told her that if I could choose, I would be Jewish. Perhaps I was moved by the story of an evolving people caught in persecution throughout the ages. She replied with certainty in her voice, "That is because you are. But we will not speak of it with your father." After that time, she created opportunities for me that gave me insight into that world and gave me her menorah. That summer I went to the Jewish camp.

She told me a story that made her feel like she had passed through a forbidden net. Her best friend while young was a woman named Ruth Brown. Ruth was a blue-blooded Protestant with financial means. Mom may have lived with their family in Connecticut for a short period while Nanny assembled helmets in New York City during World War II. On weekends, they went to the local country club. There was a sign near the gate that said: No Jews Allowed. Mom told the story as if she were telling a dark secret. "I felt so guilty being there. What if they found out? I recorded all these memories, perhaps for posterity.

It has been said that if you live with an Irishman, the entire house will function as an Irish home. If I were to summarize the influences I carry to this day from my parents, I could affirm an element known as the New England work ethic. This was a huge part of our culture. Since both of my parents came from the East, a laid-back California lifestyle did not set in for my sister and me. Idle time was never an option. I cannot just sit. I have two or three projects going at all times, sometimes more.

Glendale never felt right. I would choose to live in an entirely different place and would never look back. My family would confirm that I was unusual. I began using chopsticks for no apparent reason and persuaded my Nanny to cook rice. I insisted on leaving my shoes at the door and obtained a Hawaiian-English dictionary at ten years old and began to memorize the words. I felt as if a sheer veil separated me from a distant past and I would try to grasp it before it slipped away like a wet bar of soap.

Instead of listening to the Beatles, I started memorizing Russian gypsy music and had phonetically taught myself Yiddish and Russian from listening to Theodore Bikel and other Israeli singers. My father's taste in music was eclectic and influenced mine. For my high school prom, I wore an Indian sari the turquoise color of a tropical ocean. We'd been on vacation to the Caribbean, and I'd found a small shop that sold saris. I begged my mom to buy it and she did. When the shop owner offered to show me how to wrap it in the traditional style, I stopped her and did it perfectly. I never felt strange about myself, merely that I had landed in the wrong place and belonged somewhere else.

During our second Hawaiian vacation when I was in high school, United Airlines went on strike and the Red Cross set up cots for the long wait. A local girl slept across from me on the floor in the Hawaiian terminal. Gloria and I became instant friends and eventually pen pals. She was not even traveling, just seeing a friend off. Gloria was a Hawai'i -born Filipino girl. Her wish was to live in California, just as mine was to live in the islands. We struck a deal that upon my graduation we would switch families.

When the time came, I booked my trip to leave my home days after graduation. Boarding and departure felt like my passage to the future, and like a honu, the great sea turtle, I never looked back, only forward. Gloria and I never considered how our families were completely different culturally and financially. Gloria's mother was divorced and working full time days at the Navy PX at the Pearl Harbor Naval base and as a night barmaid at the Manila Bar on Hotel Street. Conversely, my parents were professionals, doctors from an upper-middle-class neighborhood.

Gloria moved to San Francisco one block from Haight-Ashbury in 1968, its heyday. She lived in a Catholic convent for working girls (of all places) and got a secretarial job in town. Days after my high school graduation, I went to visit Gloria in San Francisco before I went to live with her mother in Kalihi, known then as the roughest part of Honolulu. Switching families was my destiny and the beginning of my orientation to Filipino life and culture.

Movies of the day glamorized LSD and marijuana. As I walked the San Francisco streets, I saw bodies sprawled along dirty sidewalks. These were kids my own age who were off in some drug-induced la-la land. Young people coming off harder drugs were nearby in new medical rescue centers. I had no interest in drugs or the drug experimental culture. I had my sights set elsewhere and dreamed every night of palm trees, warm people with smiling faces and brown skin, and swimming in clear blue waters. I was obsessed with the move and my ambitious savings for the last four years had manifested that destiny.

As I reflect on my decision about drugs, the choice was clear because of an experience my father and I shared when I was young. As director of the Los Angeles County mental hospital my father would routinely check the wards. On occasion we visited him at work and would go out to lunch. The county hospital in midtown Los Angeles was a gritty mid-city experience. The contrast between this section of town and our well-ordered white picket lives in Glendale was undeniable. My memory of the mental wards is as sharp today as when I was six or seven years old. Even then, I felt a deep compassion that has stayed with me.

I had become accustomed to seeing the many old and confused people looking off into space or facing a wall. On one day I followed my father as he made his rounds, walking closely by his side and observing all around me. This was not the first time I'd walked with him, and as usual, I prayed for the patients during Mass. On this day, I saw the old people, but then I saw younger patients, teenagers and young adults who were well-dressed. These people looked like me, except they wandered about, lost and confused, or sat staring off into space or talking to themselves.

I tugged on my father's jacket and asked with childlike innocence, "Daddy, who are all these kids? Why are they here?"

He continued walking with charts in hand and answered in a matter-of-fact way, not realizing the impact this would have on my life. "Oh, this is from the new drug craze. These kids experiment with pills and LSD. They don't realize they won't come back again, as normal."

"Never?" I gasped; my eyes agape. "That is, it for their life? Will they ever be like normal kids again?"

"Once you destroy certain brain cells, they do not regenerate. These people will go to a home or an institution somewhere, or maybe they will die early if they are lucky, but this is life for them forever."

The word "forever" hit the hardest. I was devastated. The moment solidified in my mind like footprints implanted in wet cement. I would never take such a chance or gamble with my life in that way. I believed that drugs could never be any worse. Little did I know more powerful and lethal drugs were waiting in the wings as the new century drew near.

I once heard about an experiment that had kids walk through a prison to deter them from a life of crime. For me, walking through the mental ward in 1967 was such an experience. Fifteen minutes before lunch in a dark hospital ward was all it took.

After seeing the young people in Haight-Ashbury, it confirmed what I had seen earlier in Los Angeles. I was never tempted to experiment. At parties if someone offered me drugs, I passed. Strange as it may sound, I never felt any pressure.

I was never tempted as a teenager to drink alcohol either. At my confirmation, I took what was known in Catholic school as the pledge. You would pledge in church not to drink until you were twenty-one. This was not a hard choice since my paternal grandfather suffered from alcoholism. I saw him violently drunk, and that one episode left me terrified. I ran from my grandparents' house on Central Avenue, deserting my little sister and never returned. When my grandfather died, I had no tears. I could not bear to think of my father's childhood, imagining him living with such insanity. He must have made the same decision on some level because I never saw my parents drink any alcohol as we grew up.

My mother corrected me when I told the story. "Your grandfather was not an alcoholic; he was just Irish and drank every day!"

My family met Philip at Christmastime in the first year we started dating. To know Philip is to love him—it's that simple. My father confirmed this when he took me aside and said, "This man has no meanness in him; he is a fine person. If this marriage fails, I will hold you responsible." At that first meeting, my mother was clearly spell-bound and seemed to hang on Phil's every word. She was crazy about him then and still is (in heaven).

They shared a great respect and love for art and each other. They clicked immediately and could communicate on many levels. Through the years she bought him canvas and oils when we did not have the resources to do so.

My father's mother was quite a different story. She was haughty and arrogant. Her hair was fire-engine red, and she wore colorful print dresses made of chintz and voile on her slim figure. She exuded a sense of class distinction, different from the Irishman she'd married. When I brought Philip home that Christmas, she sat through the entire dinner and never set her black Irish eyes on him. She turned to me, asking with Philip present, "What happened to that nice Irish boy you used to see?"

Daddy loved to tease and taunt her and gave it right back. "Well, Mother, how about Philip here? He's a fine handsome young man." His comment was met with a silent glare.

"Pauley," she snapped, "do not be obnoxious."

Time can change some things but not others. When this same Irish grandmother saw my first child, Paulo, the most adorable baby, she commented, "The devil has black eyes as well."

My Parents' First Date, San Gabriel Mission, California, 1948.

I was happy and fulfilled mentally and physically with Philip. After some time, my family commented that my new husband did not seem to be physically affectionate with me. When we dated, he did not hold my hand or want to kiss me in public. Sometimes I would tug on his arm and force him to kiss me when we were out, but he was never overtly affectionate or comfortable doing this. I knew he loved me and when we were alone, he was passionate beyond my dreams. However, kissing and carrying on in public was haole style and not what he was accustomed to. I came to realize that it was unnecessary to exhibit our affection to the world.

I suspect that Philip's undemonstrative behavior came from the Asian influence of his home. He always told me that couples who "make big show, not going last." He was right. All our friends who could not keep their hands off each other in public had relationships that fizzled out in a couple of years and divorced.

I watched as his family reunited after a long separation and noticed they did not always hug or kiss. It took me years to grasp the fact that the love his family held for one another was very deep. They rarely hugged, kissed, or otherwise expressed love publicly, but it did not matter. At first, I judged them through my Western eyes and thought they were not particularly loving. I was wrong.

7 - Honolulu and Love

Modern Honolulu Skyline.
Artwork by Philip Sabado

7

 After I graduated from high school and arrived in Honolulu in June of 1969, I saw myself as a sponge dried by the sun of California, ready and willing to soak up all I was to meet in my new chosen island home.

In the truest sense, I was on an adventure, opening a door to my future. This is not unique. Everyone must have this moment or should. It is called growing up.

Trading homes, dreamed up at the airport from years before, was in full bloom. Here, I would understand my friend Gloria's roots. We'd reconnected in San Francisco after our fast friendship at the Honolulu airport and correspondence. Her prior home was at the Kuhio Park Terrace in Kalihi, a low-income housing project inhabited by families on welfare and immigrants from the South Pacific Islands. The twin towers were known as the "poor man's Ilikai," a reference to the opening scene in the *Hawaii Five-O* television show that featured a grand hotel. Gloria's family lived across the street in the lower housing, away from the two towers. Their unit was a small two-bedroom apartment on the corner close to the road.

Pauline, Gloria's mother, graciously agreed to our plan and allowed me to stay in their modest home when I first arrived. Her people came from the Visaya region in the Philippines. These were the southernmost islands, and her people had a different dialect and culture than that of my future spouse's Ilocano family. Gloria's sister, Diane, was a sweet and innocent preteen with whom I became fast friends.

In those times it was understood that you took your life into your hands by just entering the building or getting onto the elevators in either of the towers. One tower was for Hawaiians, and the other was predominately for Samoans and Tongans, or South Sea Islanders. Since fights were common between these different cultural groups it was not a wise decision to mix these volatile families together. Imagine a young blue-eyed blonde in this neighborhood and you will begin to understand.

I must have seemed incredibly naïve back then. Gloria never alluded to the neighborhood that awaited me in our letters. Clearly, my mom never knew. And thus, I never stopped to reflect on how dramatically my life would shift from the upper-class neighborhood of my youth to a housing project. What mattered to me was being in love with Hawai'i. I would often stop and gaze at the mountains and take deep breaths of the sweetly scented air. Besides, I walked to the bus at 8 a.m. and after school was back by 3 p.m. All the bad guys came out after dark. I was at peace. Deep within, I knew I was home and supremely happy. As I walked home, double crisscrossing rainbows embraced the Kalihi Valley almost daily. The nights were a different story.

The most acute damage in the housing came from those using the drugs du jour: airplane glue and assorted aerosol paint cans. Kids would climb into the trees and sniff glue and paint fumes at all hours. We would wake up to find bits of soiled terry cloth littered around the yard where they had been sniffing. This destructive habit ate their brain cells at a rapid rate and rendered them idiots, totally useless.

This was mild compared to what I'd seen in the Bay Area. After leaving San Francisco, I thought it was only my culture that had entered a spiraling decline with drugs. Alas, Hawai'i would follow suit in time.

Once, as I was looking out the back door of our little unit around dusk, I saw a triple rainbow stretching across the pali, the mountains behind us. Bands of brilliant color seemed to meet and entwine.

"Come quick, come and see," I shouted to Diane. She came running out and had a blank expression as she looked to the valleys. "Oh, you are so funny!" she said. "Dis rainbow stay in that valley almost every day." Just another slice of paradise they took for granted that would render me speechless.

Besides the twisting rainbows, another colorful aspect of Kalihi Valley was the manapua man, an old Chinese man who carried a pole in perfect balance with two steaming containers at either end that held *siu mai*, tempting chunks of red pork wrapped in a squishy white bun known to

Hawaiians as manapua. Just like kids everywhere who wait for the ice cream truck to come down their street, local kids would watch for the manapua man.

Pauline worked nights at the Manila Bar. She did her best to make a happy home. The family affectionately called me their hanai (chosen daughter). I felt safe in their warm home, even though the doors were double locked at night. We had to call the police more than once when the kids—high on glue—got wild.

To adapt to my new home, I listened carefully and memorized the rhythm and cadence of pidgin English, like a "shortcut English," spoken by everyone in my new family. Local people cringe when haoles (newcomers) attempt to speak pidgin because it sounds phony. I learned to speak the island form of English properly, listening was the key. On Molokai, Mama and Papa did not understand when I spoke standard English. Slowly, the timber and the inflections began to integrate my speech as I learned to communicate in the melodious singsong dialect.

Pidgin enables you to say what you want in a direct, clipped form. When workers and their families came to work from every corner of the world, a common tongue was necessary. The basis of pidgin in its structure and form is a direct descendant of the Hawaiian language. Compare, for instance, the structure of the phrase, "nani ka 'ala" (sweet the fragrance) with a common pidgin phrase, "nice, your house." The connective link was always the host culture.

To trade and survive, the immigrants learned enough of the lingo to communicate with those who did not speak their mother tongue. People taught each other words until they reached some common understanding. As each new wave of immigrants arrived, they added to the pidgin stew, evolving dialects flavored with words and rhythms uniquely their own.

There is a different style and rhythm to each of the different pidgin dialects, which depends on the island and cultural heritage from which you came. Every form of pidgin mixes in Hawaiian, to season the pot, if you will.

As an example, "luna" is a Hawaiian-derived word meaning "supervisor" or "boss." In the beginning the lunas were almost all from Germany, and Germans have a way of saying *ja* (pronounced: yah) after a comment or statement. This continues in pidgin. "You going store today, yah?" Some words are universal. If you want to eat a meal you say "kau kau," which is a Chinese pronunciation for the English word "chow" (so says one theory) and everybody understands. When you eat a meal among the Ilocano Filipinos you say, *"mangantayon"* (come and eat).

Of all the pidgin dialects, the most difficult to understand for me was spoken by the Portuguese and their descendants. Their pace is machine-gun rapid. One of my brothers-in-law, a Filipino, was raised in Pa'ia Camp on Maui, and when he speaks this form of pidgin, I can understand only a little. I usually turn to Philip so he can fill in the blanks.

Filipino pidgin is slower, with the rhythm of their mother tongue built into the language, almost like a drawl in some dialects.

The first Portuguese immigrants to Honolulu arrived on the German ship Priscilla. Although accounts differ as to the exact number of passengers, at least one hundred men, women, and children from Madeira and possibly the Azores were on board. They worked on sugar plantations. Though King Kalakaua officially invited them, the King of Portugal said he would only release his people if they could travel as families. He was aware that their culture thrived on their family values and connections. Portuguese were the only group allowed to bring families, and their families were large. All in all, these courageous people crossed two oceans and braved treacherous Tierra del Fuego. Not all made it.

In all, over twenty-five thousand tough workers came over on twenty-nine ships. In the beginning, the Portuguese were very strict and did not marry other nationalities. As time passed and the people of the camps mixed, their children found love with Hawaiians and other peoples. Many of the Miss Hawai'i pageant winners in the past twenty-five years have been of Portuguese descent, and our Maui mayors are predominantly so.

Philip's brother, Eugene, worked for the Hawai'i Superior Court as a bailiff. I was at his home one afternoon when he called the prospective jurors. With great ease he would swing from one pidgin to the next, depending on whom he addressed. He could speak perfect English, but to communicate effectively, he used local speech. He'd slow the speed while speaking to a Filipino man, addressing him properly as Tata, or Manong. With the Hawaiian ladies, it was "No forget, Auntie, tomorrow at nine-thirty, yah?" I marveled at how the people of Hawai'i constantly adjusted to every cultural challenge, a true tribute to the aloha spirit.

7 – Honolulu and Love

To those who are critical of my speaking in pidgin English, I pose this question, "If you lived in France for thirty-five years, do you think you would speak French?" The answer would be a resounding "Yes!" After all the years in Hawai'i, pidgin rolls off my tongue almost as naturally as if I were born to it.

A true test to see if one is fluent in a language is when you are aware of thinking in that language. Many years later, I realized I'd crossed that line on a literal and spiritual level when I worked at a resort.

A tourist came to the front desk forlorn because the door had blown shut behind them and their key remained in the room. They had missed their luau and sat in the lobby in a funk while the maintenance men formed another key. For some reason all the keys to this room were missing. It seemed strange because the sliding door was closed as well, so what blew the door closed was a mystery. After a couple of hours, we had the new key for them. As she was about to leave the lobby, she asked in a slightly irritated tone, "What are those disgusting lizards in the room?" I said they were geckos and considered them good luck because they eat the other bugs.

She retorted, "Well, I have been killing everyone I see, good luck or not!" With that, she turned on her heel and left in a huff.

My coworker was local and at the same moment we turned and spoke to each other in the pidgin vernacular. "Ai, yah. As why dat lady get hard time, she went kill da gecko, and they when get back at her!" We shook our heads and laughed at the strange logic, but as locals it made perfect island sense to us.

My mother has her master's degree in speech and drama, and not surprisingly, I can speak flawless English and so can my children. When my children work or must present themselves in the world as cosmopolitan people, they speak perfect English. However, they can be in a local situation or party with all the family present and fit in like the natives they are.

Philip and I met when we were students at the Honolulu Academy of Arts in downtown Honolulu. I was seventeen, and he used to watch me walk from class to the bus before he asked me to lunch. When I arrived in Honolulu, it was mid-June, and every day I would walk up the street in the Kuhio Park Terrace in Kalihi to catch the bus into the city. In the early morning, the cool breeze flowed from the cliffs of the pali and blew my long blonde hair in every direction. A couple of miles away toward the sea were the pineapple canneries, and the sweet smells of the sumptuous golden fruit would waft up the valley and fill the air.

Philip was in his third year of art college and had already completed his time in the Army. He sat three rows behind me in design class. He was dark and handsome in an innocent sort of way. He was friendly and popular, and his laugh was frequent, distinctive, and engaging. You could not help but turn and see who was laughing in that infectious way. One day, he asked me to lunch, but I was not interested. On the next try, he offered me a ride home. Since I was taking the bus, I accepted. When I told him I lived in the Kuhio Park Terrace, he asked straight-faced, "Can you jump out of a moving car?"

I laughed. "Don't be silly, it is not that bad." He drove slowly down the narrow roads to the housing complex, and I was the only haole we'd seen for miles. He smiled warmly to dispel my fears and generously volunteered to pick me up every morning and take me home as well. We became great buddies.

His mission initially was to protect me since I was so naïve. He asked me to lunch again, but I was still not interested. All that changed with a kiss. It happened after seeing a movie in Waikiki. Although a tourist trap, Waikiki was a great date night spot for locals. As our lips touched, I felt an electric, physical attraction to him that startled me, remembering the safety pin in the socket. Our moment turned into a similar shock wave as our lips met.

I came to learn he already had a girlfriend. She was beautiful and petite, and a Filipino beauty queen. That courtship was destined to fail because according to custom, her uncle went everywhere as a chaperone and Philip was slightly annoyed at this.

As far as the other girl was concerned, things do have a way of working out. Philip kept a hairbrush in the glove compartment of his Beetle. On the way to school after traveling with an open window, I'd grab the brush to untangle my long hair before school. She found my blonde hair tangled in the bristles and I never heard much about her again. After Phil and I married, I pretended to be annoyed when he wanted to stay up late to see if she had won the Miss Hawai'i Pageant.

7 – Honolulu and Love

My strongest attraction to Philip was his laugh and sense of humor. He never let me take anything too seriously. (He can still make me laugh at anything, and most especially at myself.) He noticed how easily I laughed. My family rarely teased or made jokes, being academic was more the theme. There was little humor unless it was on the TV. Getting to know Philip was akin to opening a window to allow the cool makani (wind) to enter my life and being.

Engaged, California, 1968.

We were passionate from the beginning of our relationship, and this strength helped me stay centered while we were on Molokai with his family. Whatever loneliness or isolation I felt in those early days was soothed in the late nights as we loved each other and began our lives together. Every moment knitted us as one, more tightly than I could have ever realized possible.

We were kids the first time we made love. We should have gone to class that day, but it looked like rain and he drove in the opposite direction to his house in 'Aiea. 'Aiea sits above Pearl Harbor. The sea was dark and the large Navy ships sat in their ports in shadow from the heavy clouds.

Philip shared the house we went to with his sister and brother. There were cousins in the back and seven other family members who lived on the second floor. Amazingly, every one of them was at work or school. We never left the bed and our day of passion, nine hours, passed in a blur. From then on, we knew we would always be together.

Strange, but from that first moment, I felt I had reunited with someone I already knew, an instinct more than love that wove us as one. I felt deep in my na'au (center of my being), that we had spent many lifetimes longing for each other. Only in this life could we know each other as husband and wife.

However, it was not until more than twenty years later that the meaning of our impassioned lovemaking would be revealed. Like a tightly bound hank of yarn finally unwound, I finally found the stray thread to pull. I began waking at night in a panic a couple of times a week for months, feeling as if I was not supposed to be with my husband who lay close, our skin always touching. It always happened the same way after we made love. I'd drift off to sleep and I would sense my body floating in a quasi-dream state. I would become nervous, then alarmed, as if I was no longer on Maui, but somewhere between worlds in another space and time. My thoughts raced, and in a blur of blind panic, a message spoke within me: I am going to be caught! Someone will find out. Here I am with him, and they will see me. *My heart pounded, and I sensed I had crossed an unseen line and placed my life in danger. In addition, I would be killed if I were caught in bed beside him, especially after lovemaking. After so many years of marriage, I wondered why I now felt this apprehension.*

When it seemed, my panic would become unbearable, a reassuring voice arose deep within me and spoke in a comforting manner: It's all right now, you can be here in bed with him. This time he is your husband; finally, he is all yours.

This knowing resonated and I exhaled a long breath as my entire body released the tension, I had held moments before. Each time the quasi-panic dream came, I would pull myself closer to his warm skin, adjusting my breasts against the curve of his back. Feeling his smooth skin was all I needed. I would relax completely and drift into a deeper sleep.

The message was clear. He was not always mine, nor could he have been then. Early on, I must have taken great risks to be with him. I had waited to have him be mine. Perhaps in other lifetimes we may have only passed each other. At last, in this life, he was the cup that would always be full. It was love, yet more, a puzzle segment that fit with all the pieces in place. I could breathe deeply, safely, and finally be at home after a long, long journey.

Years later in Hilo, a shaman helped me understand that for lifetimes Philip and I had existed as close friends. My mind had reached into the distant past and opened a door for a puka (opening to the other side). Scenes flashed in my mind, and lifetimes flew past. As my lives spun out in this spiritual encounter, I was amused to see myself as an arrogant man.

In a dream-like state, I spied upon a young couple entwined in the act of love and passion in Sri Lanka. This was us side by side in a flimsy hut fashioned from palm fronds. A tropical breeze blew in caressing circles and through the open-beamed floor. The early morning light shone through the crisscross design of the fronds and drifted patterns on our naked bodies. We were young lovers then, perhaps only fifteen years old, but in that life, we were only together the one time. I cried in my sleep, remembering the warmth and wetness of that place. The smell of the sea filled my nostrils, and I could taste the salt on my dry lips. It felt as if I was truly there, spying on us as we slept, spent from our lovemaking. I was female then, and so young. Touching base in the present, I saw even in that faraway place he had chosen the same side of the bed as he did now.

Another time, in Hilo, I went through a strange phase when for some reason I was not happy with Philip. Nothing he did pleased me. This was unusual, since after so many years of marriage we had weathered many difficult times and were always lovers. This time, all I had to do was look at him and I would start to complain. He said, "You have never been so mean to me before. Why now?"

My answer was cruel and caustic; I chastised him by calling him a loser. I remained angry no matter what he did or said. There was no reason or incident that spurred my strange outrage—one day I was fine, the next, changed. I became impatient and wild with anger when I saw him and went into a rage if he spoke to me. I was not in my body and did not see the look of surprise on his face.

After this continued, a voice in my mind awakened me in the early morning darkness and spoke: This man is a gift to you in this life, do not be silly and waste this time. He is your gift. You did not always have it this good! *The words echoed:* He is a gift.

I was so startled; I came fully awake and turned and woke him. Stuttering, I whispered the predawn message, "My mind said you are a gift to me, and I should appreciate you." I was reeling from the strong directive to appreciate my life, to be grateful he was finally a part of it.

He was groggy and mumbled something like, "That's nice." He was relieved the storm had passed from my confused state. He encircled my waist, and finding my warmth and breast, we made love in the early hours.

Later, I calculated that our fifth child was conceived that rainy morning. This voice within my innermost self-resonated and shook me into reality. My appreciation for my husband felt renewed so this next baby could find life in my body.

There is another level of sleep after lovemaking, so deep and satisfying. I was about to find that place as every fiber of my being relaxed and surrendered. Suddenly, my mind spoke again reminding me of a promise, no, a vow I had made some twenty years earlier when I had just moved to the islands prior to meeting Phil. It was like a movie reel spinning in my brain with the scene opening with me in Ala Moana Park, and at eighteen, my first time alone and on my own. I lounged beneath a large shade tree. I must have had a swim and sunned and would have my lunch and a nap. The most handsome man I had ever seen sat next to me under the tree. He was Hawaiian and amazing. He was flirting and so was I. It seemed evident our meeting could lead to sex, then or later, perhaps right there under my beach towel. I was sorely tempted by his seductive nature. Something I cannot define held me back. I begged off, saying I had a class and promised to return. He left with a smile; we both knew what would happen.

Again, I sat alone, contemplating casual sex, that could and would be my future. *Was this going to be my destiny?* I envisioned seeds strung out before me; a long line of one-time meaningless partners extended into infinity. Or was there to be more? "Okay, okay," I spoke to the tree, and I suspect the deities above. "Let's make a deal, I will skip all this and save myself if the very best one will come. Then I will not go down this path."

Was I taking a vow of chastity at eighteen? Was I nuts? What happened to my big life of independence? I heard a stronger force driving from within. Here I was, no parents, no curfew, no one would know, alone in Hawai'i with a sea of the most handsome men on the planet.

My inner voice drowned out the other temptations and physical desires. I made the deal, a pact, a vow. I gathered my towel and stood, knowing this was a new day for me. I never looked back, or returned to the tree the next day, or saw the man. Was it the next day when I turned to see Philip seated in the third row, laughing?

I had forgotten about that day in my youthful vow. This sleepy Hilo morning was confirmation—I had made that deal for life. My reward, sleeping next to me, softly slumbered at my side. I smiled, and a deeper sleep captured me.

8 - Wedding Preparations

Wedding, Preparing the Pig,
Maunaloa, 1969.
Artwork by Philip Sabado

8

On the evening after I'd met Mama, Philip was asked to go to his parents' room to "talk story." As I watched the sunlight fade in my room, it seemed he had been with them for hours. I grew anxious and weary, and succumbed to the long day by drifting off into a deep sleep. I awoke when a lone beam of light from the hallway filled the room like an arrow seeking its mark. Phil had opened the door to check if I was still awake. He would be sleeping in the parlor, as was proper.

I sat up and pulled myself together, trying to sit poised and natural, even though I was as nervous as if I'd been on my first date. The gnawing lack of confidence that lived deep within me reared its ugly head as I awaited his words. When he did not speak, I grew impatient and shoved him playfully with both hands and blurted, "Did they like me? Am I okay?" As a side comment, I added, "Your mom is sort of spooky, but your dad is sweet. Hmm, and I don't think your sisters like me much." When he still did not answer, I demanded, "Tell me now!" My mind reeled. After all, what had they been talking about for so long, for hours?

He smiled in his innocent way, laughing and rolling his eyes. "Too late to back out now. They are going to start fattening the pigs!"

This remark was truly the most local answer he could have volunteered. I understood, I had won them over and he would be my prize for life. Our life together could now begin.

I squealed, and jumped to hug and kiss him, making him fall into the bed with me. As we rolled on the quilts, his warm smooth skin and familiar smell were addictive and intoxicating, not like soap, but more akin to an aroma associated with warmth, like homemade bread. My constant desire was to wrap myself into his skin and never leave. I felt warmed and made whole when he was near me. Our physical moments were exhilarating, and I craved him. We kissed passionately and I wanted to hold him all night.

In the side room where the curtains folded in the night winds and the colorful quilts lay folded at the end of the bed, I bowed to protocol. All eyes, seen and unseen, watched us. Plenty of time for all that lovemaking, *I thought with assurance. That time will always be there for you.*

I asked about his sisters. "They smiled at me, but I'm not sure about them." As a woman, despite the smiles, I could see they were wary. I noticed passing glances. I knew I had a long way to go with these women who were devoted to their handsome, boyish sibling.

"Never mind them," he said. "Mama is the only one who will make the decisions. She is the boss, and I am spoiled by her. Besides, I am the *budidik* (youngest son)." He knew his place and rank in the family and was almost cocky about his position with his mom. Clearly, she ruled this roost, and that meant so did he in his humble way.

Molokai had a way of seducing me into another form of propriety. There was no reason why he could not have stayed in bed with me. No one would have come and scolded us, after all, it was the sixties and the hippies in San Francisco had set the paradigm. Our generation had set in motion a sexual free-for-all, yet here we observed another code to honor his family, their house, and the quaint village in which they lived to begin in a traditional and respectful manner.

A critical question loomed daily: how many pigs, cows, and chickens would be required for cooking at the party? Many nights were spent in serious discussion about whose pigs and cows to buy. How much garlic and bay leaf would be needed? Not to mention the number of dishes served. I was amazed and stood back in awe to observe the planning and discussions around the wedding and party. One point of discussion was about who would hold the honor as the main or head cook. That person would be the one to call the shots. Their choice was unanimous, Tata Basilio, an older man, tall, proper, and highly respected in the village. For payment, we were instructed to buy enough Seagram's 7 Crown Whiskey and 7 Up to make 7 and 7s for the head cook and his crew.

This family loved nothing more than a good party. In the end, we had three pigs (over nine-hundred pounds of pork), two-hundred ninety-five chickens, and two cows. The guest list would top off at over fifteen hundred

8 – Wedding Preparations

people—a significant portion of Molokai's population. It was customary then for the groom's family to pay for the wedding and the party. One of Philip's sisters gave us two hundred pounds of rice. The three pigs, two cows and chickens were gifts as well. My mom provided the whiskey for the cooks. Philip's brother, Eugene, bought our wedding cake from the Kanemitsu Bakery in Kaunakakai. The daughter of the woman I'd lived with in Honolulu would be a bridesmaid, plus she would do double duty and perform a traditional wedding dance.

After a great deal of discussion that involved a strategic mix of superstition and logic, the Chinese calendar, and calculating payday, June 14, 1969, was chosen. Townspeople would be in a more comfortable position to kokua (help) if they were not between paychecks. Mama would have the final word.

My family would order formal wedding invitations on white linen paper from the finest printer in Los Angeles. These were sent to the mainland guests, friends of my parents, and people I had known since I was a small girl. I received a large box of invitations with the double envelopes as well. They were so white and beautiful. I laid them out proudly for my husband and family to see. For a moment Phil looked perplexed and then asked innocently, "Why send? Everybody going come." Word went out about a party, transmitted on what was known to all as the "coconut wireless."

Mama and Papa had moved back to Molokai for the time being and visited Honolulu to prepare for the wedding. When she arrived in 'Aiea, Mama took us into her room and closed the door. Philip stood by to help translate. She sat on her bed and spoke in a direct manner. "They don't like you." She meant Philip's brothers and sisters. I felt momentary surprise, but I had seen this on their faces. He was the jewel in their crown. Who could pass this scrutiny? I drew a breath and regrouped. *He was my prize! Keep focused on the prize*, I reminded my spirit. *That is all that counts*. Confused, I turned to Phil, wondering where the conversation was going. He looked nonplussed.

She continued, "But I like you, and I am the only one that matters." I swallowed hard, anticipating her next words. "Your Papa and me, we move here, so no more pilikia (trouble) for you!"

She decided I deserved a chance. Only Mama would take this challenge so seriously that she would move house, home, and Papa to another island to protect and teach me. By coming to live near us on Oʻahu, she positioned herself between the family and me, physically, and I suspect spiritually, thereby ensuring that the wedding would continue without difficulty.

Not unlike other young couples we were so caught up in the planning and excitement a wedding creates, we almost lost track of the real attraction—each other. We would steal away at night in his blue Volkswagen bug to Ala Moana Park and revel in the moments of being alone. All the adults around us seemed to spin out of control with planning, discussions, and the prescribed rituals.

My mother arrived from Los Angeles two weeks before the wedding, and we were given a shopping list a mile long. On this ever-growing list was a carload of garlic, bay leaves, and onions, and the important whiskey and 7 Up for the cooks.

Parties are major events in the Filipino community. There were weekly parties being planned or anticipated gatherings at the beach to picnic or catch fish. These interactions with families and children proved to be a rite of passage where I could enjoy the moments while observing the lifestyle. In contrast, my life in California could only be told in varying shades of black and white. We had little to no family.

In this village, the parties were still held along the cultural mores of the Philippine provinces. For a home gathering, chairs would be lined against the walls with the central area vacant. The women sat together on one side of the room and the men sat on the opposite side as if there was an invisible line drawn down the middle of the room not to be crossed. The women had the children underfoot and the small ones were allowed to run freely back and forth to their fathers and mothers.

Philip explained that this custom probably came from a time in the Philippines (no doubt the Spanish influence) when it was not acceptable for a man and a woman who were not husband and wife to sit next to each other because someone might get the wrong idea.

After a number of these parties, I noticed certain standards were always observed. A lit votive candle would be in the main room on a table or a shelf. Beneath the candle was a plate of party food set aside out of respect. Sometimes a beer or can of soda would be next to the plate, untouched. This was for the departed spirits to be remembered and included in the festivities.

8 – Wedding Preparations

I asked Philip once what happened to the food on the plate. He shrugged his shoulders, and said it was left out the proper amount of time, and then shared with the family pet maybe, but never thrown out. This offering to the spirits was known as *atang* and can take on many forms depending on the family. A prayer card or statue was always nearby.

I came to enjoy these parties, but at first, I spent a great deal of time feeling alone, staring, and smiling at Philip from across the way. He was most comfortable with the men, old and young together, laughing and drinking beer, sharing a common spirit of *kabalayan*, townmates. Unless one of my sisters-in-law was with me, I sat apart, unable to speak to anyone. I became an observer. This was the grist that had molded him, whereas I was on a learning curve to have all the pieces fit. I memorized words and later asked him to teach me. Other guests were not rude and often painfully shy, watching me as I watched them with side glances. Only the boldest would sit next to a haole. I listened closely to the melodious tone of their Ilocano language. After a time, I began to hear familiar words, which I filed in my memory until I was with Mama.

Philip's parents were always around with Mama by my side. She spoke her language slowly as everyone seemed to hang on her every word. After a while, I was amazed at how much I understand. My listening was paying off, I was learning. When others spoke to Mama, I was lost. The people who were born in the Philippines spoke their dialect too fast.

At these parties, Philip would smile from across the room, his happy eyes chided me and made me smile in return. I would wave hello with a small gesture as though this was a fun thing. It was so different coming from Los Angeles in the free-forming sixties. I kept reminding myself: this was not hard, I could learn. Just knowing him made this worth every moment.

The centerpiece of every party was the food. When I sat down to eat, everyone would find a reason to pass by and look at my plate to see how brave I was in trying his or her food. As I ate, they smiled and laughed, cupping their hands over their mouths, or revealing their many gold teeth. They would comment, "Ai, yah, ading (young one), you eat dat one? Ai, yah!" Technically the ice was broken as they laughed and talked. "No more da haole eat dis kine, you one Filipina now." I was accepted because I ate their food. This was always the first step.

It would take another quarter of a century for Filipino food to become mainstreamed for restaurants and catering in America, and to be a part of Asian fusion. I revel in the memories of the good ole days when the love of family was cooked into the recipe as it was in those simplistically perfect Molokai parties.

One party made a deep impression on me, and the memory always makes me smile. I'd gone with my sister-in-law, Rosita, to the home of a newly married couple. As tradition dictated, all the men were lounging outside under a tree and the women collected in the house. It was a welcome party for the bride, a girl who had recently arrived from the Philippines, and for the groom to strut and show off his bride. This was an arranged marriage, and it was obvious she had just met her husband. Surely the village elders had exchanged photos. I wondered if he had sent a recent photo, or had this been a shock?

It was accepted that the old, as well as the young women present would help her adjust. She looked down, averting her eyes and shielding herself from the thoughts of others. Her coal-black hair was pulled tightly into a chignon and her slim body was wrapped in traditional country clothing, a dark checkered cotton fabric in amber and burgundy tones. Her husband was an older jovial man who had a constant smile fixed on his face. He had earned his retirement after thirty-some years in the fields and could bring the long-awaited, beautiful *balasang* (young girl) of his dreams home to meet his friends in the camp.

This prearranged marriage had been negotiated by relatives from the two villages. These marriages were common in the camp and the girls were known as picture brides. The Japanese, as well as the Chinese, brought their new brides, unseen, to these shores in this same manner in the early nineteen hundreds. In the Philippines and Asia, this still occurred because of the desperate financial straits of the village people in the provinces. A young girl would be married to a wealthy older man who resided in that paradise across the waters, Hawai'i. In so doing, the young girls could ease the hardship of the entire family if not the village. The marriage was a wise move on her part, and it came with an expectation that she would soon be able to bring most of her family. What did it matter if her husband was not handsome or young? She was already privileged to be out of the village and could help those she'd left behind by sending money back to her homeland.

8 – Wedding Preparations

Usually, the old men were kind gentlemen who had literally waited a lifetime to have a family. Their retirement money made them compared to wealthy nobles in the Philippines. In Hawai'i, retirement afforded them a comfortable living within their community. Once married, the old men did all the cooking, shopping, and any required planting. Their spouse did some household duties and tended the garden. When the bride had a baby, her husband would continue with the household chores. The rest of his time was spent amusing the adored child. The girl had to do very little except have babies for him to beguile and love.

When the bride smiled, she revealed her many gold teeth. They flashed in the light when she lifted her head and smiled demurely—she wanted us to see. My sister-in-law leaned toward me and whispered that the old man had paid for the gold in her mouth whether her teeth needed repair or not. According to their culture, this was an obvious sign of her husband's wealth and only the beginning of his indulgences. Soon there would be gold jewelry for her and money to buy pigs for her village. He would give her extra money to pay for the education of her family. His life up to now had been simple; he had lived on vegetables, fish, and pork for years to save for this time. Though shy, she appeared happy.

On the other side of the room sat a woman bathed in the same golden colors of the sunset. She was really enjoying the party (she also had an older husband), hoisting her beer and laughing. Already tipsy and shaking her head, she said, "Ai, yah, ading, (younger one), no worry, no matter, when da light stay out, old or young, da man feels like da same ting." Everyone roared in laughter, bending from the waist, holding their stomachs, and cupping their hands over their mouths. She continued with a thought to top the last one. "Or maybe mo' bettah! You keep da eye close if stay morning time!" Everyone begged her to stop. "Manang, please, bumbye we get sore stomach, and no can eat!"

The combination of beer, laughter, and the light in the room made this moment priceless. The young girl giggled into her cupped hand. She must have understood some English. In my childhood house no one dared to speak so blatantly. Proper decorum, and as they say in Hawaiian, kolohe (speaking a little bit naughty) was what adults might do at a party. I was a naïve kid, easily shocked and still somewhat judgmental. I think I blushed for her.

For this young bride, the camp proved to be much like her home in the provinces. Soon she would have friends. Often, they were girls like her that had also come over as picture brides. They would help the new *balasang* adjust to the loneliness she experienced without her family. Her family would cherish her for showing bravery and sacrifice. It was never easy.

On days when I sat on the porch waiting for my husband to return from the fields, I would watch the old men with their young brides pass in front of Rosita's house. I would think, *she is so young, she could be his daughter!* He would be carrying the baby along the red dirt road, and she would have bundles of laundry or groceries balanced on her head as she had done in her village. She would smile and giggle, as if she shared a secret with the older man.

She was a queen, pampered and adored. Many of the girls with whom I had gone to school had young, handsome spouses, and some were already heading for divorce. Here, the old men would spoil their *balasang* bride. I remembered thinking that some of my friends would never have it as good. But who was I to judge anyone? I, too, was entering this village.

Many, many years later, I came to understand these marital arrangements on a more intimate level. Mama passed within the first few years of our marriage and after some time Papa returned to his village in Ilocos Sur to marry a young, widowed Filipina. He was eighty years old, and she was barely in her thirties. In the beginning, the family watched her warily; some of the new brides were known to be opportunists. In the end, Manang Vicki proved to be a devoted spouse for Papa. She cared for him, and after his death she thrived in Hawai'i, bought her own home, and sent for her children, her mother, sister, and their families to live and flourish in Hawai'i as well.

Filipinos address their elders by saying Manong (male) or Manang (female). There is no dismissing this significant custom. It is a tribute and sign of respect. I noticed that Philip never addressed his siblings by their first names. He would say Manong Pete or Manang Rosita, never a casual nickname. If his sister called and left a message, she would say, "Please tell my brother that Manang Rosita called." I adapted immediately. Heads still turn when I address fellow Filipinos in this manner.

There was one secret I would keep past my wedding day. I was already two months pregnant with our first child. I had two people who had to be kept ignorant of this fact: my devout Irish Catholic father who clung to traditional ways and the Belgian priest who would marry us.

Philip's family was elated about my pregnancy. Babies were the complete epicenter of their life. I was sternly warned not to tell the priest. With wide cautious eyes my soon-to-be sisters-in-law admonished, "Be careful not to appear sick or pale, he will find out." I had to laugh because to them, with my fair Irish skin and freckles, I was always pale!

I had heard a story about a woman from the camp who had told the priest of her being with child before the ceremony and the couple was forced to marry on the church steps. In the eyes of the church, she was considered tainted and could not enter the holy ground. I was horrified! To think if my parents and Nanny came all this way only to see me married on the church steps…I was committed to keeping this secret.

Our Backyard, Early Morning Wake-up Call, Maunaloa, Molokai.
Artwork by Philip Sabado

As luck would have it, as the wedding day drew near, I was seized with a severe case of morning sickness. On some days nausea could span the entire day. I resolved to use more color on my cheeks and to stand up straight.

The wedding preparations seemed endless. Mama set forth the first directive. In the week before the wedding, Philip and I had to be separated until we met at the church steps. Various superstitions, rituals, and precautions were put in place to ensure we would have prosperity, health, many children, and long happy years together. In retrospect, I don't believe Mama was misguided.

To guarantee our paths would not cross, Philip was taken to stay at a hidden location at the opposite end of the island while I remained in Maunaloa. He was not allowed to drive a car as it was considered bad luck. I don't think he minded this custom because his time was spent hanging out with the other men, drinking, joking, and gathering flowers and the special foliage needed to decorate the wedding hall.

They were careful about timing and managed to keep us on opposite ends of the island, amazing since there were only five-thousand people living on this island then.

As in all love stories, we managed to find each other once at his niece's home near the beach. For some reason, everyone was away. I was uncharacteristically alone and then he was there. It seemed surreal, was it a dream? To this day, I am not sure this actually occurred. We made wild passionate love in minutes, and then a car drove up and he was gone. Then I was back and secure at the camp, busy with dress fittings and all the predictable details.

During our separation, the family met relatives and drove Philip to and from everywhere. Each time he was taken to the airport, a carload of family arrived from another island. I thought this amazing since no invitations had been sent out. They all showed up, the coconut wireless communicating at high speed. Often a relative would approach Phil and say, "I am your cousin from Lana'i on your mother's side. We have never met. I am here to help prepare for your party." This happened at almost every flight and the numbers swelled. It was their custom to be there as a family and support each other in both the hard times (a death) as well as happy times (marriage and birth).

As I had been told, over fifteen hundred people gathered, locally and from the islands, plus the four from my side of the family. I met his family wide-eyed, having surrendered to his world, loving it all!

During this period, there was the final selection of the pigs and cows for the party food. My father was in a photographer's paradise. His lifetime passion was on full display as he took pictures of every moment of our wedding, including the preparation of the pigs. After seeing the photographs, I am sure that had I been there, my pregnancy would no longer be a secret—I would have lost all my soda crackers. As custom dictated, the pig's four feet were bound, and a pole was set in its mouth to hold it down as a man thrust a sharp knife into its heart. They placed a cooking pot under the punctured heart as it spewed blood. Warm liquid filled pot after pot, as the life force drained from the squealing, kicking animal on the makeshift table. They took the blood to be mixed with vinegar and cooked into a dish known as dinardaraan. Some of the older men took a cupful and drank the brew on the spot.

Another cultural tradition was to drink from the bitters bag, the gall bladder of the animal. In my father's photographs I saw a great deal of bravado and camaraderie. The combination of the Filipino world and the Hawaiian nest flourished and made our time even sweeter.

Most of the time, it seemed like a whirlwind of activity surrounding us while we sat in the calm center. I heard a constant flow of Ilocano language spoken with a smattering of Hawaiian in the mix—this is how these two cultures bridged through food and language.

The soft appealing words of Hawaiian rolled off their tongues like honeyed syrup. For instance, kokua (to help or give), as in, "Tata (uncle) will kokua a pig." I learned about much going on behind the scenes: Auntie So-and-so strung the lei, another friend organized decorating the hall, another gathered the food servers, and so on. A virtual army moved behind the scenes. Who commanded it? Maybe Philip and his sisters? I never saw signs of stress, panic, or anxiety, only a consistent flow of happy and peaceful movements. True to form, there is no greater gift than to kokua your time and heart.

My parents were wonderful and took everything in stride, good sports. Nanny was the champion. They loved her and showed profound respect for the elderly. Since the Filipino family did not eat bread, they had no toaster. A fresh pot of rice was on the counter before sunrise. Nanny always had her toast and coffee in the morning. For Nanny, Papa patiently stood over the stove with a slice of bread skewered on a fork, turning the toast over the gas flame till it was a golden brown. She kept telling them, "I can eat rice with a little butter." They practically tripped over themselves to make her happy. "Ah, no, dis one no trouble, Madam." Everyone smiled and spoiled her, and happiness filled the room like the warm sun. Her coffee cup was refilled almost every other sip. Seeing her pampered delighted both my mother and me.

9 - Wedding Day

*Wedding Portrait,
Maunaloa, Molokai, 1969.*
Photo by Paul Donegan

9

 On the morning of the wedding as my bare feet touched the cool wooden floor, I detected the sweet smell of burning kiawe, a type of mesquite common to the area. The wind had shifted on this clear morning and instead of blowing out to sea, the cooking fires emanating from the backyard of the main cook, Tata Basilio, had wafted over the tin roofs in a blue hazy mist that covered the village. "Ah, the cooks have been stoking the fires since mid-morning," I whispered to no one present. The smell of sizzling garlic and fatted pork would follow from the well-oiled cooking production, silyasi as a Filipino style wok.

As I looked out the front door at Manang Rosita's, I saw people walking briskly down the red dirt path to prepare the community hall. Laughing and jovial, their arms were full of flowers and long vines with fragrant maile freshly picked from the near valleys. There was purpose and spirit in their steps that spun the day into motion. I stepped back into the shadows of the room and saw myself in the epicenter. I could see and feel portals opening and my smile returning. My mind spoke these words into my na'au (my center being), *This will all work, you will see, it will be magic!* And so, the day began.

My dress and veil awaited as did my new life. I felt a flutter cross my inner belly like the delicate wings of a butterfly. I flushed and my cheeks warmed at the reminder of another miracle, a child growing in the space between my groin and my na'au. I touched my center and the child within me knew.

Long-established traditions followed in the days to come and included Philip too. He wore a traditional sheer; richly embroidered wedding shirt called a *barong* Tagalog. It was made from fabric known as *piña*, which was smooth, yet stiff from the pounded fibers of the pineapple plant. Rows and rows of white embroidery decorated the front panels of the ecru button-down shirt. In years to come, I would see them at events in modern fabrics and tinted in shades of rose, blues, or greens. Philip's attendants also wore traditional embroidered shirts. Worn for special occasions with an undershirt, they were the norm in the Philippines, mostly because of the climate. They kept the wearer cool as the breeze flowed through, and they absorbed sweat, so the shirt stayed dry and clean.

Over one hundred years ago, the shirts were required wear by the Spanish. One never knew when a wild pig or an enemy might emerge from the bushes, and the Spanish could see a bolo knife hidden within the sheer fabric.

Pineapples were introduced to the Philippines during the Spanish colonial era and one variety, Red Spanish, was cultivated for the textile industry as early as the seventeenth century. The embroidery panels were centuries old and done by hand in the European fashion.

Originally from Brazil, the pineapple made a great impression on those who came across it. It would not take root in the cold European soil, and the fruit crossed the Atlantic Ocean aboard Portuguese ships in search of other territories with an adequate climate.

My wedding gown was made from white, delicate Japanese silk with small floral designs woven into the fabric. It showcased the traditional Filipino-style dress with peaked, rounded sleeves. This fashion, a product of colonial Spanish influence, probably dated from the 1800s. I had seen photos of the Marcoses when they reigned in Manila. Imelda's glittering gowns in every color had the same stylized sleeve.

All the fabrics for the wedding were bought in downtown Honolulu at the edge of Chinatown from Musashiya, an old Japanese store on River and Hotel Streets. Sister Lolly shopped with me and supervised my choices. An older Japanese woman smiled broadly as she helped us and anticipated our every need. She was so polite and accommodating; no doubt she'd helped countless girls choose their wedding fabric. A rickety staircase led into the bowels of the shop. An old wooden plank floor smelled of mold, and lava stone walls heralded another day when the harbor was filled with fishing vessels. What stories these old walls could tell.

I can still recall the whooshing sound as the saleswoman spun ten yards off the cardboard roll, creating a sizable mound on the table. In the end, the silken train would flow at least three feet behind me. Stiff buckram was used in the sleeve to make it stand on its own. You could strain poi, the traditional Hawaiian starch through this stiff fabric, and it was labeled "poi strainer" on the roll.

I chose the fabric for my four attendants in shades of seafoam green silk. The dresses were designed with the same peaked Filipino sleeves. They wore white lace bolero tops over their dresses that let the pale green shades peek through. A lace *mantilla* complimented the Spanish styling.

Wedding Day, Bridesmaids, Maunaloa, Molokai, 1969.
Artwork by Philip Sabado

We'd chosen to wear the traditional Filipino wedding attire in honor of Mama and Papa. This was not a hard decision; I was enchanted with all I'd seen. Why not go all the way? So many young couples in the camp had

9 – Wedding Day

adopted Western ways. Later, I realized we were one of the last couples in the family to have chosen a traditional route. The rest were Western in their dress with store bought white lace and seed pearls. We were proud to keep up the traditions.

Selected women of the camp had sewn my dress, the attendants' dresses, and the men's shirts by hand. They had sent for the *piña* fabric or had it on hand for such an occasion. They sat in a circle and sewed happily for months. There was no money involved; this was done for the sake of the celebration and out of respect and love for Philip and the family. Behind-the-scenes helpers made sure all was accomplished on time, organizing food, clothing, and party details for over a thousand people. I could have been overwhelmed. Instead, I blissfully followed along.

Another mandated tradition was selecting God parents, known as *ninongs* and *ninangs*. This was in addition to the customary Western bridesmaids and attendants. The *ninongs* and *ninangs* acted as sponsors for the bride and groom, and it was an honor to be asked. The bond and commitment to each other is lifelong. In Ilocano, as well as Spanish, these special people are forever known as *commadre* or *compadre*. In all, we had ten attendants on each side.

The space at the altar appeared crowded as we stood for photos. A snag occurred when the elder *ninang*, Mrs. Marquez, was chosen to stand by my side. My sister threw a fit, pulled rank, and insisted she take my side. This created an impasse until Phil's brother volunteered to take the same position next to his brother. When it came to these cultural precepts there was not much flexibility. This slight was the talk of the island, an intriguing collision of Western and Island traditions.

On this auspicious day, the cooks began at four in the morning while Molokai awoke. Rising early was normal in the fields, but a wedding was an exciting prospect. Prep started by cooking the cut meat in a large silyasi, *placed over open red-hot coals. The kiawe burned longer and hotter than other local wood. The cooks were older men who seemed to not have a care in the world. Younger men were willing assistants. They cut the meat and observed the masters. Breaks were taken every hour for a shot of the favored 7 and 7s. By the time the food was served they were a jovial group.*

There was no need to pay these exceptional cooks. The camaraderie and joy of the drink, family, and the community was enough. Their elated mood and contagious excitement made for an even better time. They lived for these special moments and parties. Lucky me! I came to understand we were all family. Today they would work hard for me and Philip, and on other times we would go that extra mile for family. This was a given: in the plantation, the villages in Abra, and on Molokai.

My own family experienced culture shock. My educated mother suggested with good intention that I write the story of my wedding for National Geographic Magazine at the going rate of ten cents a word. She wasn't sure where to look next as chickens and goats skittered about the dirt lanes. I had already made an adjustment, having found acceptance and comfort in this village, and dismissed the idea. In exasperation, I said, "Mom, I cannot write about them as if they were from the moon!" Just then, a stray chicken fluttered past. We were rendered speechless, aware of the two different worlds. Yet she was clearly enchanted! I could tell, both my parents were captured and immersed in the spirit of this village wedding.

My mother's innocent suggestion was not out of disrespect—quite the opposite. She looked at my life as a new adventure into a world few could enter and appreciate. I acknowledged her encouragement and the inspiration she gave me to begin writing.

Mom stayed true to her familiar traditional East Coast wedding protocol by registering me with the finest stores for the preferred wedding gifts of china and silver. Both my parents held doctorates among other degrees, as did most of their friends. The differences in culture were as wide as the sea separating this Molokai plantation camp and their comfortable California suburb. They had no economic objections to the match. The unspoken understanding was this moment in the fields was a launching pad for me, their first daughter.

Dad took me aside and casually suggested we could live on Molokai for life. I already understood the future that awaited Phil in Honolulu with another year of school, then a job in his chosen field as an artist. I could see it would be just a matter of time. Perhaps they could see how truly happy I was with Philip. My parents were wonderful, and they did their best to fit in. They, too, were seduced by the magic of Molokai and a marriage amid ripening pineapples.

On the morning of our wedding as I got dressed, Mom rolled her hair in large, pink plastic curlers as fashion dictated in the late sixties. She decided

9 – Wedding Day

to walk down the camp road to speed the drying in the hot morning sun. She was back in five minutes—horrified! She bounded into the house, her cheeks flushed as if blown in by a blizzard, her back against the door.

I stumbled toward her, trying not to trip over that darned three feet of train. "Mother, what's wrong?" I asked, thinking she had fallen, or been bitten by a goat, or chased by a chicken (one never knew).

Her cheeks reddened further, and she said, "Oh, honey, I am so sorry. I hope I haven't ruined your day."

Apparently, as she had walked down the road everyone on her path saw the strange haole woman and came out of their houses to meet the mother of the bride. And there she was, the only haole in sight, walking around the village looking like a Martian in her pink plastic rollers. We both laughed about it later and thought it was hilarious. What next?

A second, more impactful event occurred moments before the wedding. My Filipina sister-in-law, who had married Philip's older brother, was born in the Islands, and raised in Honolulu. They had lived and raised a family in California where she had been considered an outsider. Her family was from the Visayas. Her people still married those from their village or province due to language and cultural preferences in the early generations of immigrants.

An hour before the wedding, she cornered me in a hallway in Rosita's house as I adjusted my sheer veil before a mirror as old as the house evidenced by chips of flaked silver backing that left small black holes and spider veins that crept into the corners. She moved in close, blocked my view, and spoke with wide-eyed fervor. "Do you have any idea what you are getting yourself into?" Her eyes locked with mine. "This is a traditional superstitious Filipino family of farmers from the provinces." Before I could speak, she continued, "Are you a crazy person? Or have you lost your mind, marrying into this family? I met your parents. I know where they live—they're professionals!"

In the passageway with its eerie, extended shadows, it seemed like theater, akin to: "Here is your last warning before doom settles in." Her eyes bore into me like a beacon from a lighthouse. I stood frozen, rendered speechless. Besides, what could I possibly have said? She moved to the side, and I returned to my reflection. With my veil firmly in place, I fixed on my image through the flowing semi-transparent lace. When I remained silent, she shrugged, turned, and walked away, shaking her head in apparent disbelief. Our moment passed and dissolved as she walked into the daylight. I moved to an open window and watched until she was down the road with the other families.

Alone in the quiet house, I returned my gaze to the smoky mirror. I stared through the sheer veil framing my youth and heard a clear message spoken in my heart: *Have no doubt with this man.* A jolt of electricity ran from my toes up through my crown. I knew what I wanted and with whom I was to spend my life. I was sure everything would work out. I cannot explain how I knew this—I just did, from deep within my core.

My challenge was to bridge two diverse worlds and cultures. I would muster the most giving form of love. I held my spine a little straighter and told myself, I can learn, I am smart, and can adjust! This will take time, and soon I will have help. *How that last insight came in, I ascribe to another mysterious instance where my mind spoke. I was willing to wait and see. Holding me to this path was my love for Philip.*

Many years later, I asked the same sister-in-law if she remembered that moment in front of the hallway mirror. She nodded and we laughed. I think in her own way, she had to adjust to the family in her own time. She told me her own culture shock story, about escorting young Philip to Molokai. I never told Phil or the family about that moment in front of the mirror.

On the wedding day, Philip returned to the camp early. As tradition dictated, he had remained hidden from me till the moment we would meet in the church ready to walk down the aisle. Everyone was frantic on this day and yet there was one last task to be completed. It was bad luck for him to do any labor on the wedding day. On the opposite end of the camp, he ran from house to house searching for someone to press his white wedding trousers. With a melodic whine, he would plead, "Excuse me, Nana, could you press my pants? My sister was cooking and forgot." There would be no takers, "Ai, yah, so sorry boy, I no more ir-ron. See you at the par tee." By the fourth or fifth house, he found someone to do the chore. He could not come home because I was there, and it would be bad luck. What makes me smile about this story is the depth of superstition that formed this man. He could have ironed his pants, who would have known? But the truth was he knew, and to break this code was unheard of, not to mention he would never defile the trust of Mama. As the saying goes, this was the measure of a man.

On this auspicious day, I would walk down the same red dirt road as Philip and his mother. I wobbled on my white satin, one-inch heels as my perfect white silk train trailed in the red Molokai dirt. A white Spanish comb had been fixed into my chignon, and the cluster of pearls and small diamonds sparkled in the sun. I had chosen the sheerest lace for the veil, adorned with a scalloped design on the border. (Years later both my daughters would wear the same veil on their special days.) I held twenty strands of pikake (jasmine) blossoms mixed with sweet white, vanilla honohono orchids, the most fragrant flowers in the world. The flowers were strung in lei chains as long as my dress.

My entire being was filled with the multi-layered fragrance of the pear-shaped blossoms that announced my arrival and lingered in the air. The smell was so intoxicating, a person could swoon had they been in a closed room.

The moment I saw Philip again, my breath froze, and my heart skipped. Dark and handsome, he shone brighter than any other. The incredible journey I had made and the customs I embraced would be steppingstones on the path we would walk together. We stood before the church steps, so young, our hearts filled with joy and a future before us.

Fifty or sixty guests attended the ceremony at St. Vincent's church. Everyone else—all fifteen-hundred guests—were at the hall. Only my parents, my sister, and Nanny came from my side. My parents were both only children. All other guests were from Molokai or the neighboring islands. My family, being Irish Catholic, had asked for a High Mass. I am sure our other guests wondered why we tarried at the wedding since Philip's parents and everyone else were waiting at the hall for the party to begin.

As I entered the church, I saw white meatpacking paper had been laid down the aisle from the door to the altar. I tracked red dirt up the aisle and my heels made small holes in the paper. Wind swept through the small wooden building and picked up the edge of the paper and whipped it into the air. Had the mischievous wind from my arrival at the airport come to taunt me on my wedding day?

I twisted around because of the noise to see the paper fly over our heads. The entire sheet, the length of the church aisle, literally rippled up to the ceiling. I was aghast, yet no one else seemed to find it amiss. Apparently, these types of events were normal in the camp with its soaring wind. Everyone smiled when they saw my face as I watched the paper crackle and buckle as it scraped along the ceiling of the small church.

The church organist only knew the first bars of "Here Comes the Bride," and played it twenty times in a row. It was like a comedy that only I could see. How could I break out in the giggles as I stood at the altar? In truth, it was charming, and the pictures show how we beamed, so giddy in love.

The priest was from Belgium, as had been Father Damien of Kalaupapa. Out of deep honor and respect, the Belgian priesthood had continued to send priests to Molokai in homage to Damien. We had just met the priest at the rehearsal, and he was a kind man; however, he had a habit of forgetting my name! He recited the vows, "Do you...um...what is your name again? Take this man," etc. After the third time he forgot my name, I was annoyed. Each time he hit a blank, I filled it in with a stern whisper, *"My name is Christine."*

Leading up to the wedding, I felt as though I had entered a medieval time zone and worried that someone would divulge "the secret of my womb" and tell the priest why I was glowing. Fortunately, I had discovered soda crackers and I made it through my wedding day. We were properly married at the altar with the priest none the wiser.

Once we exchanged vows, Philip and I kissed, and turned to face the open doors that revealed the miles of rolling pineapple fields. Someone had been kind enough to catch the naughty white paper that had flown amok and held it in place for us as we walked down the aisle. Outside the church, my mother wiped away tears of happiness as we began our walk to the hall. I began to wonder where everyone was until I saw a sea of people before me lining the pathway to greet the bride and groom. Fifteen hundred people stood on the road, waiting for us to arrive so the party could begin. The women cried, waving, and wiping their tears, and the children jumped with joy. I recognized some of the women that had sewn my dress. They tugged at my sleeve as I passed them—one last adjustment! I had never seen so many people in my life, and I am sure neither had my family. Philip's school chums, his aunts, uncles, and cousins from different nationalities all smiled, jumped, and clapped as we passed by.

9 – Wedding Day

In June, the days were long, and shades of dusk descended on this mountain village in streams of warm gold that embraced us as we walked. Before we reached the reception hall, really an extension of the camp post office, we were met by an overwhelming fragrance of freshly harvested flowers and maile vines. A large knotty banyan tree in the center of town had been in place there for over a hundred years. It shaded the hall and the post office and served as a gathering place where everyone "talked story" when collecting their mail. We all had to stoop low to pass under this great tree to enter the hall as was the habit, for this banyan was so sweeping and beautiful no one would ever trim the branches.

Upon entering the community room, a burst of color and fragrance filled my senses. My spouse's family and townmates had transformed the red dirt-stained walls into a charmed floral palace for the reception by decorating it with strung flowers and twisted vines gathered from the Molokai forests. I saw a large roll of flowers that held special lei of a unique weave made from rare, purple Maunaloa flowers found only in this area of the mountain. The wedding party and immediate family members each received a special lavender and white lei to wear during the party.

The bakery prepared an excellent wedding cake. The owner of this bakery was of Japanese heritage and served with the 442nd Infantry Battalion in France. When the troops liberated Marseilles, he happened to befriend a baker and learned a craft for life. They taught him their secrets and the art of making French bread, which is now world famous. No one ever visits this area without buying at least one loaf of world-famous Molokai Hot Bread to take home. This shop remains today as it did during our wedding with weathered glass showcasing their heavenly wares.

Before the wedding, I saw the family huddled, fussing, and whispering about the cake, which piqued my curiosity. When I pressed the point, I discovered they were concerned about the cake arriving intact while being transported along the bumpy roads from mid-island to the mountain village. This was a valid concern. Often, a cake arrived broken, or worse, with flies stuck in the frosting. Fortunately, our cake arrived in one piece—without flies.

Mom and I bought the cake top decoration in Honolulu at a Portuguese bakery. When the Portuguese came to Hawai'i as laborers in the early 1700s, they brought ovens and recipes for fragrant breads. Soon they were among the island's finest bakers. They built brick ovens to bake *pan dulce*, golden soft sweet bread. They were at their best making *malasadas*, a delectable deep-fried round doughnut rolled in white sugar. The smell alone was seductive.

Almost all the cake top decorations had lace trim that would yellow in time. I chose a couple, arm in arm, under a heart-shaped arch. Unfortunately, they were both blonds with pink plastic skin. I used felt-tip pens to color the groom's hair black and tinted his face to bronze. (I guess I was a pioneer in interracial wedding cake tops.) Everyone wondered if I had it special ordered. Thanks, Mom, for all those Saturday morning art classes.

Wedding Day Cooks, 1969.
Artwork by Philip Sabado

Midway through the party, we ran out of paper plates. Mom had bought one thousand. The shopkeeper opened the store especially for her so she could buy an additional five-hundred plates. In the pictures, many of the guests seem to be carrying a small cooking pot from their own kitchens to take home, a feast of leftovers.

9 – Wedding Day

In one corner of the room, a "shot table" was set up. Guests could put money in a freshly oiled koa bowl in exchange for a shot of whiskey. This was a busy table with a long line.

An ensemble of old men—all plantation workers—practiced for weeks and provided orchestra music. The Mauna Loa Serenaders as they called themselves, played brass and stringed instruments, including the mandolin, an instrument from the minstrel days of the Spanish Renaissance.

My brother-in-law, Eugene, was closest in age to Philip and a professional dancer. He had been a star performer of the same Pearl of the Orient Dance Troupe where Phil had once been a member—the same dance troupe I'd seen all those years ago when I'd sat in the front row as a teenager. Eugene brought fellow dancers to Molokai from Honolulu. They danced in the traditional Filipino attire in perfect harmony. I couldn't have been more grateful of their contribution to our wedding day. Together Philip and Eugene taught me some of the traditional dances, as well as providing beautiful costumes. Philip was a seasoned dancer, whereas I was a work in progress. I never felt in sync; they laughed heartily at my attempts to work my two left feet.

I had to practice these dances for the longest time, and the steps and twists and turns were still confusing to me. I struggled to learn the unfamiliar movements that seemed natural for the brothers. It was worth the effort to see the old people smile at the special treat of seeing these traditional dances.

I am a terrible dancer, and it took courage and enormous effort for me to do the dances at all. When I showed Eugene and Philip that I could dance an Irish jig, they looked at each other, confused. "If you can dance like that," they asked, "why is this so hard?"

The *tinikling* bamboo dance was a crowd-pleaser. In this dance, two performers held hands and with great precision lightly jumped over and between two long bamboo poles that were held at their ends by two other members of the dance troupe. They clicked the poles together, separated them, and then banged them on the floor in an appealing rhythm. The clicking and banging bamboo poles were accompanied by the shouting encouragement from the performers and the watching crowd. This was a playful dance. The beat started slowly and increased to a frenzy. Only the most skilled dancer would attempt this, never fearing to have their ankles pinched or crushed between the pounding bamboo poles.

My housemate, Diane, from the time I'd lived in the Honolulu housing project, performed the Princess Dance in the Moorish style of the Muslim tribes. She was attired in a beautifully patterned silk fabric in dark striking tones tightly wrapped around her thin form. Her jet-black hair was pulled into a tight chignon, and she balanced a lit candle in a crystal votive glass on her head. In each hand, she held a candle encased in a cut crystal glass. As haunting music played, the lights were dimmed, revealing only the dancing lights and her perfect oval face.

Afterward, Eugene and Diane danced the romantic Maria Clara from the Spanish tradition. For this dance, Diane wore a soft rose-pink full skirt with her shoulders wrapped in a white, sparkling opalescent beaded shawl that whooshed and swirled as she turned and spun. Her hair was adorned with a high Spanish comb encrusted with shimmering diamonds that caught the lights in the room. They moved about the room during this flirtatious dance as if he were chasing her. He twisted and turned while she pretended to flee. Diane dipped her chin coyly at the conclusion. I was enchanted by their performance and the guests were enthralled too, especially my family. Mama beamed like a proud bird strutting her finest feathers. On this night, the feathers were her family and the culture that had formed them. The dancers twirled past her in a blur of color and light that seemed to intensify with each flurry of the *rondalla* chords. I am sure many of the villagers had not seen anything like this since leaving their homeland as children and teenagers, proved by their beaming smiles and teary eyes.

The money dance was eagerly awaited because it gave the guests a chance to bless the new couple and wish them good fortune. During the dance, giggling women and men— everyone was a little tipsy by then— placed coins and paper money in my mouth. Children eagerly waited to be a part of the ritual. They begged the parents for coins so that they could partake in the fun. Philip's task was to take the money from me with a "kiss." His hands had to remain behind him, as were mine. We leaned into each other as the music and gaiety intensified. There were hoots and hollers at each feigned kiss.

As we turned, came together, and drew apart in the dance, Philip snatched the coins and bills from my mouth with his teeth and let them drop to the wooden floor. The light caught on the coins, casting sparkles of silver and gold to fly about the room as they jangled onto the floor. The dance came

9 – Wedding Day

from the days of the Spaniards, so gold coins were a part of the custom. As the spirit of this dance caught on, everyone jumped up with money in hand to give to the new couple. At one point, a line formed as people waited for us to dance into the corners of the hall. These days the custom continues, but it has been sanitized! Little plastic baggies hold the folded cash. I guess it makes sense, but I remember sitting next to my sister-in-law, Rosita, at a Molokai wedding in Kaunakakai many years later and said, "Not the same, yah? Ours was the best!"

Before the money dance, my sisters-in-law had instructed me about the proper protocol and did so with serious consternation. "Do not look at the money," they cautioned. "When Philip takes it from you, he will let it drop to the floor. Do not ever look at the money, even when it is on the floor; people will think you are greedy if you watch the money. They will think you are counting already." I understood their emphasis. My behavior on this day was critical to the success of the marriage. Since the people at the party had known Philip from childhood, all eyes would be on me.

Throughout the wedding reception, Philip's family spoke in Filipino as they patted my still flat stomach. Happily, they were making plans for the next party, a bunyag, *to celebrate the anticipated baptism. My mother looked from them to me with a confused look. I rolled my eyes and threw my hands up, nonplussed, with a passive expression and passed it off as just another of their customs. Whew! That was close.*

I allayed my fears and formulated a plan of how I would tell my parents. I wondered if their friends would believe that a soon-to-be ten-pound baby was premature. Mother will tell them something, *I mused,* and she will reason with Daddy, she always has.

Everyone came bearing gifts wrapped in silver, white or gold paper. Yards of ribbon cascaded down the sides of boxes carefully wrapped by hand. After the wedding, the gifts were placed in Manang Rosita's house. They were stacked so high they filled the hallway until they reached the ceiling. A small path had to be made between the boxes to access the kitchen and the *banyo*.

In those days, everyone owned at least one piece of Golden Wheat dinnerware: a creamy white china with a shiny gold rim, and in the center, three stalks of wheat bending in the breeze. Back then, Rinso Blue laundry detergent had a special offer: collect enough box tops and redeem them for towels or the Golden Wheat collection. I still see remnants of these dishes. We received trays and dishes carved from monkeypod wood that had come from the Philippines. Some featured depictions of carabaos (water buffalo), the Philippines' national symbol of strength, patience, and endurance, an icon of the provinces.

Wedding Day with Full Court and Ninongs and Ninangs (sponsors),
Saint Vincent's Church, Maunaloa, Molokai,
June 1969.
Photo by Paul Donegan

Presents had arrived for months before the wedding from my family's California and East Coast friends. I felt excited when the letter carrier came with a large box. Everyone would crowd in like bees around a blossom. They would insist I open the present in front of them.

Phil and I were often sent beautiful silver from the finest stores in Los Angeles or Boston. After all the "oohs" and "aahs" had died down, there would be about three seconds of silence before someone would ask, "Okay, Auntie Chris, what is it?"

"It's a chafing dish." And then seeing their confusion, I'd have to clarify, "A silver bun warmer."

More silence, then usually one of the children would say, "Auntie Chris,...a what?"

I would explain in a way they could comprehend. After the first couple of presents, I got into the habit of telling them what the present was before the awkward silence.

My mother managed to thwart one Filipino tradition. Once Philip and I left the party, we were supposed to stay in a small house for seven days after the wedding. All our meals would be left at the door because we were not supposed to leave the wedding house. This was yet another ancient tradition to assure the success of the new couple. However, my mother had bought a honeymoon package for us in Kona on the Big Island of Hawai'i. She came up with a story after we left the party and slipped us away to the airport. The celebration continued and I am not sure we were even missed. Apparently, the lure of being completely alone with me on another island as a getaway was enough to allow Phil to break some rules—and why not?

We heard that the wedding feast went on for three days. In the midst of all the preparations, I didn't stop to think about where all the food had come from. The day was a blur, truly a mix of aromas, both food and flower that blended into a sweet memory for all time.

With the proceeds from the money dance, the gift envelopes, and the shot table bowl, we had about a thousand dollars tucked into a brown paper lunch sack. We thought we were very rich! We arrived in Kona on a Sunday when all the banks were closed and hid the money under our bed in the sack, very creased from my clutching. We were now officially married and beginning our lives together.

10 - Newlywed Adjustments

*'Ohana (family) gathering,
Honolulu, Hawai'i.*
Photo by Paul Donegan

10

 I once heard an interview that asked a simple question about marriages between the races, specifically the multicultural peoples of the islands. In truth, three out of five marriages in Hawai'i were intercultural as well as interracial. The question asked was about conflicts this relationship would impose. My thought was to question: Were there difficulties in this relationship? Some. Yet overall, not as many as one could expect. Compromises, yes, as in all marriages. Marriage is a challenge in its simplest form when you combine two vastly different backgrounds. If you allow for this, you can create a tender and rich soup that yields complex flavors the longer it stews.

When on Molokai, there was no other option for me but to listen. I had to learn to show respect for those elements and the people I barely understood.

Many intercultural marriages fail. What helped us succeed was knitted in time, patience and abiding love. For me, it all seemed simple: if you were thrown into the ocean, would you stop and think, Should I swim? *There would be no choice. You would swim or try to. I was confident that I would overcome any obstacle and swim forward. If we had married on the mainland or even on O'ahu, our marriage would have been different. The challenges of those times helped to hone and shape our relationship for the future. I can never discount the magic of Molokai acting like a salve that eased the differences in our polar worlds ready to merge as one. Molokai benefitted me in uncountable measures.*

After the honeymoon in Kona, we returned to live in the camp with Manang Rosita and her husband, Manong Perfecto. Manong Perfecto was the epitome of a hardworking Filipino man. He drove an eighteen-wheeler that hauled the full pineapple brimming crates from the main yard in Maunaloa to the Kaunakakai Harbor. Once there, large forklifts descended like a science fiction scene to lift the bounty to an awaiting barge that would take the sweet golden treasure over the water between the islands. The aroma of that golden fruit has stayed with me.

Slim, dark, with a baseball cap placed gingerly on his head and a cigarette hanging from his lips, Manong Perfecto was the kindest man, always cheerful, and cooking for the family at all hours. From early breakfast at four a.m. to the evening meal, he would be packing the day's meals for those heading out the door. He spoke English well, but with family he relied on his ethnic tongue. He used English with me, always with a melodic lilt. With his compadres, his native language poured out like syrup. He was an intelligent man too. He did the taxes for many families and participated on many community boards. He assisted the families in burial and funeral plans, wherein they paid ten dollars per month.

Sadly, he never returned home to the Philippines, mostly because Manang Rosita feared flying and leaving her alone was not an option. We knew Manong Perfecto till the end of his life when he passed in his late eighties on Maui after his wife passed on.

To live on Molokai made sense. We were young and with a baby coming we could save money. Besides, this was expected as part of a long tradition of the elders overseeing the young couples in their first years together. In 1969, Philip spent his final summer in the fields harvesting pineapple. We planned to return to Honolulu for his last year of art school.

Remembering Mama's words from before the wedding, I saw the task at hand. Immersed in a family where I was a true stranger, although now married to the youngest son, I needed to find a way for his siblings to accept me, even a little would be a huge step forward. I knew they loved Philip deeply and perhaps any girl he'd brought home would never have been good enough in their eyes. I realized that as different as they seemed to me, I must have seemed twice as different to them. I suppose it would have been easier and less of a challenge for them if he'd brought home a Filipina. Or, at least, a Molokai girl. Someone who would fit right in like slipping on a comfortable shoe, whereas I felt more like a four-inch stiletto. At eighteen, I had to stretch every mental fiber to simply fit in. I was so young and insecure, and my height, five feet nine inches, didn't help my cause.

I knew I was a mystery. I was the first haole to enter this family on Molokai. As

10 – Newlywed Adjustments

I have mentioned, an older sister had married a soldier in the service while stationed in Japan after World War II. They had moved to Northern California to live and their contact with the family was limited by distance. I, on the other hand, was a blue-eyed blonde with long streaked hair. I fit into the California mold as a surfer girl, one who talked too much and asked too many questions, especially about things they took for granted. I heard, "Das how!" over and over. Philip patiently answered me as taught by his Mama, and never criticized my naiveté.

My learning curve was tempered at night when we were alone under the covers. Even as my belly grew, our intense fervor and attraction never wavered. This lovemaking was the anchor that held me strong, his arms always sheltered and embraced me, and the passion sustained me in countless ways.

Mama made the decision for us to live in the camp after our wedding. Beforehand, Philip had what he thought was a dream job in Honolulu. Amid wedding plans, she took him aside and told him to remain on Molokai after the ceremony. At first, she teased him and told him he was becoming too 'po pa'a, Hawaiian for dark-skinned, and would scare my family.

What influenced her decision was deeper than his skin tone and more about the nature of the job he had prior to the wedding. Philip had seen an advertisement for a job opening in the newspaper for an experienced diver, someone who knew the island waters. He was the only local boy to apply, and once interviewed, he convinced them of his Molokai Ocean knowledge. He was hired on the spot and was selected to work with several other divers, all of whom had PhDs, to work on a top-secret project. His security clearance took weeks, and it took me years to get him to tell me what the top-secret project was about. He can keep a secret.

In the late sixties, the Vietnam War was raging and many of my high school friends had already perished. Philip's new job as a diver was to train dolphins to swim at top speed with antipersonnel warheads, literally a bomb attached to the nose. The mammal swam like a rocket shot from a cannon to a designated enemy vessel where it would detach the magnetic bomb from its nose, turn 180 degrees, and shoot back before the bomb exploded. All of this had to be done within seconds. Though trained to save its life by returning ASAP, the odds were not in the mammal's favor. I never learned how long the timer on the device would take. What did it matter? Innocent dolphins and orcas were being used to achieve man's destruction. Dolphins are intelligent. Could they have known their fate?

In the summer season mother sharks came to give birth in these Kaneohe waters. Every morning, the diver's first job was to lay miles of shark lines that had to be collected before they could begin the training sessions. The lines were pulled daily from the deepest blue waters and apparently, they hooked dozens of sharks. Philip would not say how many sharks were found at the ends of the large hooks. On the plus side, no one cared how many fish he caught on these diving escapades, and as a local boy and diver, what more could he ask for? Naturally, the family rejoiced and ate the freshest fish ever! To hear him regale this time, you would think he'd died and gone to ocean heaven, despite the grim task.

He did say that the dolphins he'd trained and swam with every day had become his friends. They would snuggle their large bulbous noses under his arm. He had pet names for all of them. Once in the water he could look down and see their shapes coming at bullet speed to greet him. He had to brace himself for the impact, a bump that propelled him out of the water! He laughed when he told this story, loving his giant friends.

Mama knew of Philip's work. When she found out he would be training killer whales next, her protests intensified and hardened. Even though Philip's part was small, she insisted he quit. He never could disobey her, and with his head and shoulders sagging, he consented to resign.

Many years later we saw the movie *The Day of the Dolphin*. Though fictionalized, the similarities could not be denied, and he felt he could tell me about that time. He nudged me as we were sitting in the darkened theater. He said, "Remember when I was working in Kaneohe Bay? I did that," as he pointed to the blue screen. He sounded sad as he remembered his friends who were so human-like. He also revealed a secret: protocol dictated always locking the harbor gate, so the dolphins were ready for the next day of training. One day someone forgot, and they all escaped. He never told me who it was, but he had an impish grin when he told the story.

After the wedding, my father caught my attention as we walked through the camp. A makani (wind) funneled up from the lowlands. As he looked around, he commented that I should live on Molokai forever. He was hooked, enchanted, and seduced by the simple village and the peaceful plantation camp life that to him, as a professional working in Los Angeles, seemed like an idyllic dream. I mentioned that

Philip was supposed to finish art school the next year and said Molokai would always be a great place to visit. Philip was very happy and comfortable in the environment he had always known. I, on the other hand, had to make a few adjustments. I did not know that the camp and plantation life would serve as a preface to my life.

Party—Outdoor Cooking, 1969.
Artwork by Philip Sabado

For example, eating was a celebration, the happiest time of day for the family. Men did all the cooking. They served the women and children first, and Mama and Papa. It seemed the more slurping noises the diners made, the better (an Asian tradition, perhaps?), and the cook was rewarded with smiles and appreciation.

The family had a special way of eating with their hands. Using their fingertips, they would work the rice into a mound and scoop the packed morsel into their mouths. I asked Philip about this custom. He commented that the fork I used might have been washed days before. He always knew his hands were clean before he ate. This was always done.

Some of the delicacies were unusual by American standards as family members would playfully fight over fish heads. Naturally, Mama's portion was set aside first. The white ball of the fish's eye was a treasure, sucked out and then devoured. I tried this only once and discovered a squishy, rubbery texture with little flavor. There was no part of this protein that went to waste. The soft cheek meat was another delicacy.

In my family, proper table manners and etiquette were emphasized early on. I continued to use a fork and kept a folded napkin in my lap. I took my new family's ways in good humor and considered it a great part of learning a new culture.

Sleeping arrangements took some getting used to. Philip's family used koltsons, woven mattresses of abaca fibers placed on the floor. My husband had not slept in a Western-style bed until he went into the Army at eighteen.

By the time I bore my third child, I insisted on a Western bed. It was too difficult to get up and down from the floor with a big belly. I always needed an outstretched hand to rise from the mattress and I longed to be able to place my feet on the floor once I awoke. Eventually, sleeping on a raised mattress was an adjustment Philip would have to make. I laughed to myself because whenever I was away for a couple of days, I'd return to find the bed had not been slept in; he had slept on the floor again!

Life in the camp had drawbacks. As part of our paradise, we were smack dab in the middle of a field of ripening sweet pineapple. I missed a regular bathroom with a door, not a wet piece of fabric flying in the wind. Pregnant women go to the bathroom at least twice as often. The *banyo* was located in a shed with a cold, bare concrete floor. I laughed to myself when I saw multi-colored plastic clothespins holding silky women's underpants while they dried. Everything was out in the open and unabashed.

The toilet was in a separate stall, blocked off from the shower area by corrugated tin roofing. The stall had been painted repeatedly, but it peeled from the constant moisture and was difficult to keep clean. Filipinos had a different style of bathing. They sat on a small bench and dipped hot water out of a *palangana* (large round metal washtub). They used a tako (large dipper) to splash water over their heads. I suspect it saved water and had its origins from village mountain life.

Once, before I descended the two steps to the toilet area, I noticed a shadow dart before me. The movement happened so fast it could have been anything, but I knew it was a rat! I have an intense fear of rats. I froze in place, turned on my heel, and went back into the bedroom. It was an act of extreme bravery on my part to not scream and wake up half the village.

I stood at the foot of our bed and stammered until I got the words out. "Honey, wake up! You must come with me now!" I sputtered and said the dreaded word, "RAT!"

Philip dragged himself out of bed and without comment walked me to the toilet. It became his habit to wait with me every time I needed to go, which was constantly. This was another aspect of living in the middle of a sweet crop of ever-ripening pineapples. Once the fruit was harvested, the critters would run to a place that had water and was warm and dark.

The camp people were accustomed to this routine. It was considered sport to sit up all night with a BB gun poised and ready. Philip made only one comment to me that first night when we were both in bed, "Don't worry, I will tell Manong to get his knife ready." He laughed at my look of disbelief. My eyes were wide with a new terror. I rolled over, pulled the quilt over my head, and bit the fabric.

The rats were quite creative and could enter the plantation houses in all sorts of ways: down drainpipes, through the sewage, and even up into the toilet bowl. I heard someone had been bitten on their okole (posterior) as they sat poised to do their business. Everyone swore this had really happened and more than once. Wary, I peered into the toilet before I sat down. My eyes never rested, always on the lookout for darting shadows.

The kitchen seemed to be a dangerous place as well. Sister Lolly told me that once as she stood by the stove a rat jumped onto her muumuu, and she had to beat it off with a broom. After that story, I would sit in her kitchen with my feet folded up under me, never touching the floor. On the lookout, I waited for something to peer at me from under the stove or behind the refrigerator. I was terrified! It occurred to me that they delighted in my wide-eyed terror or when I cringed in fear. "No worries," Phil advised. "I think it is sleeping under the stove. They only come out at night." Sister Rosy teased me by saying, "My husband will catch him tonight—I think!" I would smile lamely, all the while my eyes scanning the floor. Somehow, I endured plantation life and understood it would be a temporary situation.

I chose to bathe standing in a shower and always wore rubber flip-flops. The pipe with the showerhead hung inches over my head. I insisted that Philip bathe with me. He would stand aside to let me go first and then he took his shower. Once, he kept turning me around and around for no apparent reason. He was anxious and rushed me to finish. Years later, long after we had moved from Molokai, he admitted there had been a large rat hovering overhead with its long tail hanging into the shower stall.

Sometimes they must have told these stories to tease or terrify me just to see my eyes grow large. One sister told of a lump at the end of the bed and how the next morning she found a sleeping rat in bed with her. I would quake and then began to strip the bed before climbing in. I needed Phil to accompany me everywhere, even into the kitchen. I must have had a phobia or some rat disorder from all that anxiety. I maintain that in another life, I must have been in a dungeon somewhere, England, I believe.

I am sure my behavior did not add to my foreign appeal as I probably seemed like a spoiled child to them. Though these instances were not like anything I had to deal with in my former life, strange as it may be, memories and thoughts of my suburban life with my parents faded quickly in the compelling Molokai village and tropical sun.

I focused on making a new adjustment every day. Perhaps what held me strong were the nights of love Phil and I shared in that creaky little house. My body craved his warm skin and strength. I would curl close and breathe in his scent, a mixture of soap and his maleness. He never scolded or chastised me, and his devotion was overwhelming. I clung to the thought that the adjustments would be temporary, and so I managed.

Phil rose at four a.m. He never woke me, just a light kiss as he padded from the darkened room. In the hallway, he would pull on heavy canvas pants and shirts laid out the night before by Manong Perfecto. These would protect him from the pineapple points. He also wrapped a checkered bandanna around his head and neck for protection. He would slip out the door and walk down the russet dirt road with a team of men.

From the main station, the workers were transported to the fields in the back of large trucks in the dark of night. From there the trucks headed for the iron-rich roads that accessed the fields as the sun crested on the horizon. He was happy with this work and enjoyed the camaraderie in the fields. He was happy at home with friends and family—happy all the time.

While Philip worked in the fields harvesting pineapples, I would take long drives in the Volkswagen to explore Molokai. I was used to being on my own and enjoyed my independence. The memory of the constant breeze from my arrival day was palatable when enticed by teasing rainbows.

A pack of pencils and a sketchpad would keep me occupied. Anticipating our first-born was exciting and exhilarating. In these days we were like kids awaiting Christmas, knowing a great gift would arrive soon.

Word reached the family of my daily sojourns. There were some whispers and side glances, and then a directive not to do this as it was not wise to be out alone. This was not a negotiable point. When I pressed for an explanation, I was met with the inevitable "das how." I resigned myself to this prudence since Philip's workday in the fields ended in the early afternoon, followed by pau hana (work completed). He and the men would trudge up the road at two in the afternoon. I could hear them in the distance, laughing. I waited for him to come down the dirt pathway. I would sit on the steps dressed in my outing clothes, so we could go for a ride or to town. Our time alone was special and rare.

At some point in the family's earlier evolution, Mama chose to defer authority to the oldest brother, Santi. His name was a testament of loyalty to the village where Papa was born, Santiago. Perhaps Mama realized Papa's limitations early on. Even when the oldest brother lived in Northern California, family conflicts were settled by his word alone, and his word was final. I am sure Mama was aware of problems, but she could conserve her strength and prevent more conflict by delegating final authority. After her death when Papa chose to remarry, the only person he discussed this decision with was his oldest son. Since Santi lived on the mainland he was not bothered too often. He had his own family to attend to. His wife was the sister-in-law who belligerently warned me on my wedding day.

Mama must have realized this marriage between her son and the girl from a different land would need her help to prosper. I am sure their perception was: "She is a haole, you know. Brother is dating a White girl!" After the summer of our wedding, we traveled from the plantation to settle on O'ahu in the small community of 'Aiea. If you blinked, it could be missed. This town was north of bustling Waikiki and busy Honolulu on the west side of the island. Set above Pearl Harbor, it offered a clear view of Diamond Head, the ships docked at port, and beyond, was the turquoise sea.

Puakala Street dipped into a closed, insulated Filipino Community. It could just as well have been in the Philippines. We could never drive straight to the house without slowing to five to ten miles an hour to dodge chickens, dogs, and the many barefooted brown children running across the road in worn flip-flops, kicking a ball.

Being in the vicinity of Pearl Harbor, many locals worked minutes away at the large Navy base. The house where we lived belonged to Manang Carmen, Philip's father's cousin. Each of the seven bedrooms was filled with family from various branches. Their street went down a cul-de-sac and from the top of the road, we could see Pearl Harbor and the Arizona Memorial. Each day at noon and dusk, the sun would catch on the water and a zillion sparks would blaze from the sea. I was not surprised when Mama and Papa packed and came to live with us. Moving was not that difficult for them. There was always family to stay with and they traveled light, often sharing one suitcase. All Papa cared about was that he could bring his guitar and Bible. Mama's household items remained at Rosita's house, their central home on Molokai, in her la casa, the large steamer trunk.

Mama was often wary of Papa's side of the family from the Philippines. They had a habit of marrying first cousins. Mama was always pleasant to these cousins and showed respect. They treated her very well with true love and affection.

Philip and I lived in one bedroom on the second floor and paid forty dollars a month. The living arrangements were well organized. We were allocated one shelf in the kitchen cupboard and half a shelf in the refrigerator. Mama and Papa would live downstairs with Philip's brother and sister who each had their own rooms.

Everyone was totally comfortable with these living arrangements, including my new spouse. The phrase "as snug as a bug in a rug" comes to mind when I think of 'Aiea.

10 – Newlywed Adjustments

I felt bewildered in this communal living arrangement. After growing up in a family of four, I marveled at how this family could all coexist in good humor. Living together in this fashion was not always due to their financial situation. They loved to be with each other because they were family. This attitude could have come from the Philippines or Polynesia in general, where everyone seemed happy and congenial. It would be bad manners to be loud or pick a fight with a cousin. If you were having a bad day or were in a sour mood, it was best to stay in your room or to holoholo (go out for a while) and return renewed. When you were better, everyone would be waiting to welcome you back. How simple.

After we settled in, my pregnancy was the focal point of the family. I felt protected in a spiritual and physical way. I knew how important it was to take walks for exercise during this first phase so I would have an easy delivery. I did not have a driver's license, so I walked to the store or to the library, which was a couple of blocks up a hill and then down the road, in all about two miles.

Whenever I got dressed to go out, Mama and Papa became agitated. They had a discussion in Ilocano that would accelerate to pointing and without words Papa knew there was a mission at hand. He would be on his feet, agreeing. Leaving the house, I could feel the hairs of my neck rise and I'd turn to see Papa following me perhaps ten or twenty paces behind. Everywhere I went he was my shadow, even waiting patiently outside the library on the steps.

When my husband returned home, I was ready with questions. Didn't they trust me? In his kind way he replied, "It is not that." He was silent for a long moment as he seemed to choose his words with caution. His explanation was simply that his parents were afraid that I would fall or would not be safe. My intuition told me there was probably more than he was able to say.

The next day as I slipped my feet into my flip-flops at the doorway, I turned and said to Mama, "Ma, no need, no need Papa wit me." Since my Filipino was still in the beginning stages, I used a hand gesture, with my open hand turning from side to side to indicate no need. She smiled and continued talking to Papa in their language. Papa donned his hat and adjusted it to his preferred tilt as he prepared to follow me. As I walked along the path, as always, he was behind me.

I became accustomed to my shadow as Papa waited outside the store or library until I finished. He would be behind, perhaps by half a block, never being obvious, as I continued on my way. What I began to understand was that Mama had thrown a net of protection around me, and Papa was simply one of the knots that bound our family in place. He never grumbled and happily did whatever she asked.

At Manang Carmen's house, I passed Mama's room and heard my new parents singing the most melodious Filipino songs. Their voices in blended harmony created a special symmetry. They sang Filipino folk songs or church songs that became their prayer.

I stopped and leaned in closer to listen, moved by the love and beauty that emanated from behind their wooden door, thinking for a moment that it was the radio tuned to the Filipino Channel. Phil followed me into the hallway and as I turned to him with a look and a question, he smiled and said, "They are rehearsing for their church." They sang like love birds in different timber with their words intertwining as their lives had for over fifty-some years. Listening to their lyrical voices brought me to tears. I felt so grateful to be within the embrace of this family.

When Phil and I were in our room, I shared how his parents' voices had touched me. He smiled and said, "Das how." On reflection, I can appreciate that this time in 'Aiea was special, a gift. Fortunately, the "das how" came from my husband when we first met. His mother had taught him, and taught him well, all the island ways. If he picked a blossom from a tree, he always asked permission. As he departed with the flower and savored the fragrance with gratitude, he always said, "Mahalo."

In the Western world, it is typical to take whatever you want and never bother to ask, especially when the item came from nature—humans assume that they are always the dominant species. For whatever their reasons, people feel they are owed something and yet own everything. Many only respected those who have acquired and have taken. Those who have lived close to the earth seemed to understand this more.

Once when I came home to our 'Aiea family house, there was a stranger in the parlor. A haole girl sat on the sofa by herself, looking excited. They were all waiting for me to come home and were attempting small talk with her. When I came in the door, I know I had a confused look on my face. I asked her if we had met. She smiled and said she was selling magazines door to door, and that Philip was kind enough to let her in.

I returned her smile, but I turned to Philip and asked to see him in the kitchen. "Do you know this person?"

His answer was incredible, spoken with true innocence. "Oh, she is haole, too, and we thought you knew her."

He had invited her to sit down, a stranger, because he assumed we knew each other. After all, we both had blonde hair and were Caucasian. He never thought to ask her why she was there. Based on my experience on my walks, I was the only Caucasian for miles around. The Navy base was about five miles away and worlds apart from this little road above the harbor. The only other haole people I saw were on television or perhaps at the mall. I was so amused by the crazy logic; I shook my head in amazement and went back into the parlor. I had a polite chat with her and ended up ordering a magazine subscription. I realized the family was merely trying to make me feel at home.

As my pregnancy progressed, I wanted to live in my own home. As selfish as this may sound, I had two full closets of wedding gifts and the like, and in any case, was ready to set up house and begin our lives as a family. To Philip, however, this was one step leading to the unknown and nothing short of a mutiny!

I had to plan a careful strategy to convince him that we needed to find our own place to live. The dream of having my own house with my own things when our baby came would hopefully be soon.

As far as Philip was concerned, we could live among family forever. Traditionally, for this Filipino camp family, it was the custom for a young married couple to live with the family for at least the first five years. How he could broach the subject of a home of our own to his mother was a mystery; you always lived with the family. It was another "das how."

One evening the timing seemed right to speak about this subject. He resisted, but in his sweet and innocent way, he thought hard and tried to find a compromise I would find palatable.

"If I tell them not to touch your dishes, and if I buy you all new pots and pans, and if I cook for you, can we stay? I will even wash all your dishes for you."

He knew it annoyed me that Papa washed with cold water. I felt defeated. This was so shocking and pathetic. He did not get my position at all. I fought my impulse to yell. I reminded myself of the task at hand aware that I was in uncharted territory.

Again, I repeated with sincerity and without anger, "I want to have my baby in my own house."

He looked completely confused and said, "This is just not done in my family."

I was in shock! This conversation was not going the way I planned. Taking a long breath, I centered myself, looked to him with renewed kindness, and love I said, "Philip, they are no longer the family. We are your family now, this baby and me." I rested my hands on my growing belly as my gaze settled on what would be our first child. "We are your family now. They are our relatives, and we will love them always, but we are your first family. Remember, you agreed to that when we married. We need our own place to live, not just a bedroom and a shelf in the refrigerator." I gave him a warm, knowing smile. "Don't worry, you will love it. And one day you will try to remember what it was like living with all these people." As I spoke, my eyes scanned the overpacked room. Perhaps I was playing my mainland girl card, but I was at my wit's end with nowhere to go.

I glanced around our small room with its meager furnishings and overstuffed closet. As mentioned before, we slept Filipino style on the floor on abaca mats. "Once you get used to living on our own, you can never come back to this lifestyle. I promise. And you will see that."

What we had been doing was not wrong or incorrect, it was not what I wanted or expected in my married life. For the others, their way seemed to be comfortable and suitable, and fit with their culture and lifestyle. I could not compromise on this. I wanted my own house and that was final. I had made many adjustments, but the further along I was in my pregnancy, the more I yearned for my suburban creature comforts, such as a mattress and some space.

His eyes seemed to pop open in understanding. I could almost see the light go on in his head. By then, it was two in the morning. I had been pleading my case for hours and was desperately tired.

He spoke in a different tone, with confidence. "Pau already, we will move…and somehow, I will convince Mama. Ma, she from a different place, cannot help, 'das how.'"

He was afraid they would think we were not appreciative or that we were acting 'high maka maka' (high born). I suppose the assertion could have some validity. I suspected he would use the foreign card with his family.

That night I slept soundly, knowing I had scored a big victory. I felt we had turned a corner. Soon, as a couple, we would have our own place. The next morning as I sipped coffee, I scanned the Cottages for Rent section in the daily newspaper.

Every day after work we would do drive-byes in different neighborhoods. It did not take long to find a sweet cottage on Judd Street up Nu'uanu Avenue. We began packing. Once we signed the lease, a deadly silence pervaded Manang Carmine's house. One by one, Philip and I carried full boxes to the car. No one moved to help us. Mama stayed in her room and everyone else stared at the TV so as not to look at us coming and going. There was a bit of stifled sniffling as Mama tried to hold back her emotions. There was no anger, only silence that conveyed much more.

No doubt many conversations were held within the family about Philip having married outside the community, and after all, the woman was haole, and her people live alone. I imagined them shaking their heads from side to side, wondering why anyone would want to live on their own.

As we filled another load into the back seat, he spoke so they could not hear. "They are doing the best they can—'das how.'"

Soon we were settled into our cottage. The small house may have once been a garage converted into a one bedroom with a bath, but no laundry room. We found an old washer at the thrift store, a classic round tub with a wringer, two rollers at the top that squeezed the wetness from the clothing. We managed to wheel the antique into the shower space, conveniently the wash water ran into the shower drain. We would jimmy an electric line to the nearest outlet to make it work. Wisely, I chose to always wear rubber slippers in the shower when I ran the washer. I was terrified of electric shock. In hindsight, I was still pregnant and beyond stupid!

In January of 1970, our beautiful ten-pound boy named Paulo was born. The family estrangement lifted, and they adjusted to the change. A new baby always helps to mend rifts. I remember finding the name in a magazine article on Picasso whose first son was named Paulo. That was it, the name stuck.

Our lives all returned to normal with dinners at our homes. We visited the family when we could, usually for Sunday dinner. Often Mama and Papa would come and stay with us for weeks at a time. I learned how to help with her medications as her health seemed to be in decline. I could give her insulin injections.

Philip and I were happy to be settled in our quaint cottage in misty Nu'uanu Valley our first year. We flourished as a family and a couple. I possessed the skills to make our house a home and decorating was my forte. I had much to learn about living with my new husband, and to adjust to the habits he had brought with him from Molokai and the pineapple plantation.

One night we were both fast asleep—it must have been well after midnight—when I heard a dog barking outside. I pulled the comforter close in and turned over. Philip sat up in bed, paused, then stood and went toward the kitchen.

I sat up and rubbed the sleep from my eyes. "Where are you going?" I asked.

He said in the most natural way, "The dog is barking outside because of the spirits around the house that only he can see. I need to put garlic in the windows so they cannot enter the house." He saw how I came to life and saw my confused expression because he added, "If I were to go outside and take the *mucat* (the corner solution in the dog's eye), I could see them too."

I am sure my mouth was agape as he went about his task. I lay there silently staring out the window. The lace curtains cast feathery shadows on the wall as the moonlight shone through. My baby lay fast asleep in his crib. Sleep eluded me. I was now fully awake after his proclamation of spirits. I pondered this interesting family, marriage, and life that was unfolding for me. I scanned the ceiling and room as I relaxed against the pillows. The barking from the neighbor's dog ceased in a couple of moments, and it allowed me to hear additional barking a distance away. The spirits are traveling, moving away, and the dogs are barking at a distance now, hmm?

10 – Newlywed Adjustments

We seemed to live suspended between this real world and another of compromise with a spirit world for which we had to show respect. For my husband, this was the inevitable "das how," but for me, it felt as though I had entered a place very few go to and experience.

A couple of years later on another occasion the dogs began to bark, and by then we had a new baby in the crib. Baby Erin was born less than a year later, and we still lived in the same location near a graveyard. Philip rose. This time, he prepared the garlic in a small bowl of vinegar to be placed under the cribs. I never questioned his actions. These old rituals were clearly well established. He went about these tasks methodically and never complained. This time I pulled the covers closer and returned to sleep knowing this was a way he protected us. All was done in respect, and love.

I never bothered with the small bowl under the cribs. He must have emptied the vinegar on his own because I pretended not to notice. It was my way of showing respect for him and his ways, and not questioning his actions. My husband was kind and giving, he cooked all my meals, he attended to the babies every time they cried, and loved me and made love to me passionately. I could live with garlic and vinegar on occasion. Other women made larger compromises, whereas mine merely dealt with what I considered old cultural mores and superstition.

I was to explore a spiritual realm on my own. Behind our little cottage was a small backyard and over a lava stone wall the old Nu'uanu Cemetery. An ancient stone wall separated us from the graves. Here were burial stones from the early missionary days and the 1800s. At the far north end of the cemetery was a crematorium. From my kitchen window, I could see beyond the wall to the tops of the gravestones and the manicured green grass. This view seemed to elicit a dichotomy: I was a young mother in my happiest days with a marriage and a young family, looking at the ultimate ending. On certain days, when a stream of silver smoke rose from the crematorium a chill would shake me to the core. (No wonder the dogs howled.) When the wind shifted, a strange aroma permeated the small house. I said a silent prayer for those being devoured by the funeral fires.

This burial ground was the oldest cemetery on the island and many of the original missionaries from the first five families were buried there.

Mounted on the tombstones were weathered yellowed photographs protected beneath a square of a glass along with a brief history of the deceased and how they had died.

At the corner across from Nuʻuanu Avenue, there was a Japanese cemetery with black, shiny marble headstones engraved with names in *kanji* (Japanese writing using Chinese characters). A Chinese temple at the farthest corner featured a different architectural style, painted in dark forest greens with bright red trim on the tilted eaves. In these graveyards visitors would often leave a small offering of fresh fruit or an unopened can of beer and a pack of cigarettes laid out before the marble headstone. No one would disturb these offerings.

I craved exercise and enjoyed walking with baby Paulo in the stroller. The roads around my house were busy so I would go to the old missionary cemetery for a quiet place to walk. I would navigate the stroller through the high grass and read about the lives of these ancient people. It may seem morbid, but I could not drive, and this was my only outing at the time as I was pregnant with our second son, Erin.

Word of my adventures and walks in the cemetery reached Mama. On the following Sunday, she and Papa's relatives descended upon our little house. In their satchels were Hawaiian salt, garlic, and a great many ti leaves. Hawaiian customs were used to ward off spirits and protect those within. Since they had come to the house armed and ready, it appeared to be a carefully orchestrated plan.

Hawaiian salt is akin to kosher salt with large sharply angled granules harvested from coarse rocks that trap the salts from ocean water in the many lava stones on the shore. Family members reached deep within a bag and threw large handfuls in every direction. They scattered the ti leaves, both green and red, until our property was surrounded. The ti leaves were also tied in a special fashion and arranged in the corners of each room. They moved the ti leaves like a broom in a sweeping motion, never touching the floor, moving air and clearing the unseen out the door and windows. They placed peeled garlic on all the windowsills, a custom I already understood.

Under their directive, every window in the house flew open. The door could not be shut for hours as the relatives cleared out whatever or whomever I might have brought into the house with me. They spoke in a concentrated, almost silent prayer, one I could not understand.

I suspect all these elements were needed since they were not sure which type of spirit I might have encountered—perhaps it was best to cover all the bases. The Filipino spirits would surely react to the garlic, and the ti leaves and salt would affect the Hawaiians. I let them proceed as I stood to the side of the room, not speaking, not angry or even annoyed. I had made a deal with myself that this all came with the territory. I smiled inwardly, knowing the next day I would need to vacuum extra hard.

Once settled, Phil and I sat down, and I received firm yet gentle scolding from my mother-in-law. My dear husband got worse in his own language. "It is not her fault. We do not expect her to know our ways. It is your job to teach and protect your wife and children from the spirit world. We hold you responsible! She is hapai (pregnant); she carries a new life. The dead in the graves have no life any longer, pau, make (pronounced: mah kay), they are already dead. What is to prevent them from taking this child from her? She is walking over their dead bodies!"

The scolding for Philip from Mama and Manang Carmen seemed to go on forever. I listened intently and caught a couple of words and phrases. He answered her while his head hung low. "Yes, Ma. Yes, Ma." At the end, Philip turned to me and said, "Hon, you cannot go walking up there anymore, yah? Okay?"

My response was a weak smile and a question. "They have been talking to you for over an hour and that is all you have to tell me?"

He looked away for a moment overwhelmed by the emotions that had flown about that day. "Just never walk that way again…bumbye somebody going stay wit' you!"

I never told Mama that when dawn's first light crept into our rooms and I was only half-awake, I saw her—an old woman who stood by the baby's crib gazing lovingly at my sleeping child. My eyes darted from the spirit to the doorjamb still locked with a sliding latch. The old woman smiled at me and then back at the baby. I had no fear. She was clearly a spirit; how else had she gotten into the room? I noticed her beautiful, angelic face and realized Mama was correct; I had brought someone home from my walk.

Since I did not want a repeat performance at the crib from Mama and the family, I never told anyone about this incident and never again returned to the cemetery for my walk. In truth, even as we passed by, I looked away so as not to engage those who might have wanted to attach themselves to us and visit again. So, in the end, I listened and learned!

On the day the family performed the spiritual cleansing of my house, Papa remained oblivious. He hummed softly and smiled while talking to Philip. I am sure he was aware of what was transpiring. All the while he was busy cooking in the kitchen. Once Mama had completed her task, it was understood our home and all else had been returned to harmonious balance, pono.

We all sat down to bowls of steaming rice and sabau a mixture of vegetables with chunks of pork and fat in a bowl of steaming soup. Philip liked to straddle Paulo on his knee so he could eat and talk story, laugh, and make jokes as if nothing had happened. He had an endearing habit of cupping rice with one hand and pushing the grains into the baby's mouth without spilling a single grain. I was impressed, as I struggled with a small baby spoon and still needed to wipe his chin.

With everything made right, not another word was mentioned, as if a storm had blown through and no one noticed. The house reeked of garlic from the cooking as well as from the large chunks placed in the open windows to deter any more spirits from even considering entering this house.

I was not the only one who had crossed this invisible cultural line. Another time, while still living in the Nu'uanu cottage, Philip was researching Hawaiian subjects. He hiked up one of the streams in the Nu'uanu Valley and found a petroglyph of a dog on the face of a cave. It was a simple design of a dog etched into the stone, carved by the ancient Hawaiians.

He happened to have a piece of muslin cloth and some charcoal with him and found he could copy the image by taking a rubbing. To do this, he took the charcoal stick and rubbed it over the petroglyph, placed the cloth over the design, and pressed down on the flat rock to transfer the image onto the cloth. When he lifted the fabric off the stone only the imprint and design of the petroglyph remained. He brought the rubbing home—quite excited—and I remember admiring it. He had captured the profile of the dog.

Early the next morning, Philip got up to go to the bathroom. When he returned to bed he said, "I think I will need to go and see the doctor today."

This was highly unusual since he was fit and healthy, and rarely ill. I sat up in bed and asked if he was sick. He spoke slowly and carefully. "When I went to the bathroom, I *shi shi* (urinated) blood."

In seconds, I was fully awake. "I think I had better take you to the emergency hospital for tests," I said.

We debated a while longer and ended up going to our physician when the office opened that day. He went through a battery of tests and there was no sign of infection. Oddly, he did not feel ill and he had no fever, other symptoms or complications.

Somehow the word traveled, and the family soon knew. Before the day was over, Phil's brother pulled in the drive with Mama and Papa. I didn't tell them. I thought, "Oh, boy, here we go again!"

Mama's eyes had a way of looking clear into your bones. She never seemed to get overexcited or frantic. Instead, she started from the assumption that you had done something wrong and made a spirit huhu (angry). She searched like a detective for a clue as to what might have caused the problem, and then she could provide the remedy. This process seemed natural with them: another slight interruption, a protocol, then lunch.

When Philip told her about the cave and the petroglyph, her eyes flashed and grew big. Her questions flew like scattered geese after a bullet blast. Now every detail was analyzed. This time I did not need translation.

"Did you leave an offering? Did you ask permission? Did you say Mahalo to da spirit of dis place?"

Philip looked away to avoid her intensity. "Ma, I tink I forgot."

"Ai, yah!" She used her full breath to let the words escape. This expression was comparable to *oy vey*, or a serious "oops!" The riddle had been solved.

Philip wanted to show her the rubbing, but she made a loud clicking sound and protested.

"I no like see dat one. That one make pilikia for you." That was curious because he could not find it then anyway. There was no real danger, just more intense scrutiny of what must follow to unravel the knot her son created.

Mama scolded him in Filipino and in English so perhaps, I could understand her as well. "Ai, yah! You know better! Haven't you been shown how to respect? How come? You never learn dis kine before time? You must return and apologize for being so disrespectful. Go now and bring fruits to the make' man (dead spirit) of this cave and humble yourself and lie down, prostrate."

She spoke slowly and deliberately in her broken English, and when the English words were not sufficient, she reverted to the comfort of pidgin and her own Ilocano language.

"You go, bumbye, mo worse tings going happen to you. Go now! Before dis day pau, before the sun stay gone."

Without speaking another word, he rose with his head hung low and walked out the door. Mama mumbled and shook her head in dismissal. Her demeanor seemed to be partly scolding along with an undertone of prayer for her errant son to follow him on his journey to the cave.

When he returned many hours later, I did not ask him about the cave nor what he said or did. Some things are best left alone, not to be spoken of again. I did notice that he took a shower once home and changed from his now dusty clothing. Strangely, the infamous rubbing of the dog simply disappeared. He had not returned it to the cave, but it was nowhere to be found. We searched for a long time, and it was simply gone.

As time passed, I grew to understand that even the smallest plumeria blossom cannot be picked without softly and respectfully saying Mahalo. Our children learned this early from living on islands that still respected nature, and the land that gave us food and life.

While in Kipahulu, Maui, many years later, we were walking near the `Ohe`o Gulch (Seven Sacred Pools) where thousands of tourists and locals have trodden. Our children were running and laughing as they played in the grassy knoll above the pools. The sun shone brilliantly on this day, creating a sea of diamonds on each crested wave. Suddenly, Philip raised his hands up halfway to get our attention and spoke almost in a whisper, "Make no noise, do not step on any stones, pass through this area quickly and quietly, and whisper Mahalo as you walk."

We never questioned him. Fortunately, the way he'd raised the children, they never answered back with the predictable, "But, why?" They fell into a line and walked without making a sound, heads bowed in obedience and respect.

This place was an ancient heiau (temple). The placement of the stones revealed the sacred past. Only Mama and years on Molokai could teach Phil these things. I shook my head as I thought of the number of tourists who had passed through this place doing whatever they pleased, never having a clue. In deference to them, how could they have known?

11 - Mom

*Marion Louise Seiler Donegan.
Me and Mom with her
Girl Scout Eagle Pin from 1949.
Artwork by Philip Sabado*

11

 Our family had always been progressive. I am proud of my mother and consider her my hero. She was a pioneer in the early sixties and embraced the vision and cause of Dr. Martin Luther King. She opened the first Head Start in Glendale and was the first to integrate preschools. She fought this battle on many levels, never drawing attention to herself. From town protests and many community action committees she focused only on the cause. She was so discreet and subtle in this work; I never knew what an impact she had on the community until I was an adult. She immersed herself in causes of the time, always an advocate in her own right.

Her vision begged the question: If children could appreciate and accept diversity in preschool, could they have a future with less prejudice? She was proved correct in time. The Head Start Project has endured to this day.

In January of 1964, President Lyndon B. Johnson declared The War on Poverty in his State of the Union speech. It resulted in the formation of the Head Start program, and soon, Mom became the director of that program in Glendale and eventually headed the entire Los Angeles area. As always, she gave 100 percent to her work. This was the beginning of integration in Glendale via bussing children in from other neighborhoods.

It was not an easy time for a person with her convictions and she must have endured hardships. However, she held to those convictions and was encouraged through the small but positive changes she made. I owe my pioneer spirit and so much more to my mom. She passed at home on May 26, 2016. The following is a segment from her eulogy, delivered at her memorial in Glendale: "Marion Louise Seiler Donegan was a mother, wife, and true and lifelong friend to all who knew her!"

I picked up a book entitled *Road to Character* by David Brooks. In it, he answers the question: Why were people of the 1930s and 40s so different from our current it's-all-about-me selfie culture? The gist is simple. They were humble, compassionate, almost selfless individuals. It was never "all about me." They possessed strength of character.

From the first chapter, I saw my mom in his words. Her unspoken acts of kindness and charity were performed with humility. Scary smart, she attended Mother Seton High School and then Notre Dame for girls in the East. She majored in speech and drama. After age fifty, she returned to college and decided to become fluent in French. Trips to Paris followed to practice her new skill. She loved it all and made new friends that shared the same vision—all from French class!

She told a story about how in the late 1940s, she and her mother boarded a Greyhound bus destined for California from Baltimore. What an adventure that must have been. She spoke with amazement of seeing a real cowboy wearing a ten-gallon hat and chaps board the bus out in the desert. She said, "Chrisie, it was so real, not a movie!"

Once settled in Glendale, her mother, Nanny, encouraged her to join the Young Catholic Club. She resisted at first and then went to a dance at Holy Family School and it was magic. There, she met "...the most handsome man in the room." According to my sister, he told my mother at that time, "I am going to marry you." You know the rest of the story!

They married soon after and drove to Yosemite where they honeymooned in a teardrop trailer. Their pictures show they were so much in love, truly gaga for each other. I can tell you without hesitation, they were eternally committed and devoted to each other. After my sister Kathy and I started our own families, they traveled, went on cruises, and had a wonderful life, always together.

My mother had a varied career. She was the full-time Executive Director of the Glendale Girl Scouts. In the summer, we escaped the California heat by joining her in the San Bernardino Mountains at Camp River Glen where she was the director. Many will remember her by her camp name, "Si" (pronounced: sigh). Mom loved stargazing. I remember sitting in the dark on a mountain top as her finger traced the imaginary lines in the night sky as she pointed out the constellations. She knew so many: Cassiopeia, the Big Dipper—I was mesmerized and impressed by how she could pick out these wonders from the Milky Way.

11 – Mom

Real—not working—vacations came along as we grew older. My parents' favorite journey was to go to Arizona. Dad loved photography. They subscribed to *Arizona Highways*, devouring every edition. They decided to take us to Canyon de Chelly and Sedona. Most often we camped. We would stop at the Navajo Catholic Mission and donate pre-packed bags of clothes.

My dad with his favorite Nikon Camera in Kalaupapa, Molokai.
Artwork by Philip Sabado

Father was not only a photographer, but he could also build many things. He built one of the first color TVs when they first came out from a company named Heath kit. We were excited because we had the first one on the block. When the anticipated moment came for him to press the "on" button, the suspense in the house was intense. Mom was unsure if it would work or explode, so she told Kathy and me to go outside up to the corner till we saw her wave us in that it was safe to come home. Kathy and I looked at each other clueless, standing at the corner, not knowing if smoke or our mom would appear. Could our house have blown up? Where would we have gone? Did I rationalize that mom was brave and would have gone up in the flames with Dad? After we grew up, we laughed about it.

My love for books came from Mom. On a flight to Hawai'i, we read *Merchant of Venice*. I never would have read Shakespeare without her. We read all his work. She came alive with Shakespeare, as a spark ignited.

Once I had married my handsome husband and lived in a pineapple camp, I wrote long letters home about my exotic life. She kept every letter and encouraged me. "One day," she said, "you will see, this is a book." How prophetic!

Back to her character, once I came into the dining room to see she had cleared the table and had set out rows of pictures both large and small in neat piles. Thirty or forty little faces smiled up at us.

"What is this, and who are all these kids?" Many were African American or Latino.

She said, "Oh, we had school pictures taken last week, and many of my mother's cannot afford this luxury, so I took their pictures on my own and had them printed. I will pack them up tonight." She held up white envelopes and was happy doing this task. "Can you imagine not having a picture of your child?" She did not talk about this act of generosity to anyone.

My best friend in high school had to leave town. Some thirty years later, she told me that in desperation she had gone to see my mom, who just handed her some cash and a credit card saying, "Go figure out your life. I know you will be okay." I never knew! Again, silently, and selflessly, she helped others.

The Golden Eaglet Award was the highest rank in Girl Scouting from 1919 through 1939. The requirements varied over the years from simply earning fourteen to seventeen specific badges to later requirements that included earning the Medal of Merit. Starting in 1916, the best and brightest undertook projects that improved their communities and the world. This would mark the beginning of a long tradition of recognizing the extraordinary efforts of extraordinary girls.

A friend from my distant past, a counselor at the same camp where Mom was the Camp Director, called to reminisce. She said my mother had earned this award as a youth. We never knew she had earned this highest honor…such modesty, and yes, character. I remember seeing the pin in her jewelry box, a small golden eagle with wings spread in gold. She only wore it on her lapel when she was the director. It carried much significance.

One last tribute: a painting of Philip's fell, and it left a big puka (hole) in the right corner of the canvas. I used a needle and thread to sew it; we could barely afford oil paints for him. I thought I did a great job. In a couple of days, she sent Phil a new roll of canvas! She always had absolute and eternal faith in him.

12 - About Babies

Our Babies.
Left to right: Paulo, Me, Erin, and Severina in front,
Early Seventies, Honolulu, Hawai'i.
Photo by Philip Sabado

12

 Superstitions intensified with a newborn and our lives shifted significantly as the baby would become the centerpiece of the home. Now there was a link between generations, and no matter what prior conflicts once existed, all the small kine issues would melt as morning dew. The arrival of the keiki o ka 'aina (the child of the land) would soon be among us.

In Western culture, one of the primary considerations before having a child was whether you could afford this addition to the family. In island culture, you could always afford to have babies. The new lives were looked upon as sources of wealth and good fortune, the continuance of the 'ohana (family).

A kupuna (respected elder) once told me that in the Hawaiian way children are ancestors who have come to us again as our children. To abuse or neglect these precious jewels is not pono (righteous).

Many years later, a friend from the East Coast called with very sad news. While pregnant with her first child, her mother passed. She was devastated and grief stricken. She called upon my son to answer a question. "When my child is born, will it be my mother returning to me?"

His answer was so deep, connected, and compassionate, I will never forget his answer nor the words he chose to illustrate this Hawaiian understanding. "When you look into your new babies eyes you will see all your mothers and fathers from the beginning of time, but there will be one moment when your own mother is looking back to you."

When I was pregnant, the rituals intensified. Philip would be scolded if I did not wear my slippers in the house. Mama would point at my bare feet and say, "Ai, yah! Look your wife's feet, poho (shame). I tink da baby inside stay cold too!"

I loved to watch this ritual dance of theirs. He would apologize to us and jump from the sofa or chair and run upstairs and fetch my slippers or socks.

Sometimes I would protest for him and say, "Ma, no need, I stay hot already!"

She would be deaf to my defense. "Never mind, put anyway!"

When it came to meals, I was not allowed to fix my own plate of food. Mama would chastise Philip, "She get a baby, you can cook and serve her, bumbye she can find more bettah man." He would jump again and follow her orders to the letter.

Sitting back in a chair with my large tummy, I'd think, *Yes, I can live with this*. It was not that I had surrendered my independence. I enjoyed the attention, and I could be pampered like this all the time, perhaps for life. As I recall, my father rarely walked into the kitchen and never even boiled water for his instant coffee; he was always served.

When my mother came to visit us in Honolulu, she would cook dinner for us. She had always prepared my father's plate from as far back as I can remember so she automatically handed me a plate and said, "Serve your husband."

In the Irish way, this was our family custom. I considered this as I held the plate and said with a wry smile, "No, Mom, he can fix his own. Let's not let him know how you wait on Daddy. I have a good thing here. I do not want to spoil this or mess it up!" She may have thought me arrogant, but they had experienced the wedding and saw how the family customs on Molokai were now a part of my life and marriage.

Before the birth of Paulo, our first child, my sisters-in-law gave me strict instructions. With a stern expression, one of them said, "No *baen* (shame) to us." She spoke with sincerity, as a warning. "You know why? We have heard dat some haole women...," she paused as if pondering the correct way to phrase her remarks, "when dey gibe birth, dey makes da kine, big noise, and dey curse da husband and da baby for da pain." With head bowed she exclaimed, "We would be so *baen* if you make like dat." They instructed me that when the time came, I was to bear down and to do whatever was necessary—bite my lip, my hand, whatever—except make noise, and especially not to curse my husband for my discomfort. She shook her head in thought. "Besides," she continued, "so many nurses came from the Philippines, and they can see your family is Filipino name, they could tell each other about the shame for our family if you cried out." They keened together, "Ai, yah! Ai, yah!"

Their eyes conveyed their true dilemma. What would I do? Since I had yet to give birth, I promised I would do my best not to embarrass their family especially their brother. The pregnancy went well with my firstborn, and I remembered the sisters' warnings. Although it was tough with a ten-pound boy, and I did a natural birth.

According to a Filipino superstition, not a single item was prepared before the baby's birth. The crib was cleaned and assembled for the homecoming only after the child was safely home. Clothing for the baby was prepared, washed, and laid out then too. If a gift was given, it remained under my bed, still wrapped in its box, until the baby was home. I never had a baby shower since it was considered bad luck. I never felt cheated or deprived. I understood when I married this Molokai man that I would be following his ways. I learned this was not only a Filipino custom, but Greeks, traditional Jewish women, and Chinese observe this ritual as well. When I would share this story, older women would usually nod in agreement and say, "Yes, that was our custom long ago. My grandmother taught us that, but now in America, all changes."

I would adapt to so many customs and rituals in this marriage, but they intensified when it came to the care of babies. Some were radically different from my Americanized way, but they all made sense in the end.

I had one challenging moment after delivering Paulo. He had a nice full head of dark brown hair. As a new mother, I turned to the most respected source of information in the early seventies, Dr. Spock. My mom sent a brand-new paperback of *Dr. Spock's Baby and Childcare* early on, so I could study babies before the big day.

The chapter on how to deal with crying would guide me momentarily with Paulo, who I had decreed the most colicky baby ever born. The book instructed new parents to let the infant cry ten minutes for the first night, and maybe more the second night, and so forth. Philip would always be on his feet with the first whimper and pick up the baby to comfort him. Turning to me while I tried to sleep, he would ask, "Why do you let him cry and cry?" Exasperated, he once declared, "No wonder you all end up in therapy. Nobody was holding you when you were so small?" I shrugged. "Maybe."

Whenever he questioned me, I would grab the well-worn paperback and flip through the dog-eared pages of the "baby bible" and begin to read aloud from the text. He refuted the book and explained the island way of caring for a baby. Philip's words always rang true with love and concern, whereas the book was clinical and sterile. I came to trust his judgment early on as the little one would eventually fall off asleep in his arms as he rocked or slowly paced the room.

Being the youngest of twelve children, his experience stemmed from the grassroots knowledge gained from being part of a large family. They had their babies and brought them home to rear while he was still a boy. His job was to help with all the usual chores from diapering to bathing and he learned the Filipino rituals involved with a newborn. When he explained the time-tested customs, I agreed the Hawaiian/Filipino way was ultimately the best.

Once my sister and I sat on my bed with an open gauze diaper trying to figure out how to fold it. This was long before pre-folded diapers and Pampers. Philip watched silently from the doorway as we tried to fold the square bit of fabric. He came up behind us and respectfully asked us if we knew how to fold it.

Caught off guard, we both chimed in at once, denying the obvious. "Of course, we do!"

He folded the triangle and demonstrated how to carefully place the pins. He reassured us that he was not trying to show us up, (he was not being cocky). Sharing his experience, he suggested we stick the large diaper pins in a bar of soap so they would glide into the cotton. We both acknowledged his instruction as if we knew all along, saying something like, "Oh, yeah, that's how." After he left the room, my sister and I looked at each other and giggled. We were still kids ourselves. We had no clue.

Philip joyfully gave Paulo his first bath while my mom and I looked on. Cradling Paulo's neck, he whispered a blessing with every splash of clear water poured over the infant's head. At the time it sounded like "apple juice," but this was explained as a blessing, praising Apo Dios. This was again the "das how" as Mama had taught him to do with all the nieces and nephews. So many traditions were logical and well-founded that I often shook my head in wonder at my good fortune.

As the baby was removed from the bath, another ritual began with wrapping and drying. Mama stayed for some days and taught me how to massage every limb and small bone. With love, she whispered a blessing with every stroke. The daily bathing experience took at least an hour and included caressing and massaging. In those days it seemed that a mother could take more time with their babies to lavish attention on them.

In Hawaiian, this was known as lomilomi, the art of gentle massage. Years later, I saw a book on African massage showing how the village women could fix toe turn and misshapen feet by using massage from birth. To my surprise, the book illustrated exactly what my mother-in-law had taught me, and as I had seen in the hospital soon after.

Mama with 'Ohana, Maunaloa, Molokai.

Within my heart, I preferred his cultural ways to my own. There was deep, intense, loving respect for the child that I did not always see in my own Western culture.

Still, I was nervous and felt awkward with Paulo, and listened to every word the doctor told me. At eighteen, I was so young and impressionable.

We had moved from the 'Aiea house, and I was on my own. When the doctor told me that Paulo was allergic to my milk, I never doubted and sadly, believed him. I never thought to call Mama. In the end, I quit breastfeeding and had to suffer with a very colicky baby. Eventually, I learned I needed Mama's help because I would suffer without her knowledge.

In the first years, Paulo had difficulty speaking any language. He was quiet and when he would speak, it was gibberish. He seemed happy and smart enough, but we could not understand him at all. He seemed to get it, and even laughed at his own jokes, but no one else did. When Mama heard him at Sunday dinner, she advised Philip in their language that Paulo "stay all huli" (turned around inside). Her eyes showed a certain twinkle when she smiled with confidence, knowing she could fix this as well. She and Papa returned the next day. Papa never seemed to take notice and would always enter the house chuckling with an armful of freshly picked vegetables and a smile as big as the sun. Soon we would hear pots and pans banging as he set about making sabau (soup) for the family.

Mama settled in the living room and asked for the boy. She made it clear that the child should be brought to her with a key, any key would suffice. He was standing and walking by then. At first, he stood facing her as she prayed. She cupped his small shoulders in her hands and turned him slowly, three times to the right, then three times to the left. Then, with his back facing her, she held the key an inch from the small of his back, pointing it to his spine. This time the turning process repeated, except she turned the key to the left and then to the right. Soon all was pau (finished) and Mama announced, "Okay, now dis boy all fix. He can talk good now, no more pilikia."

The next day, perfect sentences and words came from him. I am not sure how to rationalize this experience. She spoke in their language as she turned him and the key, so I could never repeat anything, even if I chose to. When I heard him speak the next day, I was excited, yet not surprised, as Mama always inspired wonder. Philip was accustomed to her ways and grateful, as was Papa. These fixes where another way Mama was indispensable.

With our second son, I had an unusual awakening to the art of breastfeeding. I found renewal shortly after Erin's birth. Naturally, I was better read and prepared this time, and was determined to succeed with Erin. In the early seventies, most new moms opted for the free case of baby formula that went home with them. Breastfeeding was tough. I remember having tried and failed to nurse Erin in the first days after his birth. The pain in my nipple smarted, not to mention the contractions that returned with every suckle. No one tells you what to expect with subsequent children.

On the second day, a large, big-boned nurse came into my room. I heard her as she padded down the corridor with a determined, purposeful gait. She stood at my bedside and watched as I attempted to position my nipple into my waiting, now impatient and fussy child. She shared that she came from Kauai where the Russians came a hundred years before.

She said, "You really want to do this, don't you?" She had a strong Russian accent tempered by a local lilt and her kindness. I told her that was true, as I had not succeeded with my first.

She propped and arranged the pillow behind me and told me there was a way. She said she believed I could do this. She drew the sheer curtain around my cubicle with a sharp swipe and pressed the off button on the television remote control.

"Now," she said with fervor, "no distractions when you nurse this baby. You must focus and be clear as to the purpose for this child. Think only of how wonderful his life will be, how attractive he is, and how special the whole world will think of this young man. Do not plan what you will cook for dinner or what you and your husband argued about last night. Think only the most powerful thoughts about this boy, and you will be amazed."

Her manner and zeal convinced me on the spot! From that day forward, I did as she advised; I focused my entire being and all my hopes and dreams on Erin every time I nursed him for an entire year. I continued with this attitude and strategy with my next four children over the coming twenty years.

Once home and settled in with my newborn, I observed a custom that even with the second child would be difficult to get used to. There were to be no outings for one month. This meant Philip did all the shopping and any necessary errands. Toward the end of thirty days, I would beg to go anywhere, even McDonald's drive-thru. Philip stayed true to his customs, and I had to wait to take the newborn out. Philip was sweet and would say, "What is it you want? I will go and buy it and bring it home for you."

This custom provided many benefits. I had time to bond with my new baby. Another was to ensure my health and to have the ability to avert illness for me and my child from the outside world. The Japanese also honor this. One day, I had to run an errand (I sneaked out) after I had been home one week. A Japanese woman I knew saw me. "Weren't you hapai, (pregnant) just last week?" she asked. I was surprised she had remembered, and I told her I had a beautiful little boy. Her expression showed momentary concern before she admonished me. "Tell me, dear, I know this is not your people's custom, but how old do you want to look at thirty or fifty? You see, what we believe is that if you take the time to heal and rest after having the baby, you will never look old and will always look young. No one will ever guess your real age." Who would want to test that? She was correct. After all these years, very few people guess my age or that I have six children.

I did not work in the early years of my marriage. Somehow, we made it, and since the babies were coming almost every year, we would have barely broken even with childcare.

When I was pregnant with my second baby, I yearned for a daughter. Once when Mama passed me in the hallway in the ʻAiea house, she stopped and looked at my growing belly, almost singing as she spoke, "Dis one boy again. I know you like da girl baby but dis one boy again. Dat's okay, bumbye you get em all." She continued walking, chuckling at me and my fate.

My shoulders caved as the reality rang true. "Ma, don't tell me that, anyway, cannot tell, stay too soon!"

In my heart I knew she was correct, she always was, as was Philip. She laughed, moving her hand to conceal her knowing smile. Her eyes sparkled even more as she enjoyed my innocence. I straightened my posture and thanked my fate that such wisdom was mine.

A new baby in the family brings the consummate celebration. On the flip side, even with the adulation, the praise must be silenced. Filipinos consider it bad luck to comment on the attractiveness of a child. The moment someone says: "How cute" or "So pretty dis one," they must say in the same breath, **buyog buyog** *(pronounced: boo yag, and repeated twice to have the desired effect to dispel any curse). This custom is strictly kept. If someone was to stare too long at the baby or if they complimented the child, it was believed they might be placing a spell on the little one out of jealousy.*

12 – About Babies

I discovered another rewarding Filipino custom. When you came upon a relative or friend who had not seen the baby, they smiled warmly to the baby, yet somehow some cash would be secreted into the folds of the child's clothing. The money would be tucked into a sleeve or the space between the diaper and the pants. According to protocol, the mother was to look away and not notice what transpired. I loved the dance. Often, I would be changing the baby and tiny, carefully folded five or ten dollar bills would fall onto the changing table. I think I was supposed to save the money, but always used it to buy food and milk.

This ritual came from the understanding that babies come directly from God's hands and therefore have God's ear. This axiom was a simple example. What if a baby was to meet a relative or family friend and they were stingy? The new baby could turn to the heavens and say, "Ai, yah, did you see that one? I just met that Auntie, and she gave me nothing." On the other hand, maybe the newborn could put in a good word for this one.

I was not always thrilled by or followed all traditions and customs. There were times when I had to take a stand in my own way. In the early years, I had my babies in quick succession. The older boys were born within the first two years we were married. When I was pregnant for the third time, a conversation occurred between Philip and his sister on Molokai. She must have told him in the Hawaiian/Filipino way, "Your family and especially your wife has good fortune. "She get keiki every year if she like. Why don't you give this next child to me and your Manong? We are lonely and a new baby would be good for us. You can make one more keiki again next year." I, of course, was not aware of this conversation or possible agreement. Mama had passed the year before, and according to and being dutiful to custom, Philip could never refuse his older sisters.

Whether this was a Filipino custom, I was never sure, but I knew a Hawaiian word applied in this scenario: "hanai" (the sharing of children), which is still accepted and more common on Molokai. Many children speak affectionately of their hanai mom. This occurred on all the islands, but the Molokai way was the old customary form and common. Again, the merge of the Hawaiian and Filipino worlds.
People can only hanai a child at birth. Although many people (especially those

born elsewhere) affectionately call some local families their hanai family. Perhaps this more recent interpretation helped them feel more connected to the culture since a Hawaiian "auntie" is likely to be called a hanai mom.

If a couple is barren or can no longer have children and another family has many, they can hanai a baby to the couple to rear as their own. The transfer from one family to another should be about the abiding love for the children. Philip explained this custom to me as hanai was the true gesture of aloha. To have true compassion for another who could not have a child was the greatest gift. If done correctly, and all the parties agreed, the keiki will be the center of the hanai parents' universe.

We named our third child Severina after Mama. This was an old Castilian name not many people had heard before. An Italian man once told me that the ancient Castilian names were mostly Roman, coming from the time the Roman Empire had occupied Spain. The Spaniards, a part of Rome, carried these names to the Philippines in the 1400s.

The first time I saw Seve, I forgot to breathe. She was a beautiful baby with a full head of dark hair and mysterious penetrating eyes, the image of Mama. Even as a baby, Severina held herself in a regal way. Her eyes had a Chinese cast to them, which made her even more exotic.

Early the next morning after giving birth to Seve, the phone rang next to my hospital bed. I recognized the easy tone of my sister-in-law, Rosita, calling from Maunaloa. She conveyed greetings and congratulations from the Molokai family, expressing how happy she was about the new baby. Her next words shook me into a different reality. She said, "You probably want to keep her…since she's a girl-child." My breath froze somewhere in my windpipe as my heart skipped a beat—I was speechless! The air in the room went still and I stared at the tray of eggs and oatmeal brought to me during our call. She continued in a natural, matter-of-fact tone. "You know, Philip said we could have the next baby, but me and your Manong, we know you wanted a girl and you will want to keep her for yourself. It's okay, dats why we understand, bumbye you going get more keiki, you can gibe me another."

I stammered before I found my voice. I proclaimed that Severina was indeed mine. After all, I had fallen in love with her already. She said she understood, and we said goodbye amicably. I tried to watch TV or sleep, but

I could not. Her words stuck in my mind. As evening drew near, I could think of nothing else but what I would say, and how I would say it to my husband. I kept rehearsing different forms of the same question, "How could you?" or "What were you thinking?" I was infuriated yet needed to find the best way to approach him and this complex dilemma. I went from yelling to calmly saying, "Explain this custom again?"

At first, he looked like he had forgotten. Then, realizing he would have to confront this, he looked sheepish as he started to explain. I interrupted him, knowing whatever he said would not matter. She was my baby, and I was keeping her!

"Never mind." I spoke with an understated sharp finality in my tone. "Please understand this—I will keep all my babies, male or female. You will never hanai any of my children ever again." That was it!

We never discussed this incident again. In time, I carried three more children, six total, and kept them all. I found it curious that Severina was never happy when she visited Molokai as a child, and we never stayed for more than a few days. Being raised on Molokai would never have suited her.

I took a day to rehearse my delivery, and he did not argue or defend his initial discussion with his sister. I still find his dramatic shift in alliance away from his family's culture to be a bit of a mystery. Of course, this worked out in everyone's favor: mine, his, and our babies. I gained some leverage in the continuing evolution toward our family unit. He agreed in his quiet way that comprises would continue to be made.

Within a year, this same sister-in-law had access to plenty of babies. Her two sons had many children, and everyone was happy in the end. As a teenager, one son met a young Hawaiian girl, and she became pregnant at thirteen. No one knew until the baby's birth. The mother, because she was so young, was unaware that she was carrying a child. The young mother told me that one warm day as she hung laundry in the yard, she felt hot and uncomfortable and went into the house to take a cool shower. While she was in the shower, out came the baby! In shock, she wrapped the new baby in fresh towels and laid her on the bathroom floor, got dressed, and went outside to finish hanging the wet laundry. After her chore was pau, she told her brother about the baby, and he immediately took the mother and child to the hospital. She named the child April, as in "April showers bring May flowers." Word spread as fast as the wind that travels the length of Molokai.

When my sister-in-law learned of this baby, she knew the child had to be her son's. She and her husband went to the hospital that same day and came straight to the point with the new mother. "I know this is my son's baby, Manong and I will help you." And after a "pregnant" pause, "Besides I have wanted a baby for a long time."

The two grandmothers met and fixed a plan—they would share in the raising of this keiki. The birth mother would go on to finish high school and more, earning her master's degree. This is not a unique story on Molokai; the children always come first.

April remains loyal to our family. She is a beautiful girl and she and Severina are close in age. They became friends when Severina went to visit Molokai. Everything works out if you give it enough time.

Whenever I went anywhere with the children for any occasion, I was always concerned about their appearance. I made sure they were dressed in clean clothing and were well-groomed. My pack was stuffed with diapers and milk, I kept a clean washcloth just for wiping dirty faces and hands the moment they were soiled. Often, when I sat with the family, the subject would come up about some child that was not cared for properly. "That child of so-and-so was so pilau (dirty), I wonder when da las time he went bait (had a bath)?"

Without realizing I was haole, they often spoke of "pilau haoles." This probably originated from haole people who were known to enter houses with their shoes on, did not bathe daily, and did so only in the morning. I never took derogatory remarks personally; I was always clean and obsessively tidy.

In any event, I was wary of being judged. My children were always dressed in immaculate new clothing when we went to visit family or go on outings. They had play clothes but did not wear them out. I could be sitting with them when they spoke of the "dirty haole," but when I pointed out that I was White, they chastised me. "Oh, you know already. We do not mean you; we mean da utter kine haole. You not haole anymore. You are our family now." They always said this with true affection, but I never forgot the judgments or implications.

In my eyes, I was still a white haole woman. The only white people I saw were on the six o'clock news. The nearby shops, restaurants, and supermarket catered to locals. This was in no way segregation; it was a matter of choice. If I suggested a certain restaurant I'd read about, Phil would ask with an air of innocence but with a furrowed brow, "What? Plenty haoles go there?" He would say, "I don't want to be the only dark hair there you know." Finally, I resigned myself to my local world. Because we were so young, I often agreed. Even then, I realized I would ease him into a mixed environment. Today, this is not even an issue.

The boys were not circumcised. Paulo's foreskin naturally folded over his penis and was near black in color. What did I know? He was my first son. Soon after birth, baby boy penises may appear overly large before they go to normal size. After his birth, I was momentarily shocked. I had completed twelve years of Catholic school with Irish nuns. Philip was my only point of reference. My parents had both hailed from the soul of discretion, which was common given their backgrounds.

Once, I came upon my parents as they stood looking into the crib while Paulo slept, discussing something in whispers. Mom had just changed the baby's diaper and had called my dad over to ask him a question.

"What is it?" I asked as I walked into the room. "You look like a cat with a mouse."

They shifted on their feet, hemmed, and hawed. Mom began with an elongated "Well-l-l." Her eyes shifted as if she prepared a question. "Well, we were wondering…," Both of them looked at Paulo and removed the corner of the unpinned diaper. "Is Phil this color too?"

She was referring to the foreskin. Filipinos had no pink in their skin, the melanin in the surface membrane only produced brown or near black. Their nipples, foreskin, and the eye socket around the whites of their eyes were brown. I suppressed a smile and stuttered my response, "Yah, I mean yes, yes, he is. How else should it be?"

After my response, Mom and Dad breathed an audible sigh of relief. Mom spoke for them both and was visibly more relaxed and relieved. "Oh, okay, well, that is just fine, nothing at all, we should all move to the next room." Then in a whisper, she added, "We don't want to wake the baby." I stared at them as they left my bedroom and laughed about it.

As silly as these moments were, they bonded my parents and me. They experienced with me this new way of life I'd entered. Back in their own home, they could share stories of their daughter's life in paradise to a man so talented he would be a great artist one day, as well as a husband and father to their six grandchildren.

13 - And Then There Was Fishing

Ka Lawai'a Kahiko (Ancient Fisherman).
Artwork by Philip Sabado

13

 Between these islands, there is a treacherous stretch of ocean known as the Ka'iwi Channel that has one of the most dangerous currents in the world. A swimmer who had once swam the English Channel could not cross it, even in a shark cage. She quit when she was less than halfway across. She had the stamina to cross but lost her nerve because of the sharks that swam in masse parallel to her cage.

The only swimmer to achieve the channel crossing was the world-famous Olympic swimmer, Duke Kahanamoku. He did not need a cage. It was said the sharks were his family's aumakua (guardian spirit), so he was not afraid of the lesser ones swimming the channel.

Just as swimming against a strong current is pointless, I intuitively understood that competing with Mama would not be to my advantage, and realized soon enough that challenging Philip's love for fishing was just as futile. During the early years, apart from the children, everything revolved around fish, fishing, and if "da water stay good today."

Often, while driving down Haleakala highway on Maui, I'd be chattering away and I'd look at Philip and realize he had not heard a word. His eyes were laser-focused on a sight at a great distance. He keenly assessed the ocean still miles away to see if it was a good day. It amazed me how he could tell whether the water was flat or choppy, even when we were so far from the sea.

Eventually, he'd return to the real world, happy in the present and say, "What, hon? Oh, that's nice," knowing I had probably tried to trick him by asking him what he thought about the house fire last night.

I would counter with a smile and let him know I was on to his preoccupation. "Is the water good today?"

13 – And Then There Was Fishing

He would laugh and say, "Naw, stay choppy today, no need go." In the early days, he could deposit the children and me on a hot beach, often without a coconut tree in sight because it was a good spot to fish. This was not done in meanness. His priority was always finding the most fish.

He would disappear for hours and when he would finally emerge from the salty water, I would be cranky, sunburned, and tired. Protesting loudly with my hands on my hips, I would insist on a shady place or else we would have to go home. The children never got out of the water and did not notice. I was in danger because I would always burn to the color of a lobster in boiling water. He relented and tried to accommodate our needs while still being able to fish. For our family, this struck the perfect balance.

The first lesson he would teach each child was to love the sea. He took each of our new infants for his or her first swim within months of birth. I watched as he stepped into the tide and carefully dipped the newborn into the clear salty water. As the shiny baby emerged with black hair matted down, I would hear a squeal of delight.

The babies loved the water. They gurgled and smiled as he approached the shore's edge. They attempted to leap out of his grasp. I watched as he stepped into the wet sand, leaving deep footprints in his wake. It was as if they were being returned to their mother, the sea. After all, it was in the water where they had found life for nine months before they could see the light of day.

Philip whispered blessings each time he would dip the new baby into the water. At first, the baby would cling to him and shiver from the coolness. Then he would lift the baby to touch the sunlight. As trust was established, the little one would develop confidence and try to swim. An affinity with water was as natural as the sun shining overhead. It was not a baptism in the Christian sense. This was pono (balance) and a great appreciation for life.

Many hours were spent splashing in the clear warm tide pools that abound in the black lava ledges along the shoreline. Small black crabs, locally known as Hawaiian crabs, would skitter as the baby tried to catch the speedy creatures. These crabs were treasured and best eaten raw.

Once when our fifth child, Jackie, was in the water for the first time a large wave came and engulfed them both. From the shore, I sat up and focused on the spot from which they disappeared, no longer visible, my husband and newborn now underwater. Suddenly, from out of a moving sheet of white bubbles, the baby emerged at the end of his hand, squealing and laughing. I said aloud to myself, "Aw, she will be a water baby, for sure." Philip found his footing as the water receded and he laughed with her.

While on Maui, Philip had a full morning of fishing in the Kihei area. His face beamed as he came from the water fulfilled and satisfied. He dragged a white muslin bag bulging with fish, some still moving. He had caught enough for the family and his sister's 'ohana as well. He sat on the reef, his feet in the small tide pools that sparkled like gems with a million blinding facets that augmented his inner glow.

Philip cleaned his fish on the shiny stones balanced on his haunches in the Filipino style with the flat of his feet firmly planted. He used a spoon or a fork to scrub the freshly caught fish, scraping the utensil against the scales, and pulling away from the fish's head in rapid motions. Depending on the fish, he could often use his hands. All the while, small translucent scales flew through the air. He used a sharp knife to slit the belly and empty the guts into the clear water of the tide pool, recycling them back to the sea for the benefit of eels and other fish. Often the head of an eel would bob in the reef, waiting for the treat to drift its way in the current. Philip was seasoned to this course of nature. Out of the corner of his eye, he could see an eel approaching.

In the Hawaiian way, fishermen who did not clean their fish when they were caught were looked down upon. The fish could spoil if they were not cleaned when the fisher reached shore, and that would be poho (loss).

On this Kihei morning after he had filled his bag with the fresh fish, Philip slung the bag over his shoulder and began the walk across the hot sand to where he had placed his supplies. He heard voices calling to him and saw some young local boys sitting under a grove of shady trees in the park. They shouted from a distance. They were loud and sounded high, or maybe they had been drinking. Locals rarely shouted unless they were intoxicated.

"Braddah, we buy your fish!"

Philip answered in the local manner, "Sorry, Brah, I only get nuff for my 'ohana." As he walked away, he wondered why they could not have caught their own fish. Offering to buy his fish was unusual.

While his feet imprinted the moist sand, Philip pondered that perhaps these days it was easier to drink on the beach and wait for someone to come out of the water and offer to buy, rather than spend their time on fishing. As he walked, he shook his head and thought about why someone had not taught these boys how to fish. Maybe they had not had the privilege of finding a kahu (teacher or mentor) who could teach them the right way, the pono way to do these things. Why had their families not taught them how to survive as their ancestors had?

Fishing at Halena.
Artwork by Philip Sabado

In the Hawaiian language, "kahu" is a special word, rich with meaning and importance. It means one who takes care. In one context, the kahu is the caretaker of a kind of specialized knowledge. This person could be a master fisherman or canoe builder, one skilled in weaving baskets or lei, or one who understood the art of healing or had a special knack for understanding life. To be considered a kahu, the master artisan had to pass on his or her knowledge.

The decision to take on a student was never made lightly since the teaching was done by modeling and was a reflection of the teacher in that every flaw in a student's work was the teacher's responsibility. There is a saying: "I hemahema ia haumana, ili ka hewa i ke kumu." (If the pupil is unskilled, the errors reflect on the teacher).

It was a great fortune to have a kahu in your life. The teacher opened the door for you to gain a higher understanding of a skill and of life. A kahu was your puka, a gateway into a higher connection with the world. Sometimes Hawaiians would ask one who showed a degree of skill at some craft, "Who is your puka?"

It has been said, a kahu will always know who to teach by how the child responds. If one were going to weave a net and the child sat close to the weaver and followed the teacher's every move, then that child would be the one to teach. The child who ran all about and was easily distracted would not be worth the time and be passed over.

As a student of such a person, there was a responsibility known as a kuleana to continue the Hawaiian tradition and pass on the knowledge. Otherwise, it would be lost. Knowledge must be passed down accurately and intact so the line from one generation to the next remains unbroken; for this reason, students are carefully chosen.

Knowledge and skills were not things one person could own. The body of knowledge accumulated and evolved over time. It belonged to the community and to succeeding generations.

When we lived in California, Philip met other artists and would often ask, "How did you create that technique or mix that color?" His intention was always to admire and compliment. Sometimes, however, they answered arrogantly, "Oh, that is my secret." He was always taken aback by this attitude.

He clearly respected their right to hold on to their knowledge for themselves. Afterward, he would shake his head and tell me, "Even if I wanted to, I could not do exactly as they do. I don't understand your people; they are often selfish and think they own the knowledge, and they never know how to share." He looked perplexed as he tried to find logic in this sense of owning something, a concept foreign to him. I did not comment but knew he was correct.

When Philip was a child on Molokai, Philip's kahu for fishing was his brother-in-law, a master fisherman known to all as Brother Ray. The immensity of the oceans and their bounty were Philip's because he had his

13 – And Then There Was Fishing

kahu. Hours became days and days passed into years as the two fished the pristine waters surrounding Molokai.

This Hawaiian respect and love for the ocean were not unique to Molokai, but for Philip it brought a clear awareness that he would carry and be privileged to give to his children. It was inherent in the life of a fisherman that his heart and body would always move in perfect harmony with the rhythm of the sea. The fisherman heard the voice of the ocean in the pounding of the waves.

Philip was nine when his Uncle Ray came into his life as Euloghia's, (Lolly) spouse. He was a seasoned worker after so many years in the open sun-drenched pineapple fields. He had a seaman's weathered look and wore loose-fitting clothes stained with a tinge of terra cotta from the island soil. He drove a large harvester and worked alongside the pineapple pickers early in the morning.

Following family tradition, Philip was designated as the water boy. A water boy's job was to step behind the fishermen carrying the burlap sacks ready to fill with fish, buoys made from empty plastic containers, and various gear. Young Philip was taught to follow his kahu and not ask questions. If Reyhino (Ray) stepped over a stone, so did Phil. If he sat on the shore watching the water, Phil did too, as if he were a moving shadow of Uncle Ray's, which he did without comment—that was the discipline. They were silent, aware of an inner peace that came from being in the midst of such natural magic and beauty. Over time, a deep abiding respect and appreciation for the ocean and its many moods would stay with him.

The night before fishing was a big event filled with excitement and anticipation. Phil and Uncle Ray prepared for the next day by packing fresh water and gathering spears and goggles. In the darkness of his room, Philip tried to force the hours to pass, to relax his mind so needed sleep would come. Hours of walking on the sand lay ahead, but sleep proved elusive. He had visions of the blue sea and the lure of the treasured fish that awaited them.

While early dawn held the small village in lingering darkness, the fishermen and young Philip set out on foot. On Molokai, especially over Maunaloa, the night sky seemed blacker and the stars more brilliant than anywhere else I had been. The celestial bodies above this ancient village refracted with flashes of light stirred by an ancient wind. Even in darkness,

Philip would follow every step, every move. Only after years of watching and learning was he allowed his own spear and goggles so he could follow and learn how to catch fish the Hawaiian way.

He spent years diligently carrying water, reels, and a small pack of supplies for his mentor. In exchange, he was taught how to assess the ocean and harvest from its abundance while having a deep and abiding love for the sea—and it was all fun!

To reach their favorite fishing ground they had to walk five miles on sugar-fine sand in the predawn light. They hiked across many sand dunes in silence to avoid disturbing the delicate balance (pono). As they reached their destination, golden arrows of light pierced over the horizon.

They set down their gear at their chosen spot and entered the water. Here, the fish did not fear the fisher and swam right up to peer at them. Those fishes would either be caught, or they swam away. Even the puhi (eel) were not a threat. If the divers swam into a hole and saw a puhi, they backed off, respecting the eel's home. Balance was critical, not dominance. Philip told me many times, "If you challenge nature, you will eventually lose." One diver stayed near the hole and tried to coax the eel out. The other moved behind the eel hole and speared some fish. Back and forth the divers went, taking turns while watching the eel. The eel bit no one when they followed this strategy, and often they succeeded in its capture. The white eels were 'ono, Mama's favorite, and bagging one was sure to make her happy.

Fishing was the most sublime adventure for Philip, far better than a movie or a book or anything you could imagine. He said he even forgot about girls and missed a couple of proms because "da water stay good that day" and fishing took priority. All the absent days on his elementary and high school record were fishing days. He was never sick since Mama could always find the cure in her garden. In our first years as I lay next to him on colorful quilts, I hung on every word of his boyhood adventures.

Some of the earliest fishing memories revolved around Mama and Papa. Mama's people came from the mountain villages, as noted and freshwater fish from streams on Kauai were highly prized because most of her childhood dishes used similar seafood. On Kauai, the rivers teemed with shrimp, tilapia, and 'o'opu.

Fresh river water from the high mountains filtered through volcanic rock flowed pure and cold, so different from the salty waters of the teal ocean. The riverbanks were muddy and slippery, the trees fragrant. Days spent there were like being inside a magical forest where the only sounds came from birds, the wind, and a trickling stream. On these outings, Mama only brought rice and salt to the river's edge, knowing the stream would provide lunch and dinner. Happy memories were accented by the moist smell of the rivers and the surrounding forest.

Papa fishing for 'O'opu and 'Opae.
Artwork by Philip Sabado

These were good times because memories of the elders' childhood in the Philippines were as fresh and alive as the fish they caught. Papa fashioned his fishing gear from shaved and trimmed bamboo poles. He used the bamboo to catch 'o'opu, 'opae (freshwater shrimp), and tilapia as well. Papa was a good fisherman who also taught Philip.

Papa's favorite fishing spot was in Waialua on O'ahu, a thriving plantation village in the 1940s where the family lived before, they settled on Molokai. In truth, they moved often, settling on all the islands at some time. Most camps had been set up in the same fashion. If the family could find fellow *kakailian* (townmates), it would be "welcome home."

In the first years of our marriage, Philip also favored Waialua. Years later, his fishing partner, a locally born Japanese man, hailed from that part of O'ahu. As fate would have it, they worked together in an advertising firm in downtown Honolulu. At lunch hour and breaks, the two men would plan the next fishing outing with the excitement of young kids. These fishing expeditions meant that I would be left a couple of days at home with the babies. I protested when it became apparent these excursions would be a regular ongoing activity. To compromise, the children and I became part of the planning. It took a little more effort to organize, but never mind, they still got to fishing that Saturday. Previously, I used to enjoy sleeping in on Saturdays. When we decided to all go together, it became Phil's mission to devise a weekly plan.

Consequently, Phil was awake at four a.m. to pack our small blue Volkswagen with breakfast and lunch fixings. He strapped blankets, sheets, and a folded playpen to the top of the Beetle. The three children, including our infant daughter, were secured in their car seats, and given teething cookies to chew during the forty-minute drive north to their fishing spot.

Only after everyone was strapped into their car seats, would he come and nudge me out of our warm bed. He woke me by humming in soft whispers. "All is ready, honey. All you have to do is put on your shorts and get in the car."

The aroma of coffee percolating lured me, but I resisted. "I am still asleep!" I turned my head away and pulled the pillow over my ears.

"But, hon, everything is ready! The babies are in the car. Here is your coffee, all hot and ready. All you have to do is walk to the car." I heaved myself up, exhaling a moan and placed my two feet on the floor. With no glimmer of light, I tried to roll back into bed, but he caught my arm and got me standing. He pulled the bed together, tucking in the bedspread the way I liked it to keep me on my feet.

13 – And Then There Was Fishing

I slumped in the front seat as he drove to Waialua, my mind and body seeking sleep, still dreaming of my warm bed. I had to smile to myself as I thought of all the bribes and predawn work he did just so he could go fishing. He hummed happily as he drove along, having accomplished his feat.

Once we reached the fishing ground, he became a man possessed. He spread out the blanket, set up the playpen and tossed in the children's favorite toys.

The clock was ticking, and the sun began to reveal the warm crimson and yellow tones that heralded a new day. Flecks of golden light seeped across the dark sea and spread upon the horizon. Soon the entire sky would accept the encroaching warmth and chase the night away.

I loved the ocean at this predawn hour when the sea turned the color of liquid opals filled with light. I poured more coffee from the thermos as he donned his fins. I liked to sip the steaming brew sitting under the giant whispering ironwood trees. I learned to enjoy and look forward to these outings and it did not hurt to have a husband who treated me like a queen. By the time the kids and I were settled, Phil's partner, Toki, and his wife joined us. The men went off to the great blue beyond like two boys ready to enter nature's playground. Anything could happen out in the vast ocean, but treasures awaited fishermen who possessed patience and the desire to begin the game.

I admired Philip's relationship with Toki. Few words passed between them. Where they swam and how long they remained at certain special fishing spots was all decided simply by exchanging knowing looks. They checked how far apart they were from each other in the water. When it was a complete day and time to go in, one would simply nod to the other and say, "Get nuff already," and the other would nod in agreement and they both would swim to shore. In place of talking were subtle chosen signals. There was no need to disturb the silence of the sea.

Toki's spouse was a delicate beauty, a woman from Japan. He affectionately called her in the Japanese way, Shige-san. She was incredibly organized, and I figured she must have been up at dawn, rolling every variety of sushi. That day, Philip had prepared tuna sandwiches to share, but she politely declined my offer of a sandwich.

I enjoyed Shige-san's company in the early morning hours, but I always felt like a picture out of focus next to her. For me she was perfect and seemed to have everything together. I was with small babies who were still tired or just waking up.

Our fishing Saturdays, and sometimes Sundays, continued together for many years. This became a ritual of sorts as the children grew and learned to swim and play for endless hours in the sand under the ironwoods and Hawaiian sun. As the babies become toddlers and then small children, the ocean and land remained a constant. In time, I began to get excited about our fishing day and would get up to prepare some of the equipment and food with Philip.

When Toki and Philip went spearfishing, much of the effort was made the night before to prepare the equipment. The best fins and spear were not only important, but they were also an absolute necessity. It was understood that if fishing supplies were on sale, we would take out a loan if we had to, maybe even sell something.

One by one, I learned the rules, superstitions, and rituals that applied to fish and fishing. On one night before a fishing day, at dinner as he scooped rice from the wooden serving bowl onto the children's plates, I began to recite the fish I hoped Philip would catch the next day. "Papio," I mused, "and 'opakapaka would be ono (delicious) for tomorrow night's dinner."

Philip froze and looked annoyed. "Well, that's it, hon," he said. "They will all go the other way now when they see me swimming to them."

Fishermen, especially in the islands, are highly superstitious, and according to them, the fish could hear what we said. The fact that I had spoken their names had doomed the trip from the start. We were not supposed to talk about or even mention our fishing trip the next day, which was why he whispered to wake me. Nor would he speak as we drove because if the fish knew we were coming they would all head straight to the reef and hide. He was so strict about this, it made me laugh. However, he was serious about fishing, so I never teased him or chided him again.

The day following my comment at dinner was a whitewash with no fish caught. None were seen or they escaped the spear, as if they would swim close only to tease him. "Aha! We are on to you. We heard what that haole wife of yours said!" I imagined the fish laughing as the spear whooshed past.

Philip shook his head. "See, hon, they knew. They heard us talking, dat's why."

"You cannot be serious. Besides, we live miles from the beach. Furthermore, I saw on National Geographic that they have never been reputed to have psychic ears." He was silent. There were no words to explain this fishing sense to me. I learned another lesson, yet again, it was one of those Hawaiian realities that would keep happening.

Never again would I think out loud or discuss the fish that might be caught the next day. My mind would send a caution signal before I could make a sound.

Another superstition revolved around bananas. Local fishing custom dictated never bringing bananas to the beach. Once very early as I walked out of the house, I grabbed a bunch from the kitchen counter and threw it in the back of the Volkswagen under the buckets and toys. When Philip unpacked and saw the bananas, he gasped and slumped all in the same moment. He looked at his fishing partner and together they both exhaled long, painful sighs.

"What? What now?" I said, exasperated. Keeping up with this stuff never ended.

His partner pronounced the doom. "No fish today. Bad luck to bring bananas to the beach."

His wife walked over and when she saw the fruit, she said, "*Honto*, no good, no good. That is okay, we have fun, go swim today. We can pick seaweed instead." Shige-san was exceptionally good at making the best of an awkward situation. As they all filed past me with their heads hung low, I tried to protest, I had not known. They turned away and set up camp. Obviously, she got the karmic reality of fishing. I would learn too.

As I stood with my feet in the warm sand a part of me wanted to argue for them to at least try to catch something, but alas, it was futile. They all knew I was the only one who did not understand this connection between the ocean, the fish, the fisherman, and…bananas.

On this Saturday at dawn, we gathered seaweed as the children played for endless hours in the sand. The moment had passed, and we still enjoyed the day. However, I learned that if I played the game, we got to eat the freshest fish that night. Lobsters by the dozen often fell from their wet bags fresh from the sea. I always got the tails; they preferred the head. I blissfully went along, and the family time we spent with the children was irreplaceable and precious. I, too, learned the art of silence.

As they separated the catch, they placed a pot of water over a spitting campfire until it reached a rolling boil. Once immersed, all watched the blue-grey lobster change to a bright red orange. The meat in the head was called the "butter," creamy and savory, unique and appreciated, eaten alone with mayonnaise, this was Phil's choice. All agreed, this was "da best." Lobsters with bright orange eggs were passed over to enable future catches. I never tired of eating the firm white tails with a splash of drawn butter or mayonnaise.

In the early days in Honolulu, Phil would fish by himself. I would wait on the beach and keep an intent eye on him as he swam out until I could only see the empty, plastic bleach container that he used as a floater or buoy, bobbing in the surf. It was visible from a great distance, and I could spot it from time to time. If a diver never came back up, the floater would mark the site where he dove. If he went out so far that I could no longer see the floater, I would worry myself to a frazzle. Eventually, I realized how ridiculous this was, the futility in trying to change fate. After that epiphany, I rolled over and applied more suntan oil.

We would take the fish to Toki and Shige-san's house around two or three in the afternoon, exhausted, but the temptation of freshly caught and cooked fish was enough to renew us. Shige-san was a master with the fish, raw and cooked. I laughed when I found out the kinds of fish the Western world favored were considered 'opala (rubbish) to these seasoned island people.

Philip and Toki would sometimes catch enough lobsters, including my favorite, slipper lobster, to fill a rice bag. Slipper lobsters look like a rubber slipper and were smaller than regular lobsters with much sweeter meat. Their favored fishing ground was abundant with both varieties. The two seasoned fishermen took precautions to cover the bucket as they went to the car so that other fishers would not know of their bounty.

As stated, the rule was to catch only the number of fish you could carry, or what your family required—no more, no less. If you had a good day, you shared. Philip would drag an old cotton burlap rice bag across the wet sand and let me peek into the top to show me it was full and time to head for shore. He had caught enough fish for our family, and for his parents, sisters, brother, and any friend he could remember.

Not everyone understood these old standards. Philip told me to never reveal this special fishing ground with its pristine beach near the tall ironwood trees. If other fishermen saw their catch, they "might shamefully raid (poho) the area and maybe not enough for others bumbye!"

This was his version of fishing karma. That way, he was assured there would always be enough fish. The more he gave away, the more fish would be waiting for him when the next weekend came. He rarely froze any of his catch since it was best to give them all away, especially when you could always have them so fresh, they were still flapping. This was Hawaiian style and perhaps Filipino style too.

Back then, no one sold their fish. Their catch was for family and extended family. One bag was brought into the water, and once full, it was time to go home and cook. For some, fishing became a job, and they became greedy, laying nets with small eyes; that is, a net with tighter woven spaces. Their objective was to catch everything, even the small fish. Those small fish would never grow to be caught and appreciated properly. Philip would shake his head from side to side and exclaim this was poho (loss). It went against the principle of balance, (pono), that he'd learned on Molokai by following his brother-in-law's example. In defense, many liked those small fish. Bagoong fish sauce is made from marinated tiny fish.

In Philip's youth, the bounty of fish was staggering, and they would swim right up to you in the pristine waters curious to see who you were. As he predicted, as the years passed, fewer and fewer fish were available. His favorite local fishing TV program came on Sunday afternoon. The host was from Molokai and a former classmate. Phil would comment that his friend featured many island fishing spots, but almost never took the camera crew to Molokai since they wanted to keep those spots a secret.

When Erin went to college, he surfed the Honolulu waters with a childhood friend. He told his father about "challenging the ocean." His eyes brimmed with excitement as he spoke of finding the most awesome surf and how he would conquer it. Upon hearing his son's surfing adventures, Philip looked perplexed and increasingly concerned until he felt compelled to interrupt. "Son, you have lived in Honolulu too long and have forgotten all I've tried to teach you."

Phil's comment reflected Mama's teaching. I acknowledged the continuation of this family's culture about the ocean that had taken root in Philip. The balance of nature and sea was about age-old wisdom and an innate knowing.

He cautioned Erin to never use the words "challenge" or "conquer" when it applied to nature. With true concern he warned the boy, "You will eventually lose." He asked him to think carefully about surfing with this friend, to reconsider this term, and not conquer the ocean.

Erin nodded, understanding. He told his father not to worry and that he would be more careful. Erin's friend and surfing partner was Hawaiian and somewhat of a daredevil. Philip had gone fishing with the boy's father on occasion, and that man, also from Honolulu, did not know the ocean as well either.

Once on Molokai while Erin was in high school, father and son went diving off the eastern end of the island. From the corner of his eye through the clear water, Philip saw a shark approaching at an unhurried pace. They were about a hundred yards from the shore as the shark swam to his side. From all his years on Molokai waters he knew if they went slowly and showed no fear, there would be no problem or need to panic. All of Philip's training and inner knowledge told him to turn to shore using short strokes and to remain calm. He took slow strokes toward Erin and when they were about ten feet apart, Philip spoke while maintaining calm. "Boy," he said, "follow me back in. Swim slowly and be sure not to make any splashes."

Erin was having a good day and said playfully, "No, that's okay, Dad. I want to stay out. You can go back."

Realizing this was not the time for debate, Philip had to reveal the imminent danger. Keeping his voice even, he said, "To our right is a shark." Erin took off like a bullet from a primed rifle, making a huge splash with his departure with one of his fins.

The only word surfers feared was "shark." Phil whipped out his hand, grabbed Erin's ankle, and reeled him in. Phil locked in on his son's crazed eyes. Erin had gone pale, the blood drained from his normally tanned face with panic taking hold.

"Now, son, listen carefully," Phil commanded. "Swim very slowly, do not feel fear, or you may get us both killed, understand? Do not splash as you swim. Move very quietly and do not create even a ripple on the surface...slow and steady!"

Erin nodded his head and finding his voice, choked out, "Yes, Dad!"

They moved as a team, exactly as Philip advised. Upon reaching shore, Erin staggered onto the sand and collapsed in a heap. A huge sense of relief swept over him, and he felt like crying. Philip and the uncles had a good laugh about the "hapa-haole (half-White) boy who better listen to 'da faddah.'"

Their shark experience made a good story for the campfire that evening to be told and retold, especially after many beers. Philip said he was never worried about the shark; after all, he had never hurt a shark in his life so why would the shark come after him? "The shark was only finding his dinner, best to get out of his way." Again, there was that Hawaiian version of fishing karma.

Philip once told me about a fisher, a kid from Texas, who loved to taunt and poke at puhi (eels) for fun. He harassed them mercilessly and killed them for sport, while never being interested in eating the meat. It came as no surprise when Philip saw this friend in town one day with his arm all bandaged; the eels had attacked him all at once.

Another favorite form of fishing was called torching. At night, the fisher carried a lit torch (in modern times a propane lantern) out onto the water. The sea had to be at low tide so that the reef was exposed, and the reef fish would also be more exposed and vulnerable. The fisher would creep ahead, using his torch to illuminate the dark water. Holding his spear high, he was ready to "poke fish." The fish were an easy mark because they were attracted to and transfixed by the light.

One time Philip went torching with a Chinese friend who had recently brought home his new bride from China. His plan was for the children and me to visit with the bride and her new baby while he and his friend went torching. He neglected to tell me that she spoke no English. We tried sign language for a while as I watched the clock hands inch forward.

As the hour grew late with no sign of the men, I began to worry, so much so that I decided to call the police. The plan in my mind was clear since I knew where they went. I rationalized that all the police had to do was radio an officer in the area, have him cruise that section of the beach and tell me if he saw the torchlight out in the water. That way I would know if he was still fishing.

The police officer in dispatch did not agree and insisted on coming to the house to file a report. I argued my point. All they had to do was look out on the water and see if he was there with his torch or not! When I realized I was getting nowhere with the officer, I relented. "Fine. Come take a report if you have to, but all I need to know is if he is still in the water."

I waited outside, frantic, pacing the sidewalk. Our baby had been asleep in the playpen for hours. My mind had run rampant, and I imagined a giant fish had devoured him. Within fifteen minutes, just as the police car arrived, Philip pulled in right behind him. The officer, a tall Hawaiian man, exited his patrol car with its line of blue lights flashing on the roof. He smiled and asked Philip, "So, what, brah, you catch?"

They looked at me, shook their heads and laughed. I was tired and not amused. Philip ended up opening his catch and letting the officer select his favorite fish to share with his 'ohana. The officer walked away happy, and no report was filed.

Some of the techniques used to catch fish and other sea creatures amazed me. To catch an octopus, the fisher needed to possess great skill. First, he had to spear the squiggly creature. He had to grab the head and bite between the eyes to pinch off the main nerve, and do it fast because all the while, long tentacles and suction cups surrounded him. A great battle ensued to pull the tentacles away as the fisher attempted to find the precise spot between the eyes. And all this was done while still submerged! The object was to paralyze the creature so that none of the precious black ink held in the brain escaped. This feat was one of those macho, courageous things, to "bite the sack between the eyes" at the right moment so that the dark ink could be used for a special soup enjoyed later that night.

Once Philip was with a cousin when the tide changed to a dangerous formation—a riptide. Knowing the current could pull them out to sea, the two fishers had to push their way back to shore using their spears to pull and anchor them along. In this kind of situation, even though it was slow going, the men had to keep a clear head and not panic. Philip kept one eye on his cousin and the other one on the shifting, pulling waters at their feet. He dreaded not knowing whether his partner could handle the ordeal or not. They made it back to shore after spending hours traveling a short distance. Philip chose never to fish with that cousin again.

On another occasion, Philip's partner for a planned fishing expedition had to cancel. This was one of those rare and special low tide days and he was determined to fish, no matter what. Somehow, he recruited me, promising we would have a great adventure. We were newly married, and I was eager to please and be his partner. I was about six months pregnant with our first child. Since this baby would be born at over nine pounds, I was already huge at six months.

We went out early during a minus-four tide; that is, when the ocean sinks well below normal water levels. Water that may have been at one's throat the day before was now at chest level. As the shoreline waters subsided, the fish swam out to sea and would actually jump over the reef and create a "traffic jam" of fish. Considering the lure of a bulging bag of fish, only the threat of a tidal wave could have kept Philip at home.

We began as the morning sun crested the horizon and reached the reef by wading out in the knee-deep water. I sat on the exposed craggy shelf of the reef while he dove over the edge to spear the fish that darted in and out of the holes and reef channels.

I must have looked like a beached whale with my pregnant stomach and bikini top. Just as I got comfortable, Philip emerged from the deep. He was almost laughing as if there was something humorous, I was not aware of. He asked me to move down, just a little. This was no small feat to lumber my huge belly up and down and especially so since the reef was composed of chunky lava rock and sharp coral. As the day wore on, he would ask me to move more to the right or more to the left.

At last, he emerged again all shiny from the saltwater and said, "Okay, pau, we go now, I get plenty."

He lifted himself and his full bags onto the reef and offered an outstretched hand to help me up. We waded back to shore. I was more than ready to go. I was hot and knew I would suffer that night with a sunburn after all this "fun." As the designated water boy, I was to pull the filled bag of fish. He was the fisher, so he carried his floater, his fins and spear. As we plodded through the clear turquoise waters of Aina Haina, I noticed he kept checking behind us. He seemed a little preoccupied. Overall, I was not having fun; I was overtired, and it was work.

I can still feel the cool water at my feet and ankles with the noonday sun full upon my back, burning my tender skin. I knew it would blister from sunburn (the lotion had washed away with the first two waves). I made a mental note to take a pass the next time he begged me to go. Years later, numerous skin cancers made me remember those days under the unforgiving sun.

On Sunday, the day after being out at the reef, we went to the Waikiki Aquarium. For Philip, going to a saltwater aquarium was the equivalent of a Disneyland adventure; here he could visit all his friends.

When we reached the tank that housed the largest eels I had ever seen in my entire life, I was in for a surprise. They were gruesome with their large jaws that did nothing but open and close, revealing hundreds of needle-sharp teeth. Philip laughed to himself as if to a private joke.

"What is so funny?" I asked.

He stopped smiling, and sheepishly confessed, "Remember yesterday when I kept moving you? Well, there was an eel under you, inside the reef, bigger than that one." He pointed to the largest and by far, the ugliest eel in the tank. It was grotesque! He realized that I did not think this was amusing, but still, he nodded his head in affirmation.

I swung my handbag at his arm. "Here I am, pregnant, and you risk my having a miscarriage if I saw that thing while clinging to a sharp reef half a mile from shore?" I swore I would never fish or be his water boy again, and I have kept my word.

Fishing was the ultimate spiritual experience for him, the most natural way to reach an understanding of the balance of nature (pono). When Philip learned of his sister Lolly's death a couple of years after we'd married, he came home to tell me he would rather be alone and drove off. As I prepared the laundry the next day his pockets were filled with sand. I understood. His slippers at the door were crusted with salt and sand too. Perhaps the ebb and flow of the waves helped to wash and clear his emotions. Unlike Mama's death the year before, this was sudden. We could no longer rely on Mama and her power to protect us all.

14 - Mama Told Me

Mama and Papa Sabado.
Paulo's bunyag, baptism, 1971.
Photo by Paul Donegan

14

In her hospital room in a misty Nu'unau valley, I felt a great kinship. I had come to love Mama as my own mother. In these last precious days, she shared stories of her life in these islands and her village. My education continued in the ways of her people. The stories wove life's important messages into the fabric of my life.

All was still and cool from the night as valley shadows clung to the pali from the pale hours before. The fast-dissolving misty bands were like small fingers that tug at the folds of a mother's hem. The new sun blinded me as I entered her room. I stopped mid-step at the door, stung by the morning light that shot long shining arrows in all directions. They spilled into the room like an overflowing cup and saturated every corner of this cold, sterile place.

This was her home now—the ninth floor of Saint Francis Hospital. Though located near Chinatown and the bustling state capitol, it seemed a world away. Mama's hospital bed was by the window. Her face, worn and wrinkled by her many years of hardship, emanated a golden hue. The acrid antiseptic smells of her hospital room had become familiar. I relaxed into my favorite chair and stretched my legs, anchoring my toes on the bed's metal edge. I needed to be close to hear every word.

When Mama saw me, her face radiated joy. This was our time together, when the hours would evaporate as fast as the morning dew that settled on the ti plants at her windowsill. In these precious moments, she could relax and drift into the past so we could "talk story." I thought I was keeping an old beloved woman company, simply passing time. Her children were working. In hindsight, I see these times clear as crystal. Her storytelling manifested into this moment, for this book.

As I settled into the chair, she held my unwavering focus. I enjoyed listening to her. She gave me advice and guidance. Mama would die in this place, but not until her stories had been told. She spoke in a whisper, sensing her time was drawing near, telling me her secrets before she would pass. She leaned forward, warming to the moment. As she began, a knowing smile unfolded on her timeless face.

"When I was a girl in the Philippines, a two-headed snake hidden in the tall grasses told me that I would live on beautiful islands far across the sea and have many children." Her face glowed as the ancient recollection crossed her mind. The snake, known as the *papapal* was magical. Even the word, *papapal* sounded lyrical and seductive. I never stopped to question how a snake, no less a two-headed one, could speak to this extraordinary girl who would ultimately become the mother of the man I would marry and *Apo Baket* (grandparent) to my children.

My daily morning excursion was to see my husband's parents, old, yet strong in spirit. After the babies woke from the first nap, I would put Paulo, now eighteen months, into the stroller, and strap infant Erin to my back, papoose style. I would pack diapers and milk and treats for my babies, and fruit and a sandwich for me. I walked with my babies on misty Nuʻuanu Avenue to the hospital, almost a mile up the Valley Road from the cottage we rented on Judd Street. In the warm blush of the early morning, the mist in the valley seemed my constant companion as I pushed the stroller up Liliha Street.

Many Chinese and Japanese families had made their homes in the Nuʻuanu Valley. I enjoyed the beautiful old homes and manicured yards. I could see how the houses reflected a unique mix of East and West. Some houses had roofs with uplifted corners, positioned this way to release trapped spirits. I loved the many colors. Reds and forest greens accented the undersides. The entrances featured heavy wooden doors brought on great ships with the missionaries from New England.

When I arrived in the lobby of the hospital, Papa would be waiting. As usual, he began his day early. Mama hated the American meals they served at the hospital, so he prepared their food at home. That way they could eat together as they had for all the years since they had first met as teenagers in Hilo. He always dressed in the same dapper button-down aloha shirts, freshly pressed, showing scenes of old Hawaiʻi with red hibiscus and hula dancers in grass skirts. His hat was adjusted and pushed down with a suave, slight tilt.

He smiled when he saw me pushing the stroller into the lobby and affectionately patted my shoulder as I placed baby Erin in his lap. He'd prepared a sack of Filipino goodies for the children, usually sweet mochi rice called *kankanen*. Papa mixed his confection similar to what was available locally, but he used his own special recipe, rich and golden with butter, brown sugar, rice, and coconut milk that he had braised over a fire wrapped in banana leaf. He used a banana leaf to wrap the sweet dessert and tied it up with a string. After all this time, I can still recall the taste of Papa's *kankanen*. Other versions never matched his recipe.

Papa stayed with the babies while I visited Mama. I knew the boys were fine with him even when they raced about. Papa would chuckle and never bothered to get up to chase after them. The kids knew he held the treats, and they would pull at his trouser pockets in a playful taunt, looking for the sweets he hid till the moment he could "surprise" them.

In her room, Mama shifted her weight by grasping the cold silver bar of the hospital bed as she leaned against one arm to find a comfortable position. Years of illness and a struggle with diabetes had taken her physical strength and her frail body now weighed a scant eighty pounds. She winced once or twice never commenting or crying out.

Once settled, a smile lit up her face. She spoke in broken English, then would revert to Ilocano, the language of her native mountain people. I had paid close attention in the first months of our marriage as my husband translated for me. In time, I would wave him away because I could understand her. If I got stuck, I could always call for a nurse who spoke the same dialect. "Ma, try wait! Repeat dat one. I never understand you. Try one more time," I would plead.

A passing nurse lingered to translate. "Ai, yah, Nana, I remember that place too!"

Mama would cover her mouth and laugh, scolding me as she waved her hand in good humor. I was grateful for Mama's sharp mind and her keen wit.

The Chinese say a fine red thread binds all life. It reflects the prevailing wisdom that we are held together by one fiber of understanding. All who came to these island shores sought fulfillment of a singular desire—a new beginning and better fortune. As I sat in the cool Nu'uanu Valley and listened to her stories, I realized the courage and resolve required to depart from one's homeland. To separate from your mother, father, and the siblings who nurtured and loved you must be the most bitter, and yet, the most promising task. All the immigrants of this time were courageous pioneers who believed that somehow, in the end, their sacrifices would help those left behind as well as those who came after them.

The distance between the two island groups of the Philippines and Hawai'i was not as far as many would believe. A strong, ancient connection between Hawaiian and Filipino culture exists.

My brother-in-law learned on his cruise from Asia to Hawai'i, the Chinese called the Hawaiian Islands set in the Pacific, "the land of the fragrant trees." His comment upon returning amazed me. "Before we could even see the islands on the horizon," he said, "we could already smell the flowers." The Chinese were correct in naming it. The Philippines was known before Spanish Colonization as "the land of the tattooed peoples." When you see the tattoos from the South Pacific and compare them to those on Hawai'i, one does not need to reach far into the distant past.

In the early 1900s upon her arrival in Hilo, Hawai'i, Severina, also known as Paning, was told by her *kakailian* (townmates) of a man, Felix, who was constantly in trouble because of his drinking and fighting. The plantation rules were very strict. Troublemakers were rooted out and returned to the Philippines. This man's combative technique was the Filipino stick fighting art known as *escrima*, in which he was highly skilled. In this martial art, two sticks—one in each hand—are wielded with amazing speed. His fighting combined with heavy drinking earned his exile home to the impoverished rice fields of Ilocos Sur, where he would soon be sent. Felix's people who had come from that same mountain village, pleaded with the émigrés from Mama's village to meet and marry off this man so he could remain in the islands. After the ceremony, the bride would be free to go her own way, or so they said.

In the quiet town of Hilo, Paning met Felix (pronounced: fay leez) at the church steps and they walked to the altar. Felix was meticulous in his appearance, wearing his customary beige or white fedora angled to the right. He always dressed well and wore a colorful aloha shirt with the sleeveless white *kamiseta* (a knit sleeveless undershirt). As the divine and fate would deem, the two were married, and Mama chose to stay with Papa. Twelve children later…

Papa was a charmer with a hearty laugh. Mama was a woman of silent power and rare beauty that could always turn heads as she passed. Full of energy, Papa loved to walk and was always on the move somewhere. Their first children were girls, Magdalena, and Loretta. The third, a boy, was named Santiago after Papa's hometown.

Unfortunately, Papa had an accident early in the marriage that prevented work in the fields. The poisonous tip from a pineapple punctured the white of his eye, rendering him disqualified from the fields. Once recovered, he occasionally found work. He grew vegetables and was a good fisherman. Anyone who knew the basics of fishing and gardening could survive in the islands then. The barter system would sustain them with a little pork, some vegetables, and fish. There was always "nuff" to go around. They lived in poverty without the steady income of the main provider. He brewed a pineapple wine that he shared with his compadres. He was a modest man with simple needs.

Mama was industrious and creative. To support the family, she took in laundry from the single men of the camp. Philip's older sisters quit high school to help with the family laundry business. Only the last children born were able to finish school and graduate. And only one, Philip, would complete college.

Four girls were born in Hanamaulu, Kauai and each were given melodic Spanish names. Most would later use English names that were more cosmopolitan. My husband would be the last child born to this family of twelve. To his mother, he would always be known as Alipio. His school chums and the camp kids knew him by his English name, Philip, and his nickname among friends on the country roads was "Honu," Hawaiian for turtle.

A Filipina woman once told me that she knew my husband was a Sabado before I introduced him. She had spied him from a distance and with a knowing smile she said, "If you were to visit the Philippines, you would see your husband's family has a distinct look, they all have a rounded face." I can see this feature in our children who favor my husband, the others have my Irish chin.

Plantation life for this growing family had them going from camp to camp as they traveled from island to island. Wherever they went there was always family or *kakailian* (townmates) to help them settle in. Marriage and children did not change Papa's wild ways, and time after time his drinking would push the family to the next camp or island.

Faced with a growing family, Papa found a new career in brewing pineapple wine. Large porcelain vats used for storing rice were suitable for the potent wine of fermented pineapple called "swipe." Quite often there would be a sampling party by fellow villagers in the pau hana hours. The so-called "gypsy alcohol" would take a toll on the sobriety of the camp and a move to the next camp would become necessary.

Single men were recruited by the thousands, and their plan was to work at the camps until they could return to the Philippines and marry. Their objective was to be wealthy enough to afford a family. Some of these men worked for thirty and forty years before they could allow themselves to have a family of their own. They would visit the Philippines, choose a woman, marry, and bring her back to Hawai'i for his well-earned retirement. It was assumed he would support her family, and eventually bring them over to live in the islands.

In the early days the camps had special names for the settlements: Manila Camp, Spanish Camp, and Maunaloa Camp. When the Sabado family first came to Molokai the small plantation community was on a dirt road that faced the open Molokai Channel looking toward the back of Diamond Head on O'ahu. This was known as Spanish Camp.

At the same time Mama and Papa were boarding their respective ships in the Philippines in the early 1900s, folks from all four corners of the world were on the move. Across the continents of Asia and Europe, millions boarded ships with the same hopes, a better life for themselves and their children, born and to be born. They came to well-known points of entry in New York Harbor, San Francisco Bay, and elsewhere. Like the villagers from the Philippines, these immigrants sought sovereignty and safety from oppression, a release from poverty, and above all else, freedom.

The Chinese were first to arrive in "the land of the fragrant trees." They came in the bowels of dark ships as human cargo and as indentured workers. They understood there would be no returning to the villages of the mountain Haka people and the Punti of the lowlands. As was often the case, the men came as laborers accompanied by very few women who had to be wed. This was why the picture bride business took off. Being of one mind, the immigrants meant to carve out a future in these islands.

It was reported that most of the Chinese laborers remained in the fields for less than one month. These industrious people pooled their minuscule wages in what was termed in Hawaiian as a hui. Their objective was to buy out their contracts when they could. Chinese-owned shops, restaurants, and gambling dens began to appear in the towns that skirted the plantation camps and across the other islands.

James Michener, in his book Hawai'i, wrote about the short time the Chinese stayed in the fields. They were organized and prepared to make Hawai'i their home, and moreover, support their home villages as well as each other. Each Chinese family had an ancestral village that was supported through a broker that made sure a percentage was deposited in their ancestral shrines. Some Chinese maintained a wife in China as well as Hawaiian Family.

The Japanese sailed from bitter cold shores, but their goal was to work hard and save their earnings in anticipation of returning to their ancestral villages. The Japanese stayed in the fields longer than the Chinese, but they found the heat of the fields oppressive. Eventually, some of the first waves of immigrants did pay off their contracts and return home; however, most remained in the islands to create strong cultural communities. In modern day Hawai'i, Chinese and Japanese descendants have wielded great influence on the political, financial health, and welfare of the islands.

In later years when the Japanese formed their huis, the family cooperatives nurtured doctors, lawyers, and political forces for the future; almost all had come from camp people. In a hui, every family member would invest a monthly or yearly sum. The accrued amount after years of saving would be sufficient to finance selected individuals for medical, dental, or law school in the mainland for all the children in the hui. Both the Chinese and Japanese employed the hui system. Doctors flew in once a week from Honolulu to the small populations of Molokai, and because they were a product of the huis, they were tolerated by the old-timers. Language and an understanding of culture acted as threads that tied the community together with open communication, and pidgin English became the common language.

The next group of workers was much smaller than the first to arrive. The Portuguese had been invited by the Hawaiian Kingdom and primarily came from the islands of Madeira and the Azores with the blessing of their monarch. Leaving their homeland was not as dire for the Portuguese because they were allowed to bring their large families with them with the supportive mandate of their sovereign that stipulated: Families or no workers. The

Portuguese brought ukulele's, and many aspects of their homeland with them. Clay ovens to bake bread were well-received and still appreciated by the Hawaiian population. The beautiful orange and blue spiked bird-of-paradise flower came originally from Madeira with these first pioneers. Other Latin groups followed from Spain.

Puerto Ricans and Mexicans came to work on the land and taught the Hawaiians the sublime pleasure of riding horses. Hawaiians took to the horses with a passion and their love has continued with renowned paniolo and pa'u riders featured in parades. Ranches on Molokai and the Big Island have continued to support this lifestyle. Rodeos are ongoing on Molokai, Maui, and the Big Island.

Filipinos proved best suited for the fields and long hours under the unyielding Hawaiian sun. They remained employed by the sugar and pineapple companies in the fields long after their arrival. They were happy people who thrived on the hard work the tropical Hawaiian fields had to offer. Only when the hotels began to open their doors for employment did the Filipinos move from the fields to work as domestics. Once their children were educated, doors opened for management and professional positions.

In the early years, farm workers wore clothing that covered every inch of exposed skin, including the face, with an added shield for the eyes to prevent blinding. The needle-sharp tip of pineapple leaves was known to contain poison, as Papa experienced early on. The women wore a conical hat with ruffles around the brim, reminiscent of the hats worn by pioneer women of the American West. Drive by the fields, and you may still see this attire worn by workers.

Pineapple and sugar barons of the plantation system soon realized the enormous value of these Filipino workers. The first wave of immigrants had strong and capable men and was so successful that scouts were dispatched into the distant provinces of the Philippines to recruit more workers. To this day, the Filipinos are considered the oil that keeps the machine running. Hospitals, nursing, and elder care facilities would be sent scrambling without these dedicated, hard-working people.

One of Mama's favorite stories was how Papa found salvation and changed his errant ways. Most Filipinos came to these shores with a lifelong devotion to the Catholic Church. Many chose to be Protestant after their arrival for their own reasons. High on that list was the comfort of speaking their native tongue. The Hawaiian Catholic Church did not respond well to the trials and challenges of the immigrant group. Small factions of Protestantism found a ready congregation in these newcomers. As in all her stories, Mama began with a smile that would fill a room and illuminate her face from within. This story was her favorite because she was so proud of Papa.

"One night I had dis dream. I see your Papa. He stay all in white, he get on one white hat, white pants, shirt, jacket and socks, and shoes. From head to toe, all over he stay in white." She nodded her head as her memories sharpened. Inhaling deeply, she continued, immersed in the moment from all those years before.

Understanding the symbolism in her dream, she went to the store to buy these items for him, including the white hat, shoes, and socks. She spared no expense because she had ultimate faith in her visions. This was the same woman who set the table for visiting spirits. As she saw it, every item had to be new and spotless. She arranged the new clothing on the koltsons (abaca mats) on the floor, and then called him into the room.

"Dis one all for you," she said with pride.

He was very happy, his eyes wide with approval. As he reached for the crisp white hat to try on, he stopped and paused with his hand mid-air before placing the hat on his head, knowing the caveat to come. There had to be a catch as he waited for the rest of the story.

"Last night, I had a dream," Mama explained. Papa knew this was not always a good sign. "I see you all in white, so…I go buy all dis white kine clothes for you. All you have to do, if you like all dis kine," she gestured across the new assortment with the tags still attached, "is go church with me…only one time."

As a man who took pride in his appearance, this was an easy request. There was singing and food, so Papa did not hesitate. He loved to sing, and he could play his guitar at this church of hers. Plus, so many there were *kababayan*. To have all these new clothes, he would accompany her dressed to a T!

Smiling now, she repeated, "All you gotta do is go with me one time, and all dis one for you!"

According to Mama's story, that was all it took. She had discovered the

Way of Salvation Church. The church members all spoke Ilocano and there was great camaraderie. After this vision and the one-time religious experience, Papa never drank another drop and would outlive her by many years. He became devout and was never seen without his Bible. He wore his white hat as he went to and from the church. After he found his faith, his only vice, if it even qualifies, was a simple spoonful of apricot-pineapple jam aside his rice as a treat.

I knew she craved her time with Papa. I would see them talking softly as he would stroke her thin, skeletal hands. They always held hands these days. How beautiful to live a long life and still grasp the hand you had held from when you were a teenager.

Many people came to visit Mama at her bedside, and she would talk with them for long periods of time. If she wanted to visit someone, everyone and everything would stop to accommodate her wishes.

Once while standing at her bedside, I commented that Philip was on a diet and could not eat too much of the *kankanen*, the sweet mochi rice Papa had made the night before. She laughed and said, "Dis one, no can help, he always going be little big. When he small I no can find da white cockroach."

"The what, Ma?"

"Da white cockroach."

I laughed and said, "Ma, what are you talking about?" I pulled up my chair from the edge of her bed to make sure I didn't miss this story.

"When Eugene (Phillip's older brother) was small boy, I give him da white cockroach. Dat why he never going get fat. Only dis kine cure for the boy baby." As an afterthought, she added, "Bumbye, I tell your Papa to go find for your keiki."

Apparently, she had found a white cockroach and fed it mashed up in Eugene's food when he was an infant so that he would be thin all his life. He has stayed thin. Everyone else struggled with weight. The rare albino cockroach (yes, they exist) was supposed to be good luck and ensures thinness for boy babies. I drew the line on this one, passing on the offer to find one to mash into the boys' baby food. Papa never found any, but per her instructions, no doubt he was on the lookout.

The week before Mama died, I went to visit her. Our "talk story" times had become shorter. She smiled as I entered the sterile room. I had slipped the children past the nurses, and we all sat in the warm sunlight that poured through the window. She loved the babies, and her eyes followed them as they played. Seeing the children always gave her joy.

Being in the hospital was torture for her when it seemed they kept finding ways to inflict more pain on her frail form. She suffered from the advanced stages of diabetes and her circulation was very poor. The solution seemed barbaric. The nurses attached long strips of hospital tape to her paper-thin skin and then ripped them off to make her arms bleed—this was to increase circulation. The sores never seemed to heal completely because diabetics heal slowly.

She grimaced in pain as she rolled over on her side. Gripping the cold aluminum bar, she whispered, "I like make (die,) at home, dis not home. I'm ready now." We all heard her, but she never made it home.

The visit with the children and me in Mama's hospital room was short that day. The shadows hung longer in the sterile hallways, and she was growing ever tired. Perhaps the spirits who guided her were growing impatient waiting for her to pass over. She turned onto her side, an indication our visit was pau for the day. As I left, I thought about how much more I could learn from her if only she would live longer. I still knew so little about her family and cultural ways.

I never wanted to think about how much I would miss her when she passed. She had become like my own mother, teaching and guiding me through the ways of Molokai, Filipino ways, healing, babies, and marriage.

15 - Herbs, Circumcision, and Coconuts

Ka Niu, Coconut Tree.
The wonders of the coconut tree.
Artwork by Philip Sabado

15

 *Mama's garden was a practical place. It was not always picture-perfect, but every blade of grass and plant had a medicinal purpose or was used in cooking. The family never considered using the services of the company doctor who came once a month to the settlement. Mama's plants and teas always did the trick.*

"Da haole kine doktor, what he know?" she said.

If her remedy did not do, there was always the kahuna who lived by the large banyan tree on the shady corner five miles from Kaunakakai where you turn up the road to Hoʻolehua. Both Mama and the kahuna administered their remedies with care, respect, and aloha.

Once when Philip was very young, they attended a party. He played with the other boys, but somehow a fight broke out. Another boy threw dirt at him, which burned and swelled as shards cut into the white of his eye, preventing him from seeing. Mama called him over, held her long black hair to his eye, and blew smoke from her Toscani into the affected eye. The grit of the dirt disappeared, the eye magically cleared and was not even red.

"No need doktor, we get our own kine already." *Mama knew what to do, and her garden of strange-looking leaves and fruits usually did the trick. Phil never saw a Western doctor until his exams for the military.*

Camp people generally were in bed by eight-thirty or nine at the latest. Evenings were spent "talking story" in the kitchen. Tradition dictated drinking one last cup of cape' (coffee) with a hunk of soft bread, and *pao duce* (Portuguese sweet bread) was on hand to dunk into that last steaming cup. Often someone would start to strum the ukulele (kanikapila), and everyone sang (mele) their favorite songs together. The atmosphere was uncomplicated and sublime. Imagine the only sounds being the ukulele, the wind, and occasional rain falling…paradise!

At four in the morning as darkness held the village houses and dirt pathways appeared as black strips, sleepy villagers rose before four to prepare the kau kau (food) tins for the most important time of the day, the midday meal. These tins consisted of two round aluminum bowls stacked with a cover and a twisted wire handle. Kitchen lights illuminated the men's breakfast as coffee and sometimes eggs and rice were prepared.

As grown adults, Phil and I ate eggs at breakfast. He reflected to a time when eggs were a privilege and sometimes a rarity in the camp. Back when Hawai'i was still a territory, eggs were never imported. Not many families raised chickens, and there were only so many eggs to go around.

In the misty predawn hours, my new husband let me sleep in, but I could hear the clap of the screen door as the workers filed out. They sat on the porch step to strap on their gear and put on their heavy work boots before padding down the red crusted steps to meet their day. Phil geared up with the heavy canvas clothes of the fields purchased from the field owners at a nominal cost. He liked to twist a red bandanna about his neck in a cocky fashion. Before long, he kissed me goodbye in the quiet darkness of our bedroom. The heavier canvas chaps used for arms, legs, and body were donned at the truck station, and for good reason: the pineapple points and spines could not penetrate the thick material.

Still half asleep I could hear the stream of workers shuffle down the red soil road, women and men moving as one force. Dressed alike to meet the fields, they headed for the loading truck capable of carrying twelve to fifteen people to the harvest area. They were a jolly group, full of life. They viewed working in the fields as "good fun," and more so, a privilege to be working.

Outside my bedroom window, I could hear the women teasing and laughing. They were all so happy—even at that ungodly hour. Someone would tell a joke and they would all howl as they walked. My sister-in-law was renowned for her pilau mouth that could make anyone blush. "Ai, sista, no talk like dat. You da same too!" The laughter became more distant as they disappeared down the road, like waves cresting and ebbing away. Stillness followed and then the birds in the front avocado tree inevitably erupted in a chorus. I pulled the blankets close as the quiet of the small village returned. I fell into a deep sleep until the heat of the day would force me awake. Soon the noise and laughter from children heading off to school replaced the sound of the workers.

At lunchtime, the workers would find a place in the field, sit in a circle and place the top portion of their tin into the center of the circle. This was the *sida* (see da) main entree. The bottom portion of the tin was always filled with rice. Everyone would enjoy the midday meal together, sampling the many main dishes. Lunch was never boring.

I was determined to be a good wife and since I could sleep in, I would make my husband's lunch the night before. Every day, I made him either a peanut butter and jelly or tuna sandwich with chips. He was so tactful, or maybe he never knew how to broach the subject, but he never told me about the kau kau tradition. I learned later that all the men felt sorry for the boy who had just married the haole wahine. They would smile and say, "Come boy, no shame we feed you, see, we get plenty!" With open arms and hearts, they would wave him over to their makeshift table in the center of the fields.

I got wind of this and said to Phil, "You could have told me! Let your manong get up and make your kau kau tin." Then I asked, "By the way? What did you do with all those sandwiches I made?"

He grinned sheepishly and said, "Always get plenty of camp dogs that are hungry."

On one overcast day, Philip saw a man sitting off to the side, not eating with the other workers. He wondered why this man was alone as he seemed friendly enough. When he went to sit with him, the man informed him he was eating dog. Philip, not wanting to be rude, sat with the old man and shared his lunch anyway.

Phil told me he had eaten dog with the old man to be polite, and the meat, he said, tasted like goat or deer.

"In the *banyo*," I said, "there is mouthwash. Please drink it before you come anywhere near me!" I was making a joke—kind of. If he ever ate with the old man again, or if he ate dog, he never told me.

Old country rituals and traditions were maintained in the camps. One of these rites for boys was circumcision at age thirteen. Most first-generation Ilocano boys of Philip's age had not been circumcised. After hearing of the process from a Visayan relative, Philip was glad his time had still not come. The relative told of going to the beach where an old man sat ready, meticulously sharpening his cutting edge with long, steady strokes on a leather stropping belt. The old man gave each of the boys guava leaves to chew. The leaves were not to be swallowed but used for their numbing effect when applied to the severed skin.

When their turn came, each boy was to place his *boto* (penis) on the tree trunk, and the sharp blade would be quick and final. The chewed guava leaves were then placed and held (with a shaking hand, no doubt) on the severed area and the boy would be told to run into the ocean so the salty water would dull the pain and cauterize the bleeding.

As he retold the story, the memory was still as sharp as the knife intended to do the deed. Philip recalled standing in line with the rest of the boys and watching them step forward one at a time. He became more nervous as the boys before him winced and staggered after the final cut as they ran into the water. He saw his friends standing for the longest time in the waist-high surf shifting their weight from foot to foot waiting for the pain to pass. His turn drew near and after careful consideration he said he waited for the right moment and bolted from the line, vowing not to return no matter what anyone said, not even his mother! When we had our babies, he decided the boys would be as he was, uncut.

A Filipino girl told me that she was only five years old when her family began the journey to Hawai'i. Before leaving their province in the Philippines, her mother stopped to scoop a teaspoon of the fertile ground from her village soil and put it in a small pouch that was sewn into her satchel. Her mother explained that often when one travels from one land to another, illness could strike. She believed that in her small parcel of rich soil, she carried her homeland and the protection of her village ancestors. Their family guardians traveled with them to the new land in the little pouch that held the sacred soil. The purpose of carrying the native soil from her homeland was to secure the welfare of her children and the entire family. Once they found a home in Hawai'i, the mother released the soil onto the fertile land of her new island home.

When the time came for them to build a new home in Hawai'i, my friend told me they had made an offering of two boiled eggs and a scoop of sweet mochi rice. These items were placed in the middle of the new land before they broke soil to begin building. The food signified the family's longevity and prosperity on the land.

Many years later, the family returned to the Philippines for a visit and continued the custom in reverse. Her mother carried a pouch of Hawaiian soil to be discreetly placed outside the home where she stayed for her holiday.

All went well on their visit to their home village. No one became ill as a result of the difference in food or water. As my friend explained it, in a subtropical climate the heat often causes constant thirst. Her family did not suffer this distress. She told me with an air of pride that she thought her mother was the wisest woman she knew. Another abiding ritual occurred whenever this family went to a park or beach for a picnic. Whether in Hawai'i or in the Philippines, a handful of cooked rice would be thrown as an offering to appease the spirits of the area so all would be well.

Innocently, I asked if the birds ate the thrown rice. "Oh, no!" She exclaimed, amazed that I would ask such a question. "It was not theirs!" The protocol and respect for the sake of the living spirits made a deep impression on me. I was reminded of Molokai and Mama.

On a sunny summer afternoon as I sat in Mama's hospital room, she told me quite casually that I would want another man. The hot sun against the glass window radiated heat and the temperature in the room became significant because she'd made me blush.

Horrified, I spoke in her dialect and in pidgin. "Ma, no talk dat kine!" I protested. "You know, I only like Philip. We are in love!"

I gulped hard and waited for what she would say next. She knew how devoted I was to Phil. I also knew her well enough to know there was a hook. Her expression grew serious, and ignoring my protest she said, "I know dis one, dis when happen to me one time wit your Papa. I know how to fix when dis happen to you."

Aha! Now I understood, this was one of her lessons complete with a cure. Without prompting, she told me a story that took place when she was in the hospital on Molokai. My mind shot to a scene—Philip once showed me that old hospital. "The spooky one," Philip whispered in all seriousness, "where get all the spirits."

Mama said she felt attracted to a male nurse, yet believed he was some sort of devil trying to sway her and intending to cast a spell on her. She did not hesitate to speak to Papa about this. She had fallen under the nurse's spell

15 – Herbs, Circumcision, and Coconuts

and gave Papa instructions on how to break it.

She pointed down the hall at the male nurse. "You see dat man? I tink I like him now…and not you."

To her way of seeing, she was under a kahuna, a magic spell cast by the man. In her way, Mama always knew how to respond and find the antidote. After all, she was from a powerful place, too, and not easily swayed. Accustomed to her insights, Papa understood he would be given a mission to fulfill. He was to find lemons, as many as possible, and concoct a juice for her to drink for seven days. He dutifully squeezed lemons by the bucketful each day and brought them to her to drink until she lost her feeling for the man.

She shared this remedy so that when I was in this position, I would know what to do. Whether I ever needed the lemon cure will be my secret. Mama was a wealth of knowledge in what is known in Hawaiian as la'au lapa'au, the art of healing with plants and herbs.

At times, I was never sure when she was really trying to teach me or tease me. I made it a habit to watch her eyes because they always told the truth. Once while standing outside her room in a darkened hallway, she said. "I have bones in my room." Another time she said, "If somebody kahuna you, I can take care." I was young and did not fully understand what she was trying to tell me. I never asked her what kind of bones she kept in her room. I never saw the bones and I chose not to know more.

I had suffered from bladder infections off and on for years since I was a teenager. I never drank enough water. My usual solution was to go to the doctor and obtain an antibiotic, and then drink gallons of water. Mama and I were sitting in the kitchen as I filled yet another tumbler with water to down the large white pills.

Mama asked, "How come you take da big pills? You get pilikia (trouble)?"

"Ma, when I go *shi shi,* I get an infection, so burn down there." I indicated my groin. "The doctor, he give me dis one medicine, I have to take all dis one." I held up the amber-colored cylinder of fat white pills.

"Ai, yah," she exclaimed. "Dis one no need! Mo bettah you tell me about dis kine pilikia, dis kine I can fix!" She launched into a dialogue with Papa in rapid Ilocano, giving him instructions.

Sometimes, their language sounded like a flock of clucking chickens being chased by a dog. In the beginning, Philip would translate. If I heard a new word, I'd ask him and practice rolling the unusual sounds off my tongue. If the word was in Hawaiian, I'd look it up in the Hawaiian dictionary or ask for an explanation. If it was pidgin, then I'd remember it. After a while, when Philip translated, I would say, "Never mind, I already got that." The most important thing was not to be rude and interrupt a conversation for an explanation of a term. I would store the words like a mouse hiding a crumb and look it up or ask when we were alone.

To help me with my affliction, Papa was now a man with a mission and on the move. He had his bucket and bolo knife in one hand, tilted his hat, and flew out the door.

Oh, boy, I thought, *what did I start now?* Mama and Papa were old and enjoyed their quiet time. I did not want them to make a fuss over me.

Soon Papa was back in the house with a dozen or so green coconuts. Placing them in the middle of the kitchen floor, he unsheathed the long knife to open the green and amber coconuts. I felt worse for making them go through all this effort. The work involved removing the inner nut, no small feat. The fibers have a stranglehold on the brown nut. Once the nut was removed from the outer husk, it had to be pried open to reach the young coconut meat, called spoon meat. The texture of this meat was squishy and had not developed the inherent coconut flavor. The water inside the nut was still clear, not milky. I was instructed to drink cup after cup of the medicinal clear coconut water mixed with chunks of the spoon meat. This entire experience took an endeavor to accomplish, and I did it so I would not offend Mama.

Beyond my expectations, the bladder infection was completely gone by the next morning. I was amazed with the result.

Mama asked how I was doing. Happy to make a great report, I announced, "All pau," making the "no more" sign by waving my hand to and fro.

A smile lit her face. "Never again you going get dis kine," she said with a little chuckle. "Dis one cure, you no more dis kine pilikia now."

Forty-eight years ago, I stood in her kitchen drinking the coconut water and the cure worked. I have never suffered from this infection again. Whether it was her magic or the cure, it all worked.

At times Mama would catch me off guard. I really didn't have a clue. She loved to tease me and make me laugh. We were close like that, but more often she had a lesson in every story for me to keep safe for the future when she would not be there to guide me.

With all her natural instinct for the spiritual, the Western world often eluded her, or perhaps she did not care either way. When American astronauts landed a man on the moon, we all sat mesmerized before the TV. Brother Eugene and Anita tried to explain the idea to her. She only shook her head in disbelief. "No, no can."

Erin was born with an inherited family trait common to peoples of the South Pacific, his legs were turned in and bowed. The doctors at Shriners Children's Hospital diagnosed his condition as "toe turn." For three months he wore heavy plaster casts that extended up to his thighs. A team of doctors advised me that all my children would in some way be born with this condition.

While in the hospital, Mama saw the casts with baby Erin straddled to my hip. She sat straight against her pillows and asked me, "Why you make dis boy dis kine!" as she touched the cold plaster cast.

I answered as simply as I could. "Ma, cannot help this one, the boy's feet funny kine when he was born."

I showed her my hands with my fingers pointing at each other. She exhaled a long breath, making many quiet clicking sounds in her mouth and shaking her head. She was not happy with me at this moment and spoke in a firm and scolding voice, "All my babies like dis, but I fix." Exasperated, she grabbed the casts and pretended to show me the art of lomilomi, Hawaiian massage. "You can fix dis one!"

I had never noticed Erin's feet until a doctor pointed out his condition on a visit and told me he would need to have his feet fixed. I should have spoken to Mama first, but my Western way was to go straight to the doctor. In my husband's family, there were always the kahuna la'au lapa'au, healers who used plants and massage to consult first. The doctor was the last resort.

Erin's treatments began when he was only five months old. He went through a grueling ordeal of being held down by at least five nurses while they wrapped both legs in the plaster-dipped gauze. The cast hardened and extended to his groin area. It weighed at least fifteen pounds. I think the cast weighed more than he did. He could only have the cast on for two weeks and then it had to be changed. To remove the old cast, a power saw was needed. I never in my life heard a child scream with such terror month after month.

I finally called the family together and announced, "I quit!" I couldn't listen to him scream one more time. It was killing me. Family members chose to take turns going to the hospital with Erin.

When he was eighteen months old, the casts came off. A physical therapist trained me to massage the legs straight. I was amazed to see that it was exactly what Mama had taught me when I had my first child, Paulo. If I bathed Paulo when Mama and Papa were visiting, she would help dry him, and taught me her lomilomi technique of massaging the entire body, including the limbs.

Erin was not supposed to learn to walk with the casts, but he did. He dragged the casts around until he pivoted into an upright position. After he started to walk, the doctors put rubber disks in each heel and toe so he could balance.

I called Erin Tarzan, when he was little because he could go from limb to limb when he climbed trees as a boy. He developed a tough attitude and upper body strength from hauling the plaster casts around for over a year. It was successful, but I would never put any of my children through that ordeal again. My third child, Seve, was born with the same condition. I massaged her and settled for corrective shoes that she wore during sleep. For two years, when we went to Shriners with Seve, Erin stopped at the door and said, "This is a bad place. I won't go inside." Philip waited with him in the car and we never took him back there again.

In hindsight we were very grateful to Shriners, but the ordeal for the child was so difficult. Present day, my daughter's children had the same condition. Doctors no longer do the casts.

16 - A Passing

Fishing at Kapuaiwa.
'Ohana fishing near coconut grove.
Artwork by Philip Sabado

16

 I knew Mama's time drew near. I became more sensitive to little changes. The lights in her room were changing as well. Elongated shadows reflected the passage of time with the sun hiding in the Nuʻuanu Valley and showers drenching the ground. Her hand reached for mine, sometimes as she faced the wall not seeing me, searching to hold with a squeeze from her spindly fingers.

Two weeks before she passed, she told me of her visit to the other side. Her face beamed like a child's on Christmas morning as she told me of a dream. Her words flowed like warm honey of how very beautiful it was in her dream place, and how everything glowed and sparkled in celestial light. She leaned toward me and held both my hands in hers. Her hands felt frail in mine with skin like a soft tissue that slid over her tiny bones. Her eyes danced as she spoke her language. The Filipino nurse had come into the room as Mama spoke and lingered a moment longer to translate. Mama's face was aglow as she described visiting Moses and St. Peter. In this place, they had come to carry her like a baby to Heaven's gates where she was rocked to sleep in the arms of Moses. Listening to her brought tears to my eyes. I blinked hard and was quick to wipe away the sudden emotion with the palm of my hand. She was prepared for her passing, at peace, with no fear whatsoever.

Dusky shadows slowly filled her room as the last shred of sunlight lingered a moment longer, warming her corner of the room. As I was about to leave, Philip joined us. She turned her attention to him and held his hand. "Alipio, you get food?"

He tilted his head quizzically and their eyes locked. Love had always served as the conduit between them. "Why, Ma, you stay hungry?"

She turned her head from side to side, making the slight ticking noise she used when annoyed and repeated her question in another way. "What I like know is if you get house and get nuff food for your family?"

16 – A Passing

"Yeah, Ma, we get, we get nuff food, and we have a home."

Her gaze stayed centered on his eyes. "Nuff, then, you will stay happy, dis all you need!"

The idea was too simple for me. I wanted many things my Western upbringing had taught were the marks of success. My dreams centered on a house we would own someday and possessions for the children and the family. For Philip, Mama's words made sense. She wanted us to understand that the simpler we made our lives the happier we would be. Not that the material things did not matter, but in the larger picture we should remember the uncomplicated lessons she had tried to teach all her children. Over the years, I think it is interesting how many times we have remembered this wisdom from those shadowed moments in her room.

Perhaps she felt she could now pass, having imparted the essentials of life, spoken so simply by not such a simple woman. Her words have returned especially when I felt slighted or jealous of others with fancy things and new houses. A roof and enough to eat was all we needed. The happiness and love surrounding us, and the children had no price tag.

We knew she would cross over soon. On one particular visit we had the babies in the room since it was already late. Erin had been playing on her bed and drifted asleep on her frail body, fully relaxed against her with his heart resting on her heart, their breathing in rhythm. Their chests rose and fell, each deep breath as one. We needed to go home. I placed my hands on each side of my baby to lift him from her. With eyes closed she wrapped her thin arms around him and hugged my child closer.

I bent toward her and spoke in a soft whisper, "Ma, we gotta go. Stay late already. Da baby's sleeping."

She clasped Erin tighter. In a strong clear voice, she said, "You never going take this boy from me. I like keep dis one!"

My eyes went from her to Philip and sought his support.

He echoed me. "Come on, Ma, we got go put dis baby in his own bed. Look, he stay sleeping already."

Mama unwrapped her arms and released him. "Dis boy mine, I going keep dis one!" She closed her eyes, allowing sleep to come and take her pain where her spirit would join the spirits that awaited her arrival. I told little Paulo to kiss Mama, his Apo Baket, goodbye. He did, as did we. I felt strange as we left her room, as if a shift happened that I needed to understand. That time, I knew Mama was serious.

On the day she died, I had not been to visit. One of the boys had a slight fever from a routine vaccination. That morning was cloudy with rain, and I chose to skip the walk up the valley. My parents were visiting and staying with us. I considered seeing Mama later. It was still early morning when Philip got the phone call from his older brother that Mama had passed. He accepted the news well since it had been expected. After she had shared her dream, I understood she was ready to let go. I believed that once she knew what was waiting for her and that it was her time, she could pass peacefully.

My parents were sensitive to my husband's situation and felt it might be best for all if they cut their vacation short. I said it was not necessary, but she reasoned that with the family coming from the neighboring islands, I might need room for relatives. My mother changed her ticket to depart the next morning. Philip was quiet that evening. Their bond was beyond my understanding. She had worshiped him, as he did her.

Once, when Mama was ill and still living at home, Phillip's brother had to carry her to the car to take her to the hospital. I was there, too, and saw how she fought him, crying, "I only want Alipio. Put me down. I can die here but bring me Alipio."

My heart was mournful, and my soul wept deeply for my husband and our loss. She must have known this moment was coming when we first met on Molokai. In the short years since our first meeting in Rosita's house, I felt she had passed the banner to me to support Philip.

Philip came to me on the night of her passing. I was sitting on the bed, folding the sheer gauze cloth diapers for the boys. He spoke slowly and with a deliberate tone. "I am going to tell you some things and I don't want to explain them now, but if you could, please speak to your parents for me." He collected his thoughts and took some deep breaths before continuing. "No matter what, no one is to open any door in the house tonight. If there would be any sound at all they must first look outside through a window to see who is there." He paused again and swallowed hard. "Under no circumstances are they to open that door, not even if someone calls their name from the outside, and especially if someone calls from outside!"

16 – A Passing

My eyes widened as I nodded. I looked away; it was painful to see his despair. His face had a heartbreaking ashy cast and his entire body seemed bent with the weight of grief. There is a bridge we must cross when a loved one departs, more so with a mother. I went about my task and placed the folded diapers in their caddie. With as much compassion and respect as I could manage, I assured him that I would do as he asked. "Okay? Go to bed now. You look spent and you must be exhausted. I'm going to help my mom pack, and I'll come to bed soon."

He nodded and turned to go to the kitchen, intent about his business. He placed garlic in the windows in compliance with ritual, earnest in his actions. On this painful night, the one he was shielding from us was a vital part of himself.

After he settled into bed and I had the boys in their cribs, I went to the parlor and spoke to my parents as he'd asked. They were sympathetic and nodded as I explained his family's customs and rituals. I added that from the time we had first met, I'd never heard him speak with such certainty and focus. We could only respect his wishes. They both nodded numbly, conveying the weight of the moment.

As I have noted, this little cottage was in the heart of the Nu'uanu Valley and the bathroom was far in the back of the unit. The graveyard filled the back as well as the entire end of the block. For some reason, Mom and I ended up packing their bags in the bathroom, setting her cases on the closed toilet. My father went to bed early. They slept in the living room on a futon, a fold out mattress. Mom and I jabbered away as we packed their clothing along with numerous boxes of chocolates and gifts. We finished around one in the morning and went to bed exhausted.

Six months later, Mom and Dad chose to tell me what happened that night. All seemed normal as we said our goodbyes at the airport. They seemed in a rush to leave, but I felt they were being sensitive to our family's grief. They said they both waited until they were on the plane before they turned to each other and said at the same moment, "I have to tell you something." My father said that when Mom and I were packing in the back of the house, there was a loud knocking at the door. He recalled three loud distinct raps. He cursed under his breath, thinking Mom might have gone to the car and locked herself out. He reached for the front door handle and stopped cold, remembering what I had asked for Philip's sake. He paused, and with the tips of his fingers, moved the curtain aside. The house had old-fashioned windows in wooden frames that enabled a clear view of the front door and anyone standing there. He searched for whoever could be at the door, but his gaze was met with silence and darkness—no one was there. My father, being an Irishman, said he swore under his breath, "Goddamn! I'll be a son of a…" He returned to bed shaking his head.

As their plane soared through the clouds, Mom recounted her tale as they stared at each other in disbelief. Her story was strangely similar. She was awakened in the hours just before dawn by someone loudly pounding on the door calling her name. She thought it must be Eugene, my brother-in-law, who loved them and sometimes gave them Filipino records or candies for their journey. She assumed he wanted to say goodbye. In the hazy morning light, she darted to the door not wanting the loud pounding or the calling to wake the family. Just like Dad, she hesitated as her fingers started to grip the doorknob. The cold brass was like an ice cube in her palm, and my words of Philip's warning returned. Pulling the curtain to the side, she saw the drive, now lit, as the long fingers of dawn reached into the day. The doorway and the front entrance of the little cottage were in full view, yet no one was visible. She returned to bed, debating whether she should tell anyone—even my father.

Philip's family flew in from the other islands and the mainland to prepare for the funeral. A large family is like a quilt, so many textures and pieces blended into one larger piece. Mama was the thread that bound this family through poverty and the good times. Each section of this master quilt was unique unto itself. Some pieces were sewn into the whole at special times with care only an expert tailor—a mother—would know.

I stayed on the sidelines. There was enough for me to do with my two small boys. All the major decisions were discussed among the older siblings. Besides the funeral, there was the wake, and naturally, the food. How many pigs would do? Would they serve goat? Planning an event, whether for a party or a wake, was taken as a serious matter. The menu was important, but the planning and activity created a distraction from the reality as if an ominous cloud had settled on the family.

Great attention was given to Papa, who would now be alone. We took comfort in knowing he had his religion and the connection to a strong

16 – A Passing

congregation. I was confident he would contend with the loss in time, albeit with difficulty.

Without her, I felt like more of an outsider. As much as I wished I could have been a part of this complex and amazing quilt of culture and family, it really was not mine, nor could it be. I could only admire and enjoy it. With her passing, my shield against the unknown was gone. Her moving to Honolulu from Molokai and staying till her death was for the express purpose of being close to Philip and me, and in a larger part, protecting me.

I remembered her words again when I was new to the family and feeling vulnerable. I tried hard to impress others and always looked silly, even to myself. Only age and maturity would build my confidence. As soon as Mama and Papa were settled in the 'Aiea house, she often took me into her room and closed the door to give me her guidance. Now that she had passed, who would teach me as she had? I watched from the sidelines as her family prepared for the ordeal of living with her passing and the funeral.

The last rites were held in the country, away from the bustle of Honolulu. Kaneohe is on the windward side of Honolulu and provides a vista of the mountains and the O'ahu coastline north and south. I chose to bring the children. Many questioned this action, but I felt that birth and death were both sides of life's coin. To hide from them their Apo's passing made little sense to me. The babies were fine, and the funeral went as expected.

Their church friends sang songs, and the minister was in great form, switching from Ilocano to broken English with an occasional gesture of holding a dog-eared Bible high above his head for the desired effect. Philip got through the difficult day because he had the children and me with him. I was confident I could fill to some degree the void of her passing.

On the morning of the funeral, I did not feel well, as though I had the flu with an upset stomach and strong cramps. It was not my time of the month, so I did not give this too much attention. However, at the funeral, I felt as if I could have buckled over once or twice. I excused myself and sat outside. Philip was a pallbearer and was occupied with the funeral.

When we reached the house for the wake, I felt worse. I held my stomach with one hand and needed to sit and rest. A relative spotted me and started jabbering in Ilocano. I wasn't paying much attention and soon I was seated with Philip, Papa, and a relative. They had all been watching me carefully. I learned that according to their beliefs, Mama's spirit had entered my body and was hanging on because I still had life and maybe because I had Philip.

We were asked into their room and Papa closed the door behind us. Papa began speaking slowly to her (within me) in Ilocano. From what I could understand, he was addressing her spirit in my body. He spoke lovingly, as a prayer, urging her to move on to the next life and not to "bother this girl." He said, "She does not understand our ways, leave her alone." He inserted enough English, so I got the gist of what was happening. Phil sat by my side, silent, with his head bowed and his eyes closed, listening to the last conversation his father would have with Mama. I distracted myself by looking at our two boys, each so small with limpid brown eyes and Erin's brown curls tipped in gold from hours in the sun. I never knew if they understood what had taken place, but somehow their presence was required.

The rest of the family was not aware of the conversation going on behind Papa's closed door. I certainly did not want any of them to know what was happening to me. It was my choice not to draw any attention to myself. All I knew was that I did not feel well, as if I had been hit hard in the stomach. Before we left the room, Papa reached into a sack in the corner of the room and gave Philip an article of Mama's clothing, a pink and white floral robe in a soft flannel. She had been wearing it when she died. It still smelled of her in a pleasant way. He instructed Phil to take the garment in the paper sack, so that when we left the wake the garment would not be seen by the siblings. We went home early, telling everyone we needed to put our babies down after such an emotionally difficult day. Once home, I went right to bed. I felt weak and craved sleep. Philip pulled the gown from the sack and handed it to me saying, "Try wrapping this around your middle and see if it helps your pain." Too weak to argue, I did as he suggested for three nights. The pain had lessened some, but not entirely.

On the third night, both babies stood in their cribs and pointed to a vacant corner of the room. "Apo! Apo!"

My pain intensified, and I bent over with a new wave of cramps, a pulling of my gut. This was not nausea or the runs, or other effects like a fever. My gut felt like someone was wringing the water from a mop head.

Philip sat up in bed and addressed the spirit according to Papa's instruction, who said Mama had to be "out" by the seventh day. Sadly, he began this arduous task. He spoke in English so I could understand.

"Ma, you have to leave her now. Your life in this world is pau, finished."

16 – A Passing

His eyes brimmed with tears. "You need to leave my wife. We must go on with our lives. We will always love and remember you, but you no longer belong in this world, you must go to the next world. We are the living, and you are make' (dead)." Being the gentle person, I know him to be, I knew it broke his heart to tell her to go.

As Philip explained, they believe the spirit will remain for seven days and then must depart or be destined to wander the earth; and if the spirit could have a traveling companion, all the better. Within moments of his speaking, I felt a release, as if a heavy veil had been lifted—the pain was gone. The boys looked at us and said, "No more." We knew then she had gone and the air in the room changed, similar to when a window has blown free. A fresh, cool breeze cleared the air. We turned off the light and fell fast asleep, and all slept very well thereafter.

Mama had taught me how to live an island lifestyle and about life by her example. Over time she taught me about babies and superstitions, and with a generosity of spirit I have rarely experienced. Even after she passed, she taught me lessons in the spirit.

Three months after Mama passed, one of our young nieces, Marlene, Lolly's daughter on Molokai, had a dream. In her dream, she saw Apo's casket in the sky. Above her casket was a smaller casket. Marlene saw the old woman's spirit leave her casket, go to the smaller casket, and remove a baby. The spirit of the old one lovingly and carefully carried the child to her own casket and reentered into it. The lid closed and clouds surrounded until the scene disappeared into the clouds. The young girl awoke and told her mother her dream. "The baby was Erin," she said with excitement in her voice. "The baby was Erin, Uncle Philip's baby boy!"

Our phone rang early the next morning. Lolly reported her daughter's dream and advised Philip not to take his eyes from the child, not to drive anywhere and to even take off from work if need be. Philip described the call and the dream in vague terms, saying little. He was distracted and when I tried to question him, he waved me away. I knew this gesture well enough and stepped back, knowing it was a Filipino thing I would decipher later on. I suspect Philip and his sisters agreed to take turns watching over Erin for a week. We never left the house. I was not told everything, and I knew not to ask too many questions.

Filipinos believe the dead never choose to go to the next world alone. They understood that Mama chose Erin to accompany her on her journey. I reflected on that evening in the hospital all those months ago as he slept in her frail arms when their two hearts beat as one. I remember her comment about Erin going with her and the questioning look I gave Philip, that strange moment when my eyes searched his. Now I understood.

17 - Ancient Understandings

Ka Ulu Niu 'o Kapuaiwa
(Kapuaiwa, Coconut Grove.)
Artwork by Philip Sabado

17

 *Sometimes a moment will freeze in the mind's eye. It has been said there is a perfect time in one's life when you hit the axis, that period when you have achieved the pinnacle of your own beauty. It has nothing to do with age, your body weight, or possessions. It's about an inner beauty that only comes with contentment. Philip's sister, Lolly (Eulogia), had it all on this night, and I was the lucky one to see it.*

We all piled into Uncle Ray's car and went to a party outside Kaunakakai, Molokai. Lolly sat in the front seat as we drove the mountain roads. Philip and I were in the back with the windows open on this summer's eve. I was struck by Lolly's beauty and happiness, and I complimented her on how pretty and happy she looked on this special party day. She wore a classic missionary muumuu cut with a lace bib, and she had on the exquisite black and gold Spanish hoops that I had given her. The gold glinted in the light as we drove to Kapuaiwa Coconut Grove, a special place on the beach on Molokai near Kaunakakai.

Lolly was joyful. Overall, this was a good time in her family's life. They had four daughters and the son she and her husband had wanted for years. The family called him "Boy." The party was a baby luau, a special event on Molokai. At least a quarter of the island's population would attend.

In sister Lolly's house, all life and energy revolved around her and the children. Not unlike the planets that spin about the sun, she was the center of their universe. She had a special way of making each of her children feel loved.

While Mama lay in the hospital bed in the Nu'uanu Valley, she felt she had sealed Lolly's fate, and related why in the story she told me. When Lolly was a small child, a spirit had come to Mama in the deep night with a proposition. The spirit said, "Give me this child," and tempted her with offerings. Since Mama was the *anting-anting*, meeting and conversing with spirits was not anything new, it had been going on since she was a child in Dolores, Abra.

Mama referred to the spirit of these visitations as her commadre, her friend. The spirit wanted to take the child to the next world. Each time, the persistent spirit asked for the child in a more convincing manner. "Release this girl to me. She is sickly; let me take her." As an enticement, the spirit made a promise. "To ease the family's suffering, you can have riches and a life of content," it pledged. "No more trouble or worries. Let me have this one."

The spirit came three times and with each visit the deal sweetened. Mama would never have to work again, or surely not as hard as taking in laundry from the single men of the camp, which kept her busy at that time.

"Just this girl's life…I'll take it."

Mama had powers, too, and she said it took all she had to fight the demon and its temptation. She was adamant in her refusal, even as she went to great lengths to please the spirits with compromises. She understood she was forfeiting any chance of an easy life for her family.

One of Philip's sisters said that on many occasions Mama would prepare great feasts. She would set food out on a table as a peace offering with the express purpose to appease those who cannot be seen by the common man. The food she prepared had to be the best, nothing cheap or shoddy, all for pleasing the spirits. As the mealtime approached, Mama would be the only visible person at the feast, even though the table was set for many. The family ate elsewhere, while Mama took care of these unseen spirit guests.

This was all done to keep her child. Her life of poverty continued, but she was at peace—her choice irreversible.

Lolly passed from this world precisely a year after Mama's death. Lolly had been born with a bad heart, yet her life's story was one of persistence and courage, and love for her children, husband, and family. On the day of her death, she awakened early to prepare breakfast and see the children off to school. She felt strange, not quite well, so she returned to bed. She suffered a heart attack mid-day and passed away in the arms of her daughter. The Western medical explanation for her death was the failure of her rheumatic heart.

Philip received the news at work when we lived in Honolulu and came home. He pulled into the drive; his face ashen. He wanted to be alone for the rest of the day. That evening, I shook sand from his pockets and realized he'd gone to the ocean to sit and remember her. He had been away, alone, for hours.

We returned to Molokai. On what turned out to be a cool afternoon, I chose to sit outside on the wooden walkway and look at Lolly's prized gardens surrounded by her blooming orchids. Each of her daughters approached me separately and spoke lovingly about their mother. Without exception, each would lean in close and whisper to me their secret. "You know, Auntie Chris, I was my mother's favorite!"

Each time, I smiled and said, "Yes, I know, I could tell." Later on, I reflected about how rare it was for each daughter to feel that she and she alone was her mother's favorite child. I marvel at how a mother could convey this tribute to each one. That was a special talent she had.

The funeral and burial were painful, more so because Lolly was very young and her passing sudden. Her passing was a devastating blow to the entire 'ohana, especially her five young children. Our disbelief and shock were numbing. The custom was to leave the casket in the house for three days before the funeral. I had never experienced anything like this. Family members knelt in the living room with rosary beads in hand, repeating Hail Mary's, and Our Fathers in succession. The days were long and difficult, and there was no escape from the overpowering grief.

When the casket was removed from the house, the pallbearers stopped at the foot of the steps. They lifted it to a height where we could all pass beneath, and then they rinsed their hands in a mixture of water and lemons. In so doing, it was believed that the one who died would give them protection.

As the line formed to bend and pass under the casket, I was intently aware of being surrounded by her flowering plants that bloomed in profusion. I smiled, realizing this was a fitting tribute to a wonderful sister and mother, and underfoot, the red Molokai earth that nurtured us all.

Philip and I and our small boys were held back and told to pass twice under the casket because of the incident the previous year with the dream and Erin. This had been discussed and it was hoped the spell on our family would be broken. All eyes centered on baby Erin. Philip carried him and washed his hands.

I could not look into the faces of the family at this emotional time. Instead, I gazed at her thriving plants and prize orchids that flowered in a myriad of colors. Her life still breathed forth in them. As the wind gusted from the lowlands, the blossoms seemed to bend and bow in deference to her.

The gravesite in Maunaloa was high on a hill overlooking the camp and West Molokai. The last time I'd gazed at this view was on my wedding day four years earlier. The cemetery was near the church. I remembered thinking that since Philip was the youngest, we would walk this path many more times, and in my heart, I knew this would not ever become easier.

On this sad day, Philip and his other brothers were the pallbearers. Later, the brothers commented that the coffin seemed to grow heavier and heavier as they walked. According to Philip, it felt as if she was resisting the inevitable. One sister had to be restrained from throwing herself onto the casket before it was lowered.

I had to look away and held tightly to my children's small hands. I made them turn their heads. After this experience, the oldest brother said he would refuse to be a pallbearer for any other family member—it was just too painful.

An afternoon cool breeze blew, the makani that embraced us all. As one, we left the grave and returned to the camp by the same red earth pathways beneath our steps to attempt to go on with our lives. I found it interesting that the priest at her funeral advised in his sermon that only the living can hurt you, spirits cannot. Hearing him acknowledge spirits surprised me. Even then, I could not agree with his message.

18 - Mad Dogs, Spanish Camp and Selling Frogs

A Passage of Time.
Artwork by Philip Sabado

18

As the years passed, I found certain rituals woven into daily life intensified on all levels. In the first years I had two close pregnancies. I became pregnant four months after Paulo's birth. Family superstitions arose surrounding the well-being and safety of children, and I accepted these rituals as the norm. I was told never to hang clothes at night and to take laundry off the line by three in the afternoon. The accepted belief was that as the skies darkened the spirit could seize the article of clothing and cast a spell on the person who wore it or on the family. Keiki were especially vulnerable.

I was never to sweep at night, the logic being that you might have to open the door to sweep the dirt out and you never knew who might feel they were invited in. If someone were to call to you in the night, you were never to open the door, and with Mama's passing, I knew that one already.

During one of my conversations with Mama while visiting in the hospital room, she mentioned a place down from Maunaloa known as Filipino Camp. In those days the camp names were often determined by the nationality of the inhabitants. Mostly Filipinos and some Portuguese and Puerto Ricans lived in Filipino Camp. Philip's sisters also mentioned this as the first camp they lived in when they arrived on Molokai. As we drove to their favorite fishing ground, they pointed to a distant field and remembered the old spot where the plantation camp once stood. Brief glances passed between the siblings followed by heavy sighs and an uncomfortable silence.

All I had ever heard was that the place was "too spooky." Apparently, there were more accidents and deaths in Filipino Camp than one would expect, and the belief took hold that it was not the correct place for a settlement.

Within a few years, the first immigrants were moved to the present location a few miles up the West Molokai rise and renamed Maunaloa Camp. Straight rows of pineapple had been planted in the old spot interspersed among the high grasses that strong ocean winds bent to the beat of an ancient time. If you were not aware of the location's history, you would pass by without a glance. The family knew. We never drove past without someone commenting, "Dat the place we used to live."

In the first camp, in Waialua, O'ahu, Loretta, one of Philip's sisters, had been playing down the road with other neighborhood children, a simple game of chase using a semi-inflated ball they kicked to each other across the path. Small tufts of red dust billowed in that breeze as the ball bounced from one child to the next. Sounds of children laughing and playing in the late hours of the day filled every path and lane in the camp. Without warning, a growling dog joined them. He wanted to chase the ball, but he latched his teeth onto the calf of the nearest child, Loretta. She collapsed and fell into the road.

Everyone knew the dog. He belonged to the cranky old Filipino man at the corner house. On other days, the scrawny creature slept under the man's large mango tree, quite content. That day, he had been transformed. His eyes showed crazed madness as he bit Loretta.

At first, the other children withdrew in fear. Then they came to her rescue all at once. One boy, quite brave, grabbed the snarling dog's ears and pulled him away. One swift kick from another boy sent the dog squealing and limping back to the corner house with his tail between his legs.

Blood poured from the fresh wound as Loretta held a part of her skirt against the punctures to suppress the flow. Her friends helped her to her feet and provided their shoulders for support. More friends followed behind the whimpering girl. Loretta made her way home, wiping away tears with her dirty palm that left streaks of red dirt from her nose to her ear in a pattern that resembled war paint.

Mama saw Loretta coming up the path and knew what to do. Her first steps were into her garden to gather the herbs she grew in the far corner next to the new pumpkin leaves under the old papaya tree. With bunches of thin dark leaves in her hand, Mama led Loretta inside and began to clean and dress the wound.

As she mixed her potion she asked, "Now, tell me one more time, which dog? Da one that went bite you?" Loretta grimaced and quivered as Mama plucked a chunk of red sandy dirt from the wound. "Ai, yah, you know, the pilau (dirty) black one at the old man house?"

Loretta held her leg out straight so Mama could finish dressing the wound with the pasty green poultice. Her playmates stood at the closed door, peering past the gray screen.

Slightly annoyed, the girl answered, "No, Ma, not dat corner, da one stay down udder side camp!"

The children at the door all sang out in a chorus, "No, Manang, da brown dog by da uddah side camp at da cranky man house."

Ka 'Ohana Sabado (The Sabado Family).
Color tint, Baby Philip in his Mother's arm,
Waialua, O'ahu, 1945.

Mama spoke under her breath, bellowing her anger. "Ai, yah, I know dat one. He da one dat always stay by the tree." Then, in an even softer voice only her daughter could hear, "This dog will not live to see another day."

Only Loretta heard these words spoken with somber conviction. Mama focused on the bandaging that would hold the poultice in place, using clean strips of fabric from old cotton rice bags.

Mama turned and saw all the children pressed at the screen door. "Ai, yah! You kids, go home, go eat, bumbye your Mama going call you."

Like a troop of elves, a shuffle of small feet scampered down the steps. The children expressed their thanks, goodbyes, and well-wishes and were gone, replaced by the sound of the wind in the trees and tufts of dirt from the road.

Something about the way Mama spoke piqued Loretta's curiosity, but her thought was interrupted—she had forgotten her books and her homework at her friend's house, which was due the next day. She limped to the door.

"Ma, I going be quick, still get nuff light, my books stay at my friend's house."

Mama saw her push past the door and spoke to the wind at her heels. "Be quick, almost going be dark!"

Though her friend's house was close by, at the corner Loretta made a quick decision to tempt fate yet again and pass the scene of her struggle with the dog. She could see him from a distance, resting as usual under the old mango. She slowed her step. "Ugh, I am sure he is sleeping after all he did to me!" Drawing near, she saw the old man down on one knee, shaking the dog with his hand.

He looked up and saw Loretta staring. "Ai, yah! I tink dis dog went natay (dead)!"

Loretta half-ran as best she could across the road to her friend, who stood on the porch holding the book pouch. As she climbed the three steps to the verandah she said, "Go look, the dog dat went bite me, he stay natay!"

Both girls stared at each other, speechless. The orange glow of the setting sun seemed to burn all it touched. Forgetting her injury, Loretta flew home with the wind and her mother's words a breath behind.

Once when the family was living in Kauai, Philip heard someone calling his father's name. Without thinking, he opened the door, and without warning his father came from behind and slammed the door so fast, it sent a pile of newspapers flying into the air. When Phil turned, he saw the old man's eyes were wild as he looked at his son, who had just returned from the Army and had forgotten the island ways.

"Spirits are very clever," his father admonished. "If you open the door, you invite them inside. They can trick you!"

Philip's answer was, "Ya but Pops, you friend is selling frogs."

This Kauai house situated close to the pounding surf was the same one where Mama advised everyone to be in before dark. "Many eyes are watching." She repeated this often and her eyes would shift to the window that faced the mountains. The family would always refer to this house as "that spooky house where Mama and Papa had lived in Kauai."

Ancient understandings and superstitions remained profound no matter how many new generations were born. We have an amazing portrait of the Goddess, Tutu Pele, at the studio. When people look at this painting with Her ilio (dog), they often nod in a sign of respect and do not speak Her name. The braggadocios had no idea what they were talking about and should have been cautious.

A friend, a Filipino girl, petite and almost doll-like, told of camping and drinking with friends, being loud and raucous around a campfire in the volcano area. On that starry moonless night, glowing embers colored the ohia lehua branches a burnt orange as the group danced drunk and stumbled around the spent fire. They sang and pretended to be the Goddess Pele, but also chastised Her in their rants. Even with generous amounts of wine and beer, no one slept that night as She appeared and chased the one who had voiced the loudest criticism of Her beauty. Now when this friend mentions Her name, it is in whispers. At the conclusion of our talk, she leaned into the small space between us and said in a hushed tone so no one could hear, "She is real you know!" Of course, I knew, we both knew this to be true.

The menehune (little people) are known and respected as an unseen part of the Hawaiian culture. Menehune are not an invention for tourists, they are akin to the leprechauns of Ireland or the gnomes of Scandinavia.

The summer Philip and I married, we lived with his sister, Rosita. One evening I felt like taking a drive to Kaunakakai about half an hour away. Most of the day I sat by the window, watching the road for the men to be finished in the fields. I'd peer through the checkered curtains and listen for Philip's unique familiar laugh. He loved to laugh, and sometimes I could hear him as he turned the bend that led to our red dirt lane. Usually, someone was telling a joke or a story that would cause a hearty rapture of laughter, the same laugh that made me turn to see him on that very first day.

After he was done in the fields, I craved our privacy and the drive down the mountain to Kaunakakai was especially pleasing. I was expecting Paulo and craved an outing. As I sat on the porch, I asked, "We go riding?"

Manang Rosita nixed the idea. Looking at Philip she said, "Not tonight brother, there is a full moon and the menehune will be playing ukulele on Mo'omomi Beach."

My eyes widened and, in all innocence, I said, "I would like to see that. Why can't we go?"

Philip and his sister each shot the other a glance, and in that brief second each had a look of panic and knowing. Clearing his throat, Philip stuttered the words "No one can see the menehune and live to talk about it…'das how.'" Sister Rosita nodded in agreement.

My curiosity piqued, and being slightly cocky, I decided to explore this. Sitting up with my back straight, I said in an exaggerated tone, "Well, if no one has seen them, then how do you know they exist?" This was pushing the cultural envelope.

Again, my husband and his sister shared that look, this time with more alarm. The energy was palatable as if it flew across the room. I had gone too far. I withdrew my question by shrugging my shoulders. Not showing my defeat, I avoided their eyes, slumped in the chair, and sighed, "Never mind then, we will stay home. I guess I am tired anyway."

They exchanged looks of great relief and their shoulders relaxed accompanied by strong exhalations as if some small victory had occurred. They agreed. "Yah, more bettah for you. You get baby as why, go rest." Again, that line of what was Hawaiian and Filipino merged to affect daily habits and ruled the day.

Later that night after lovemaking, Philip and I lay in the dark of our room wrapped in the colorful handmade quilts that smelled of the dampness of an old camp home. Rain pounded our tin roof. Philip could tell that I chose to live with that evening's revelation. In turn, he moved close to my ear, and I sensed he would tell me an intimacy. Perhaps this was his way of building a bridge of understanding only I could cross and only in the dark of our room. He spoke quietly, almost reverently of a memory that was sealed in time but never forgotten. He decided to share his most precious secret at this opportune moment, a story about a planned fishing day.

He and his Uncle Ray set out on foot in the early dark, laden with their equipment. "It was just before dawn, and the fishing grounds were five miles straight ahead. We walk on the wet sand on the west side of Molokai." They had walked this stretch of unblemished sand hundreds of times. No other humans, only sand crabs and the occasional herd of deer would cross their path or had access to this secluded stretch of beach.

"Just as we came around the bend, in the dark we saw a shadow in the wet sand. Brother Ray goes first. He is cautious and walks slow, then stops and I see his eyes come big. I look down and can see what he is staring at. "Hon, there are some plenty footprints, all the kine baby footprints everywhere. It was as if tiny feet had run into the water and back and forth along the beach. There were dozens of the prints. In my mind, my first thought was where is the mother? There should be larger footprints too! After all, she would be chasing the small ones."

Being Molokai men, both Philip and his uncle came to the realization in a split second. These were the small footprints of the menehune fishing in the early dawn. The two exchanged a quick look. No words were spoken. They both turned on their heels and retraced their steps in the sand. They did not fish that day and remained silent as they plodded the miles homeward in wet sand with no fish.

I hung on every word and had sat up, supporting my chin in the cup of my hand. He paused as another gust of rain beat at the roof. I waited as he looked out the window.

"That's okay, though," Philip said thoughtfully in the quiet of our room. "When it comes to Hawaiian kine, best to show respect. They were here first, and they don't want us to see them."

I relaxed into the quilts and closed my eyes. The rain outside intensified and the branches of the avocado tree beat the sides of the simple wooden house. Gales echoed from the old shingle thatch to the roaring splashes in the muddy garden puddles. What a special place I had chosen to live my life.

This story still amazes me. It speaks volumes about culture and respect. Had I reflected in my Western perspective, I may have called National Geographic or the Discovery Channel to photograph and investigate! Not here. I could visualize them loaded with all that gear, spears, and jugs and all, and merely turning away in silence and never speaking of the moment again. In private, after many beers, they may say, "Hey, brah, you remember those keiki footprints?" They had so much respect for the land of Molokai and that is why it cannot and will not change as long as these fine men exist. I cannot speak for Molokai today. In 1969, that was our world. I hope this is still true.

19 - For the Love of Molokai

Kipikipi, (Mound Taro Patches).
The Hawaiian system of kalo (taro) and 'uala (potato)
mounds grown in fishponds.
Artwork by Philip Sabado

19

Molokai had a unique distinction in ancient times as a place of great power. A kupuna (elder) came to an art exhibit on Maui that featured Philip's work. His paintings were magnificent, strong images that portrayed the history of the Hawaiian people through their mo'olelo, their ancient Hawaiian stories. On this evening, his paintings seemed lit with the golden inner light of the evening. The kupuna, an elderly woman, linked her arm through his and they ambled away.

Without preamble, she leaned in and said, "You know, brother, when you go Molokai, you must walk softly, and talk softly."

She smiled and disappeared into the crowd. When he looked to find her again, no one present knew who she was or had seen her. Perhaps she only came to give him this advice.

On Molokai early one morning, I sat beneath the coconut trees in Kaunakakai with my fourth child, Ian, who was six. Looking beyond the waves, our eyes fixed on the reef situated a half-mile out. Cresting waters sparkled like faceted gems and leaped from the waves. He looked to the water's horizon and then to me with his sincere brown eyes and said, "You know, Mummy, when I wake up in the morning and I am on Molokai, everything in the world is perfect, there is no wrong anywhere in the world. When I am on Maui, it is not the same."

I thought long about his words. Not everyone takes to Molokai, and I cannot explain why. I needed years to grow into the island spiritually and to be able to appreciate the nuances. For others, it may be different, yet somehow the Molokai people see this in you before you understand it in yourself.

Once when I was with Philip at a community center in Kaunakakai, I sat on the side watching the women. They fascinated me. They were a strong and tenacious lot. It was as if they were gripping the edge of a cliff, hanging on, and they were fine with it. In fact, they loved it that way.

From ancient times, before Western recorded history, Molokai maintained the reputation for being a land of plenty. Ancient fishponds on the eastern end were perfect sanctuaries for growing fish. A multitude of fishes swam and flourished in these turquoise blue waters. According to legend, the menehune were credited with the construction of some of these ancient ponds and their brilliant, half-moon crescent designs can still be viewed today. Here an abundance of all types of fish: mullet, moi, awa, papio, aholehole, and weke could thrive in a safe haven where black lava boulders strung a necklace of stone, safeguarding them as they grew. A gate, known as a makaha, would allow fish to swim freely in and out by slipping through slats of wood until the fish grew fatter. When ready to catch, they would be accessible to the ʻohana and the village.

In the early nineteenth century, literally dozens of these fishponds lined the eastern and central coastlines of Molokai. Arriving from Maui by air, you will inevitably fly over the eastern tip. From above, the fishponds appear like beaded necklaces that loop along the shore—their numbers will truly amaze.

When Philip and I were not yet married, we took a drive on the eastern end of Molokai at sunset. As we passed the ancient fishpond, we saw a phenomenon that I had never seen anywhere else. We'd planned a drive to Halawa Valley, once an ancient settlement and thriving community on the farthest end toward the Lahaina side of Maui. In this pristine hidden valley, the people farmed kalo (taro), and ʻuala (sweet potato), and fished the plentiful water. It was an idyllic life for the thousands of Hawaiians who called Halawa Valley home. Tragically, on April Fool's Day in 1946, a tidal wave wiped out this community and others across Hawaiʻi as well. The kalo industry there was pau.

Philip lived in this valley for a short time when he was a small boy since Mama had church friends there. He remembered fondly one Hawaiian girl, perhaps six or seven years old, who would always come to find him. The entire valley was her playground and they spent many days exploring the terrain holding hands as she led the way through dense forests and thickets. He told me how she knew all the secret caves and special spots of this forest paradise. His eyes softened as memories filled him with emotion—and of magical Halawa Valley.

My brother-in-law asked me if I was going to mention that Mama and Pop were fluent in Hawaiian. He informed me that at times they lived in the Halawa Valley on the far eastern side of Molokai. Eighty to one hundred years ago, Hawaiian was the dominant language and naturally, they conversed in that language. In my early years on Molokai, I remember some dialogue that wasn't Ilocano. Many people came to Mama to remove a kahuna (a spell or jealousy), and Filipinos as well as Hawaiians would seek her out. I thought back to when she told me, "I have bones in my room," and "If somebody kahuna you, I can take care." Their speaking fluent Hawaiian was a new revelation, but in hindsight, it made perfect sense.

As we drove the narrow twisty road, we realized darkness would soon descend and we abandoned our plans to continue all the way to the valley. The one-lane road can be tricky. There were many turns and with no streetlights and we decided to make a U-turn. On our way back, we rounded a corner just past the lookout to Turtle Rock. We were so close to the pali (cliff) that we would honk the horn as we approached a curve to warn an oncoming car. The sun continued to descend and disappeared into the sea. On the radio, we listened to the rich timbre of a famous Hawaiian singing about a distant time. As we rounded the next bend, our eyes were drawn to a translucent sky the color of ripe tangerines. From far above to the shore, there was nothing but this intense saturation of color. The sea mirrored the sky and together had become a solid block of color. We had a hard time making out the horizon since everything was a solid block of orange. I caught my breath. On shore, palm fronds danced to an age-old lullaby in the evening breeze, making whispery swishing sounds, and the greenish-brown lines of the coconut trees made a stark silhouette against the vibrant sky as if created by a master artist's hand.

We traveled miles along the road in awed silence. The combination of all the elements burned the moment into my na'au, my center of being. This became Molokai to me. The color, the voice in the music, and the gentle makani woven together caused us both to gape in awe and wonder.

A relative, one of the nieces I'd met on my first day on Molokai, would come to live on the eastern side and marry into one of the large Hawaiian families holding rights to the ahupua'a (land from the mountain to the sea). I told her about the orange sky and that amazing day. She said, "Oh, yes, Auntie. That is the time when the sky and ocean become one." She had seen this many times before and agreed that only on Molokai had she seen this spectacle.

A kupuna told us a Molokai story that adds depth to this phenomenon. In ancient times when the orange-crimson skies appeared, it was the signal to all the kahuna, the people of knowledge, to return to Molokai. There were kahunas on all the islands, and once the saturated orange sky summoned them, a molo (waterspout) would go to each island to whip them into the molo and transport them to Molokai where they could hone their skills. They were transported across the kai (sea). That is why the island is known as Molokai, churning, rolling water.

A kupuna told me that when the sky embraced the ocean in golden hues, the halaus of the seven neighboring islands heeded the omen to come to Molokai. Seven terraces were on the hillside of Mahana, representing the seven islands. It was here the surface was prepared for them to dance and celebrate the hula.

At a Hawaiian celebratory event, a question from the audience was posed by a young Hawaiian man. "Why is Molokai pronounced two distinct ways?" You might hear people say the name with a diacritical, guttural stop: Molo ka'i (mo lo ka ee) or more often Molokai (mo lo kai: the last syllable rhyming with "sky"). The panelist who chose to answer represented the Molokai newspaper. He said, "I have no idea. Both ways are used, and I guess they all work!"

While pregnant with Alipio, our last child, I worked for Air Molokai. I observed that Molokaian's pronounced the name of the island without the "ee" sound at the end. Everyone else, locals as well as tourists used the "ee" sound. I posed the question to Phil at dinner that night. "How come people say—"

Before I could finish my sentence, he jumped in with, "Because they're all wrong, Molokai people know!"

Because of the mo'olelo, "kai" means "sea." There is no such word as ka'i in regard to Molokai. Ka'i in general is used to be a guide, or to guide. Pronounce the name as the people of Molokai do. More to the point, Auntie Harriett Nea writes on the first page in *Tales of Molokai*: "Please correct this error."

I made it a rule to always ask the family if it was okay to go to this or that place on the island. Apart from going to Kaunakakai to shop for groceries, their answer would start with a momentary pause and then spoken slowly with consideration. "Why don't you wait for Philip? Then you won't lose your way."

One reason never mentioned, but one I felt nonetheless, was the fact that I was clearly the outsider. In their own way, now that I was a part of the family, they were making sure no one bothered me. Even when I went to the store, they advised taking the children. Their presence would validate that I was part of a Molokai family. I did not look like any of them but being together made us family and in that way, they provided me a certain protection and understanding.

I never ceased to be surprised by one thing: whenever I met someone on Molokai, the first question inevitably was (spoken with aloha), "Who is your family?" This established your identity, a reminder of the ancient custom of reciting one's genealogy upon meeting a stranger.

Once a link was made, the person would say, "Oh, you are so-and-so's son. I know your Auntie Rose…" This was common among the Hawaiians, but I found it happened more frequently on Molokai than on any of the other islands. Molokai was one of the least populated islands and there was a significant chance that any one person would know one of your relatives. Once your place was established in the chain of 'ohana, the rest was easy. Recognition and familiarity established comfortable relations. If a discussion continued long enough, the other person would inevitably find they were related through a distant family member. Smiles and hugs affirmed. "See, brah, we cousins."

A handsome young Hawaiian boy told me that he would sit near his mom at a party while he checked out all the girls to see which ones he could date. Some may have turned out to be family and not distant enough cousins. This happened when Phil and I went to Molokai with a group of friends and rented a van. We were in the central part of the island with no time to drive up to Maunaloa. I asked Phil, about visiting his sister and all his relatives who lived up camp.

"Naw, no need, we will slip in and out."

We were not sleeping overnight and left the kids home since they had school. About mid-day we got a phone message. "Philip, this is Manang Rose, call me! Are you here? My friend said she just saw my brother crossing the street in Kaunakakai!"

"Busted!" I said. "You should know better on Molokai."

Another time on Kauai at a family party, my fifth child, Jackie, was walking past Molokai relatives, and one of the boys asked in a charming, inviting way, "Who is that?"

The boy's mother (my husband's niece) slapped his head. "That's your first cousin!" That ended that! Smiles and knowing laughter were accompanied by the blush on the boy's face. He continued his search for who else was available.

20 - Kalaupapa

*Mokumanu Seabird Sanctuary,
Kalawao, Molokai.*
Artwork by Philip Sabado

20

Ships came here in the early twentieth century to deposit the most tragic cargo: 'ohana (family). Men, women, and children were tossed into the deep waters of the bay in the dark night. Their fate if they survived the treacherous shark-infested harbor was certain, for upon the black stony shore more horrors awaited. Only one man, known to Hawaiians as Kamiano, would be there to serve them. In time he would be known to the entire world as a saint. Nations would speak in humble respect of Father Damien from Belgium.

In a book by T. N. Jagadisan (1965), *Mahatma Gandhi Answers the Challenge of Leprosy*, Gandhi talked about how Father Damien inspired him to help the people of India. "The political and journalistic world can boast of very few heroes who compare with Father Damien of Molokai…It is worthwhile to look for the sources of such heroism." Damien's life and work was an inspiration for Gandhi's social campaigns in India that led to the freedom of his people and secured aid for those who needed it.

Father Damien's mission was not complicated. He was there to help the displaced people of Hawai'i, to remind them that God had not forgotten them even if the world had. His first priority was attending to the sick and dying.

Those afflicted with Hansen's disease, leprosy, had been transported to Kalaupapa from 1866 until 1969. According to the records, some of the first patients came on large ships in 1886. Nearly twenty ships were recorded at that time. Patients upon arrival, were then put into smaller vessels and rowed to shore in Kalaupapa to walk the three miles to Kalawao.

Of all the special places on Molokai, the one that called to me from the first moment my foot touched the island as a young woman of eighteen, was Kalaupapa. Seeing the layered bands of color in the rainbow, my heart was tempted and seduced by the sublime beauty. It was from the misty forest of Kalae perched on the pali lookout where you can see the small sliver of land jutting into the sea—Kalaupapa. Standing against the lava rock wall, I was resigned to gaze at the settlement that had been there for years. The feeling of being drawn like a magnet resonated from my toes and traveled up my spine to tingle at the nape of my neck. From the first day as a bride, the Kalaupapa lookout called to me. The energy was relentless. Yet, like so many before me, I was destined to only stand and gaze from afar.

The drive to Kalae, Molokai had a twisting road past grassy uplands and dense forests that spotted the hillsides on either side of the road. Cattle and the occasional dog broke the canvas of verdant green. To reach the lookout, I walked along a narrow dirt path where the roots of the tall eucalyptuses and pines protruded from the earth at every step. I focused my eyes downward to mind my step as my foot crunched pine needles. I teetered on the uneven roots though I tried to move between them. The only other sound was from the whipping winds that funneled into the topmost tree branches, whistling like a siren, an eerie cry. Light caressing showers fell intermittently and with the trees so dense, the mist could not find the earth, a true rain forest. A thick blanket of dried ironwood needles sheltered the damp soil, snapping and crackling underfoot like strands of uncooked spaghetti. An abrupt end to the shadowy pines yielded to a shock of sunlight. I felt the wind lash out from behind like an errant child as the vista of Kalaupapa lay before me. Molokai is known as one of the highest sea cliffs in the world.

I always think of this moment like being in a movie theater. After the lights dim, the darkness explodes with light as the show begins. It has always been the same for me—Kalaupapa reveals her beauty every trip, every moment unfolds in this way, like returning home. From the lookout, the Kalaupapa Peninsula appears as a narrow finger jutting into the bluest azure sea. A small airstrip and rusted tin roofs atop the homes are visible from this vantage point. A dark ribbon of gray that goes straight then turns and disappears to the Kalawao side appears to be the only road. A trail snakes below the lookout. Many tourists have held their breath while riding the popular Molokai mules that masterfully navigate each pothole along the well-worn path. Often visitors keep a steady gaze forward. Looking below the sheer drop is daunting.

Lava stone walls and an iron railing at the lookout separate the viewer from the sheer drop to the sea. From the first day I stepped onto Molokai, I knew I would come here to repeat the experience of looking down the sheer green slopes at a natural Hawaiian village on the Kalaupapa Peninsula. Though I felt it, I could never understand the magnetic draw. As the years passed, I would look at faded photos and see myself as a young woman, always standing in the same spot at the lookout. In one photo, I am smiling between my mom and my sister, all of us so young with fresh faces full of excitement, promise, and happiness; I would be married the next day. In the distance was the infamous colony known for its inhabitants, the poor souls who suffered with the dreaded Hansen's disease, formerly known as leprosy.

The Kalaupapa Peninsula is beautiful, yet even the word "leprosy" makes one stop and quiver with forlorn and foreboding. The Bible first recounts dark caves with the afflicted covered in rags. I think of the scene in the movie *Ben Hur* where he finds his family and his wrenching pain on seeing them. Even now in India, where Mother Teresa labored, some have improved but not much has changed.

I answered the beckoning rainbows of my arrival day and went to this place each time I visited Molokai. When I was younger, I would drive there alone, sit and listen to the wind in the trees, and spend hours looking toward the old colony, never understanding the draw and fascination. Visiting this vista that clung to the edge of the cliffs became a ritual. As a chill wind came from the dense forest behind me, I would stand in the dirt walkway before the worn picture of Father Damien and the sorrowful faces of the children. Being there tore at my soul. I was aware of my present moments yet catapulted away from my reality to a no man's zone of space and time, teetering between the past and present.

Long ago, ships loaded with their shunned human cargo left from Honolulu Harbor, and on certain evenings, the wind carried the sound to the sleeping city for all to hear the wailing of family members and the discarded loved ones bidding their final aloha to their 'ohana.

One time in Honolulu, we passed the harbor at night after a late arrival. My gut twisted as we drove by the boats tied to the dock bobbing in the inky sea. I turned to Phil and said, "It was here, I was here. I am terrified and feel ill." This had never happened. Bile churned and rose to my throat where it tightened to a stranglehold. I could not push it back down to my gut. The sickening knowledge would not remain quiet a moment longer.

The realization of the story settled to a dull ache; a turn of my stomach as deep unquenchable sadness felt like the cold forest wind that had found my brittle bones. It churned memories of what occurred on this sliver of land, a mere one-mile-wide strip, where over eight thousand were forced to come to endure the effects of Hansen's Disease. They were without the care of medical staff or sufficient caregivers, until recently. They struggled like castaways. Some had kokua (helpers), but they were rare and indeed, extraordinary people, all who should be considered heros, saints, or anointed ones.

A memory that helped me adjust to this forested place occurred the first time I walked to the lookout with Philip. He leaned in close and in a hushed tone cautioned me not to speak or make loud noises in this sacred forest. As he walked, he held his finger to his lips. His eyes darted in all directions. He looked to the sky and the thicket of branches where birds watched us pass by.

"Best not to disturb the quietness of the spirits that abide in this place," he said as the errant wind came from behind.

Still a stranger here, I obeyed without question. Like a true enchanted forest, every particle of life was alive and observant. Once we passed through the forest, the vista opened and a few more steps revealed the weathered plaques at the precipice. They told the story of the rigors of Hansen's disease, and of the kokua who came from afar to aid the dying and bring order to the insanity of this terrible place. The plaques were weather-tarnished and scarred from the beating of wind and rain. On future visits, I felt moved to go off the path and sit quietly. I was not sad, but reflective, and moved to pray sincerely for all who perished there. Never once have I gone to this place and not been moved to pray. It is my ritual.

I turned away from the lookout and trod upon a fresh blanket of needles cushioning the path in the opposite direction. Larger roots from the majestic ironwoods broke up the red dirt passage leading to the Phallic Rock, another landmark. This rock is a large fertility stone covered with moss, a perfect replica of an erect penis and large testicles. In ancient times, a woman wishing to conceive would straddle this stone for the desired effect—

pregnancy. It seemed everyone had a photo straddling this strange rock that jutted into the air. I have one taken with my children. The shape is unmistakable—it is what it is. Many years later we traveled again with the family, and two of my daughters-in-law took their turns on the rock. Interestingly, both conceived their first-born child within two weeks of each other.

I got lost twice trying to find the trail to the Ka Ule o Nanahoa (Phallic Rock). The skies were mostly cloudless, and I could see very well. Occasional swooping branches of the ironwoods shadowed the path. On both occasions I was alone. As I walked deeper into the woods, the path vanished under thousands of pine needles. I searched for an indentation in the needles, but the path under my feet was undisturbed. I heard a voice in my head, a whispered warning: Take care, turn back now, if you do not, no one will ever find you—you will disappear forever. *I stopped and turned on my heel. After that moment, I made the decision never to walk alone in this mysterious forest again. I shared what happened that day with my husband when I got home, and he looked at me with wide-eyed consternation. Years later, on my third attempt, I was with Philip and the children. He easily found the correct path. I still wonder how I had gone wrong.*

On another visit to Molokai, I was with the children without Phil. We were on the main road to the forest and the lookout when I saw a narrow dirt road engulfed with tall grasses off to the right. Without thinking, I turned and was halfway down a small one-lane dirt road when a feeling of foreboding came upon me like a creature crawling up my spine. I could feel it and taste it, and knew I made a grave mistake. In a twist of my gut, my mind told me to turn around. To either side, I saw thin slivers of barbed wire that held cows at bay while they grazed on the tall grasses that grew as high as the car. Just as steam from a boiling kettle erupts, within seconds a cloud of fine white mist descended on the small road and our blue Volkswagen. I heard the wind and the cows and swallowed down my panic to rid myself of the fright rising in my throat.

My children picked up on the energy. They became antsy, then nervous, and then fearful. Little Erin's sniffles turned into a whimper, and he cried. I got the VW bug turned around with great difficulty and shifted into drive, but the car was stuck. The back tires spun and spewed soft mud all over the windows, and between the mist and mud we could barely see.

My panic increased. I was in the middle of a sacred forest with three small children in a dense fog, stuck in the mud with no one around for miles. I pressed the gas pedal hard, the wheels spun, and the mud spewed even higher, dispensing another shower on the windows. I remember calling out to the children in a white panic, "Everyone pray! Don't cry!" And as if by magic, the tires caught. The car jumped in the air with a jolt. I tore up the road, leaving a spray of mud and stones in our wake. When we reached the highway, my stomach returned to its natural place.

When we arrived at Maunaloa, I told my tale of woe. My niece's spouse, a Hawaiian whose family had lived on the island for generations, stayed silent as I spoke of my misadventure. Usually a man of few words, he scolded me gently. "You have been in this family long enough to know Molokai better than that. You should know not to take chances and go places alone." I took my reprimand stoically and could not argue, numbly bobbing my head in agreement.

I was an outsider and if I took stupid chances that no local would take, I was told I'd be sorry if "I never listen and learn." Simply put, on Molokai you must have respect for what is. The island is too powerful to be blundering about without thinking. I knew of others, not unlike me, who had been lost forever. I resolved to never again go out on my own to explore.

In the spring of 1995, after years of viewing the colony from a distance, I planned to go to Kalaupapa with my husband and parents. This would be a special journey for my parents and me, because due to a hardship in 1993, we'd not spoken for a little over four years and our time together would be an unparalleled reunion.

The original plan was to go to the settlement with Philip's brother Eugene, who had many friends there. He was a staunch Catholic as were my parents. Eugene had traveled to Belgium as a kokua with the Kalaupapa residents to celebrate the beatification of Father Damien who would now be known through this ceremony as Blessed Damien. The ceremony for sainthood was still years away. Eugene was thrilled to tell us that the Pope had joined them in Belgium to celebrate this holy man. In a newspaper photo captioned "Pope learns to speak Hawaiian," Eugene stood before the Pope.

20 – Kalaupapa

The Pope gave him a rosary that years later Eugene believed gave him amazing luck in Las Vegas. After that trip, Eugene was invited to return to Kalaupapa by his new friends. Eugene was very popular with the residents; everyone loved him. He was welcomed to stay overnight, an honor and a rare privilege, and then extended the invitation to Philip.

Phil turned to me after hanging up the phone and said, "This place has always held a special spot in your heart, why don't you come too?" I could not explain the dull ache that registered in my gut. It was a mixture of fear and desire, a yearning not unlike unrequited love. I did not accept at first and promised to think about it. When Mom called, I shared news of the invitation and off the cuff asked her to join us. Her answer was immediate, they'd be thrilled. Even with my parents scheduled to go, I vacillated. I felt overwhelmed by a gnawing dread that seemed to envelop me, yet somehow it seemed I was destined to go—the pull of a magnet.

The week before the departure date, a scene erupted in my mind while doing my morning and evening prayers. It came as regularly as clockwork: a heartbeat-like opening, a portal, a dark bay with people bobbing in the black water. I saw outstretched hands as the forsaken struggled to stay afloat, the wind and waves tossing them about in the rough seas. The dire souls were so terrified and forlorn that even as they fought to live, they understood that death would be imminent once they reached the hostile shore. A chilling fear gripped my insides as I held them in my gaze. Tears welled in my eyes, and I blinked hard to hold back the emotions from overtaking me. Each time I closed my eyes for prayer the all too surreal image reappeared, and as much as I tried, I could not dislodge the chilling images or the terror I felt. In the gathering dusk, I saw the form of the dark ship and the castaways, just offshore, never docking. Overhead was a silver ghost of the moon's shape on the water. This scene never left, like a scratched record repeating the gruesome images, it played morning and night as the date of departure drew near.

Once while turning a corner in town onto the harbor road, the eerie ocean scene came into focus again, this time with more clarity. This was bizarre. I was on the open road, not in front of my altar, yet there it was again. In this dismal vision, I was bobbing in the water with the others I had seen moments before on the ship. I saw myself in black and white accented in sickening shades of gray. There was no color in this place. I was a young

Hawaiian girl, perhaps fourteen, on a small, flimsy red dinghy floating in the bay at Kalawao. As I wearily lifted my head, I saw the towering wind-hewn cliffs of Molokai. Women holding their babies above their heads screamed and moaned in concert with the sound of the wind. I saw a form near me. A girl in the cold dark water disappeared in a sudden jerk as the faint silhouette of a shark's fin moved past. I felt shaken to my core. My stomach turned. I shifted my gaze away as a chilly wind blew off the razor-edged pali, sending an ominous siren through the deep valleys. The sound bounced from the sea cliff to the water. The current thrust us forward and we caught the wave's movement. There was no fighting the tide.

The ships left Honolulu at two in the morning so the public would not know how many were being taken. There was another small island in the midst of the harbor known as Moku Mano home to the `aumakua mano, the guardian shark of Kalawao Bay. When the ships came there, it was "feeding time." I could not have known this, yet what swam beneath and around me was hell on earth! Every cell in my body felt petrified in fear. As the camera lens of my mind moved closer and sharpened, I could see myself and knew my panic-driven thoughts. I debated: If I jumped off the dinghy I could drown or be taken away by the circling sharks, or I could go to Kalawao. A couple more waves would pull me forward. I was confused, my bones were tired, I was weary. Others held on as long as they could to a log or each other and then they sank. Only small bubbles from whence they held on to life remained on the surface, the last of their existence.

Many Hawaiians and others, even the ones without leprosy, were discarded to waste and die on this small splinter of land. Feeble hands stretched out for naught, for it seems the gods had turned away and could not answer.

The tide pulled me forward. I did not have the courage to surrender to the sea as the others had. My fears mounted as the small boat inched toward the shoreline. My mind reeled, I needed a plan, any plan. How could I escape? Where could I go?

The bottom of the dingy crunched onto the sand near shore. I rolled out of the dinghy and my belly chilled as I laid impotent in the cold water. My clothing was so loose it fell away in the surf that slapped the wet sand. With each roll of the waves, my skin scraped against black stones. My nostrils filled and I spit out a mouthful of salty seawater. I could see from the illumination of silvery moonlight. Many were with me on the shore. I shook from the chilled water and a nauseating fear twisted my gut. I was aware of losing my mind as well as my life in these critical moments!

I adjusted my gaze to the moonglow and desperately searched the shore and land. There, in the distance to my left, I could see a thicket and a mat of bushes to either side of our landing place. I slipped away as a sea snake would over smooth wet rocks toward the bushes on my left. I saw no one else there. My mind screamed: Crawl quickly. Be the crab and hide! *I knew the stories of gruesome men with mottled faces, some with no noses or fingers, who would carry you off to unspeakable horrors. And in the end, you would become one with them in madness and death.*

In my mind's vision, I clearly saw it all. As the sand and stones clawed at my nakedness, I scrambled to reach the thorny bushes and once in the prickly shelter, trembled in such a way that my flesh might have fallen from my bones. I did not know what would kill me first, this awful fear, or the disease that would soon take its toll on my limbs. I could not see more or bear my demise. As my mind departed from that gruesome scene, I saw a more immediate death was possible. I slumped against the thorny bush, hoping the thorns would pierce me, causing me to bleed and die. Overwhelmed by the pain and fear, I collapsed at the base of the bushes.

The vision I had witnessed in this leprosy colony of Kalaupapa faded like an evaporating mist, though the outstretched hands and wailing never left me. Morning or night within my prayer, they were waiting for me. The family trip was coming in weeks. Within my na'au (my center of being), I already knew—I would go.

Still, I vacillated. I had an ongoing debate inside my head. A part of me had already chosen not to go on the trip. My visions made the prospect more challenging by adding a layer of foreboding fear. Until I had reached Kalawao, the separate district of Molokai that made up Kalaupapa, would I understand these visions? As fate would have it, the day before the proposed trip Eugene called to cancel—he had a bad cold and chose not to risk air travel with a stuffy head. At that point, Philip made a special point of persuading me to make the trip.

My mother was especially happy we would do this together. As the four of us departed Maui, the small plane reached the clouds and the wings dipped with the winds that buffeted the sheer slopes. We traveled on a commercial aircraft not unlike the one I'd traveled in those many years before as a girl to be married. At the Molokai airport we switched to another smaller Piper that transported us to the peninsula. For this leg of the trip we needed to be invited, which required paperwork in order to stay in Kalaupapa. As we descended, I could see the lookout in the distance where I had stood peering into the future, that became a mere dot. As we came in for a landing, my heart pounded and I felt overwhelming emotion, rising, brimming like a combination of acrid nausea and a bubbling cauldron. I could not contain my tears and donned sunglasses to hide my eyes. I patted my cheeks with a napkin so others would not be aware of my erupting emotions and see the traumatic effect of the journey.

Above us loomed the towering pali, the lookout, and the east and north shore of Molokai, all inaccessible except by helicopter or the steep trail. Behind the peninsula were the misty outlines of the razor-edged cliffs that held lush verdant valleys, the hidden north side of Molokai. The small airstrip was before us, and I felt my heart would leap out of my skin. The pounding so violent, I feared others could see my chest moving. I reached for my husband's arm and held his smooth skin firmly. He did not turn to me and could not know what I was experiencing.

The small peninsula had flat land with grazing horses and errant dogs scampering to either side of the runway. As the wheels from our prop plane touched the tarmac at the airport, I heard a skidding sound and felt the natural pull of brakes that eased up as we made a smooth rolling stop. At first glance, I noticed a few individuals leaning against a white picket fence as they awaited their friends. They held onto the slats as their hair blew in every direction, their clothes plastered to their bodies from the strong gusts. After alighting from the Piper aircraft, we took the short walk to the terminal. The small terminal was painted in the plantation colors of time-worn sage green, and the picket fence made it seem like a simple country cottage community. Inside, the one-room building displayed a photo history of Kalaupapa. The photos revealed sad faces and the rigors of Hansen's disease.

We were informed upon arrival about rules all must follow. No photos of any patient were allowed without their express permission. Privacy and respect for the residents were of the utmost concern. The settlement allowed no visitors under the age of eighteen. There were no children anywhere in the settlement.

In times past, according to one book I'd read, patients were treated like guinea pigs. Doctors would come from all corners of the world, not always with the best intentions, and patients were often treated as less than human. Patients were prodded and poked, their lesions scraped, and they were held in isolation. Many experiments were conducted and some sought fame and fortune at the expense of the patients.

Many would attempt to escape up the trail in the dead of night, or the brave could try to scale the sheer cliffs and try to integrate topside Molokai before the rigors of the disease became obvious. A Molokai friend told me his uncle was positioned at night with a shotgun to pick them off from the pali or the switchback trail. Their concern was real. The highly contagious disease could be a risk to their own families. My friend explained that once sulfa drugs were known to be an effective treatment, he laid down the gun, refused to lay in wait on the cliffs ever again, and assisted the patients instead.

A resident family comprised of our host, a patient, and her non-patient husband, who worked for the state, sponsored us, a requirement to stay overnight. Eugene had made this possible and since Philip was from Molokai, we were able to enjoy privileges not always afforded to the public. At the time of our visit, there were fewer than one hundred remaining on the peninsula. Our host was one of the youngest residents, the last to be taken there as a young girl when she'd contracted the disease.

Most tourists and other visitors to the settlement came for the tour and to ride the mule pack down the winding path that accessed the peninsula. The only other visitors were hunters and fishermen invited by the patients. All visitors were closely observed. There had been accidents with some of the fishermen and hunters that unfortunately resulted in their deaths. The residents were so upset, out of true concern they watched each visitor to make sure they were safe. Life was more precious than anything here.

On that first day we were given a tour of the small settlement. The freshly painted houses and grounds were meticulously maintained. The style and the ambiance of the architecture reflected the war years as if time stood still in the 1940s.

We drove around the community in an old green pickup truck. I sat in front with our host. The windows were open, and the wind tore through the cab, attacking anything that was not nailed down. My parents, Philip, and our hostess sat in the back of the truck laughing and spreading aloha. I was thankful for my husband's happy disposition and his easygoing way. He broke the ice and soon we were all friends.

I mentioned to Mom that without Phil we would have had a far different visit. There is an unspoken Molokai way that cannot be taught or even learned—it just is. I have observed this phenomenon for years and always bowed and gratefully surrendered to this timeless Hawaiian way. Phil had a way of giving effortlessly. I saw it often; people would want to know him and be near his happiness.

As we stopped to enjoy a vista, I turned to our host when we were alone to pose a question that had gnawed at me from the onset. "Why no children here?" I missed the presence of children.

"It is out of respect for the old ones." His gaze remained out to sea.

The absence of children's energy was profound. In the "before" time when someone got pregnant, they were not allowed to keep their baby. All the newborns were taken for hanai (adoption) to be raised by relatives on the other islands or topside Molokai. Ultimately, all the women were sterilized even though they were Catholic. Sterilization was imposed by the state agency that supervised the administration of the colony. Tragically, those who were pregnant had to surrender their children for life. Stripping parenthood from the displaced of Kalaupapa was another ruthless injustice to these prisoners of circumstance.

As for the present ban on children visiting the colony, our host reasoned, "They would be a painful reminder of what the patients had been denied." To compensate for the lack of children, the patient's pets were precious. Everyone in the colony knew each other's animal's name. As we rode in the back of our hosts pickup truck, we would round a bend and a dog would bark. Our host would wave and greet each animal by name.

On that first day, the sun shone brightly in Kalaupapa, and a magical feeling wafted around every corner in the road as the dusty pickup moved through town. Everywhere we looked there were gravestones, from one end of Kalaupapa to the other, a continuous graveyard. There were also numerous monuments to the kokua, the helpers who'd made the supreme sacrifice in the name of love and filial loyalty.

I felt awed by the sublime beauty and peace, yet my knowledge of what had transpired remained as constant as the wind that whistled through this small sliver of land. I reflected on a comparison of other recorded world

20 – Kalaupapa

tragedies. If one were to visit the concentration camps at Treblinka or Auschwitz they would be met with a cold, dank, gray reality. No matter how the outlying areas may have been improved, the weight of their history would be overwhelming with the tragedy of human degradation thick in the air.

In Kalaupapa, the pali reaches to the heavens and the clouds clothe the peaks in white vapor. One cannot be seduced by the amazing beauty into forgetting what happened here, it is not possible. Clear, pure water surrounded the peninsula. I needed time away from the beauty to contemplate the reality of what had transpired. I found it difficult to fathom how the remaining patients lived day in and day out. Imagine being surrounded by innumerable graves. Yet these were their friends and family.

I have come across a tiny ash-green succulent, the hinahina (from the Goddess Hina) that reputedly only grows on Molokai. During our trip, I found a patch of these on the Kalawao side that stretched for miles, its white blossoms as far as I could see. I bent to look closely and saw the tiniest flower in the center shaped like a miniature plumeria. Twisted and woven in a certain fashion, this special plant can make spectacular lei. As I knelt to pluck a few flowers, my father picked up an object off the ground—a bone. Was it from an animal? "No," he said, "it is human. A femur."

We stared in silence at the weathered white fragment, dry and brittle, as he replaced the bone. I whispered a prayer, aloha to all the spirits who had died here. We were deeply moved and did not speak of it to the others.

Crimson clouds etched the skyline in dramatic strokes, and we retired early to have a fresh start the next day. Our living quarters were basic, set near the water's edge, a simple old wood-frame building akin to a dormitory with one central kitchen and bath. The walls were painted the cool green of the plantation camp house era of the 1940s, and the wooden floors polished to a deep burnished umber with the stain of kukui nut oil that creaked with every step.

The beach was steps from the house and smooth black lava stones filled the shore. Across the way, a perfect black sand beach welcomed each wave that crashed with a surge of spray, bubbles, and foam that absorbed as it landed. Peering toward the cliffs, I saw the lookout where I had peered down on the settlement so many years ago as a young bride, and now I was here…again.

Within the cabin were fresh linens and a stack of gray blankets folded in squares and placed neatly at the end of each bed. More blankets were set on the top shelf in the closet. There was one lamp on a nightstand and a single naked light bulb shone overhead. Our cost then was twelve dollars a night.

We chatted a bit with our hosts as we settled into our accommodations and asked them to join us for dinner. In a brief exchange of glances, they readily agreed and said they would bring food. Exhibiting telltale smiles, they asked if it was all right to bring friends to join us. As the sky glowed in sunset colors, we all prepared to share a meal. We'd brought a cooler with the basic supplies of bread, buttermilk, soda, and sausages. The evening before, Philip had supervised our shopping since he knew best what was practical and what local people liked. Mom and I chatted away not ever noticing all the food he'd placed in the shopping cart. He knew what would work, simple and unpretentious fare so everyone would feel at ease. I cannot explain why, but the apprehensions I had prior to the trip eased and the excitement of traveling with my parents replaced my fears.

I saw our hots during the meal and the days to follow as kind, precious people who had been dealt a tough life. They had come to our little wooden cottage with bright shining faces. Their arms were full to overflowing with food to share. They were eager to talk story with new friends and our evening took on a party atmosphere. I was later told that the patients would watch to see if you showed any fear in their presence or when sharing food. I was oblivious to this point as we sat down to a simple dinner of rice, chicken, and teriyaki beef with a fresh salad.

My mother was what I always referred to as a class act. She was East Coast proper, kind, and polite to everyone. She felt strange about eating before our guests joined in. My parents laughed, Dad with his beer and Mom with her wine.

Mom asked, "Aren't you going to eat too? It really is so good!"

They seemed quite happy as they reached for the bottle opener for another brew. They would wait to see if we enjoyed the food before they would partake.

I leaned close to Mom and whispered, "This is Molokai style. They will eat only after we have."

My own introduction to the family in Maunaloa and my first meal at sister Rosita's house returned in a flash. It seemed a short time ago when in truth it had been some twenty years before. Eventually, our host grabbed plates and ate. After the meal we all relaxed and settled back into a mode of talk story time.

Our host spoke up with excitement, "We have all heard each other's stories so many times it is our good fun to hear your stories, since you are from the outside world."

Saying "outside world" caused the words to hang in the air a moment as I pondered its meaning. Entranced by the beauty of this confine and the kinship of our welcoming guests, I had not considered their suffering or sacrifice to live here. I realized the enormity of the life they led, still feeling segregated from the natural world beyond their shores yet being happy.

My mother's stories were a treat for them since she and my father had traveled to Rome, Israel, and most of the Catholic shrines and holy places. Mom had a cache of prayer cards and pictures of all of her favorite saints in a small plastic baggy and doled them out like candy. The holy cards of Mother Mary were a favorite item. The cards from Fatima in Portugal were a close second. As if in a sacred card game, Mom would shuffle the cards and pass them around. There were "oohs" and "aahs" as they pressed the small bit of polished paper to their bosom.

Mom beamed as she referred to certain cards. "No, you can keep that one. I have another."

The evening was indelibly imprinted because everyone would remember the kind haole woman with the holy cards. They loved my mom. She had a genuine way of spreading her own aloha. Our evening drifted past midnight and our hosts continued to drink beer while my mother and I enjoyed our red wine. We were not kept up too late since we had plans to travel to the opposite side of the peninsula in the morning. Our new friends left and promised more fun for the next day. Since my mother and I had not seen each other in four years, we were not tired and chose to stay up talking until almost two in the morning to catch up on our lives. All that had separated us in that time no longer seemed to matter. It was as if we had not missed a beat in those four years.

While we talked, the wind blew hard and there were occasional bursts of rain. The old wood-framed house bent and creaked with every gust as the wind found its way between the old planks, and surrounding tree limbs brushed and whipped against it. We would pause our conversation, thinking we had heard something, then look around, glance at each other, shrug our shoulders, and continue talking.

When I am up late, often Philip will come and say, "Hon, it is late, go sleep already!" I kept thinking this would happen. Mom and I were chattering away, and we heard footsteps approaching on the wooden hallway floor. Anticipating Philip or my father, we would stop talking, expecting one of the men to appear at the doorway to scold us about the lateness of the hour. No one was ever at the kitchen door.

After the third time the footsteps drew near, I whispered as my eyes darted from corner to corner, of the room. "There sure are quite a few things here that go bump in the night, aren't there?" I scanned the room again as the wind whipped around the small house, pelting the planks with broken twigs and debris.

I rose from the kitchen table and walked to the darkened hallway. I looked up and down the plank floor with its dull gleam of oil and heard nothing. I walked to my room to check on Philip, and then to my father's room; both men were in a deep sleep, Phil snoring away as usual. What seemed even odder was a strange calm that permeated the rooms, peace and tranquility prevailed.

My conversation with my mom was far more important than the unexplained sounds. We never discussed the impasse of the past years. Clearly it was still a raw wound that festered within my heart. I am not sure why we never crossed our bridge of painful memories. Though I felt sad about our fractured relationship, we were attempting to rebuild after a long separation. In retrospect, I realized a much larger canvas was being painted in the background. Being with her in Kalaupapa was enough of an emotional leap forward, and all we could handle then. Mom and I agreed to call it a night. We both slept well, and mysteriously, when we were in our beds the wind died down.

We managed a quick breakfast as we prepared for our trip across the peninsula. The goal was to tour before the tourists arrived. Our new friends were helping to load the truck with supplies. I shared our strange tale of unexplained sounds from the night before.

My father said, "You know, I was not going to mention this, but yesterday, when I awoke from a nap, the same thing happened to me. I thought you were all back because I heard footsteps in the hallway and got up to see you, but no one was there." He shook his head and smiled.

Our hosts exchanged glances. "They are only niele (curious)." They looked away from us. It reminded me of Philip and sister Rosita with their tale of the menehune, giving each other a side glance, but knowing! "Das how" was Molokai through and through.

The following morning my mother said that when she reached down for her purse, which was on the floor, someone slapped her rear! She straightened up and turned, expecting to see my father, except she was alone in the sunlit passageway. Mom said she smiled to herself and just shook her head.

Soon we were all loaded and rambling down the rocky road. A tremendous wind blew the white mist off of the cascading waves and sent the salty spray high into the air. It seemed the sheer veil of white mist would be carried to the opposite side of the peninsula. Like a wedding veil, pure and fine, the shower misted us as we bumped and bounced along the red dirt road. I felt exhilarated. Then, another wave would break, the spray would lift, and be carried by the wind, it often smacked us in the face like a bare hand. With each crashing wave the predictable spray came. I was mesmerized and watched as each feathery cloud glided over our heads as if in slow motion to descend as a fine mist.

We traveled the narrow isthmus, turned a bend, and headed toward what was once the community of Kalawao. The early morning sun bore down on us in vengeance as we almost tipped while riding over the boulders and white sun-bleached stones. We reached the inlet at Kalawao where the ships deposited people to fend for themselves. This area cannot be seen from the lookout on the pali. Continuing on, the road led us to another lookout set on a precipice surrounded by giant ironwood trees. There was a resting place here with a small picnic table. As I looked at the mountains and two small island landmarks, I was struck by the realization—this was where the horrific scenes took place against the Hawaiian people, the precise spot where people were thrown into the treacherous waters.

My vision from the prior days had now manifested before me. I knew this place. I knew these waters. I felt the chilling fear and agony clench and turn my stomach with a twisted sickening nausea. These ominous ships were now long gone, yet for the briefest moment, I could hear their cries.

A railing at the lookout had a sign telling the history of the area. I curled my hands around the iron rail as I realized this was exactly as my apparition had revealed. I was here. The waves pounded like thunder in my ears. I did not feel fear but a deep sadness and a knowing that had lived in my bones for a very long time. I gripped the rail until my knuckles turned white. My mother was at my side, her arm around my waist. She seemed to clue into my torment as if she had read my thoughts and entered that hellish vision. Only as a mother can, her presence brought me back and centered me in the moment. The perfect azure of the ocean, of all things, grounded me in the present.

Ocean colors were a reflection of the sky. On cloudy days, the sea was gray and mossy green. On clear sunny days the ocean was alive with opalescent blues. The deep indigo and clear cerulean blues in the Hawaiian ocean are profound. Being married to an artist helps me identify these colors.

There is another blue, perfect in its way, a clear aqua. When I see that color, I feel as if I could jump into the blue and allow the surrounding water to heal my body and soul.

An incident in 1993 had shaken my existence and torn at my heart with unmistakable anguish and pain. After a moment of reflection and centering on my feelings, I could take the next measure and knew this feeling was affecting us all. Like a poultice, the small sliver of Molokai's peninsula wrapped us in her folds and embraced us as a mother holds a crying baby. In a strange way, the intense blue of the water lifted the darkness that had injured my soul. This color seemed to rise from deep within the waves, not from a reflection of the sky.

For those living in the Molokai plantation camps, being frugal was a constant reality. Philip was about seven years old as he sat coloring on the floor of the old-style plantation house. He merged green, blue, and white to create a brilliant turquoise. Seeing this, Mama knew—this one had talent. Despite their hardships and twelve children she always found money for paper and crayons. Philip explained the mixed color revelation to me, and as he spoke, his happiness, excitement, and passion were palpable.

"All my childhood," he said, "I have been surrounded by this blue. It has been my second home. In my Molokai waters, fishing has always been my whole world."

There was another blue, a clear and perfect turquoise. When I saw that color, I could imagine jumping into the blue and allowing the water to surround and refresh my body and soul. This color seemed to come from deep within the waves, not from the sky. I saw this in the harbor as if a vat of dye had been dropped into the center of the bay. Even the normally white froth of the waves had this tinge of color. I was so amazed, I squeezed Philip's fingers. "Philip, look at the water." I pointed to the crashing surf. "It is your blue, the turquoise in your painting."

Kanehunamoku (The Hidden Land of Kane).
Artwork by Philip Sabado

Philip had completed a painting of a mystical island that year. He had seen it while fishing in the early morning with his brother-in-law, Reyhino. Philip had told me about this island, it was one of the first stories he shared with me in the first months of our marriage. He whispered it as we were about to drift off to sleep as if someone could be listening and he shared a great secret. The wind beat against the house, raining twigs and branches against the tin roof as we snuggled under colorful quilts.

In mythology, this island was known as Kanehunamoku (land of Kane). Not commonly known or spoken of. Legend told of a floating island that would appear in ancient times to transport the spirits of the Ali'i (chiefs) after their passing to the next land.

Philip smiled knowingly as he explained the color revelation to me. In his painting the floating island was in the distance, illuminated with a burst of light and executed with dramatic strokes. He had captured the same color of the turquoise waters of the Kalawao inlet as I saw it before me. The color of the water that surrounded the mystical island of Kanehunamoku, and the meaning of what I saw overlapped with the reality of what I had been shown in my daily prayers, morning and night.

At first, the painting was so powerful, I could only look at it for a few minutes a day. In time, I became accustomed to the Goddess who sat to the right of the floating island. To me, she seemed like the island's protector.

When the painting was first shown in an exhibit, a Kupuna, Uncle Leslie, sat on the floor with his legs crossed. He looked at the image, and murmured in a deep tone, "Maika'i, Maika'i, good, good." He seemed to be addressing the picture and not us. He smiled and his eyes, brimming with joy, reflected his understanding. "Do you know what this blue place is?" He pointed to my favorite spot of pristine turquoise water that surrounded the hidden island.

Knowing how I was drawn to this place I asked him to please explain. "In ancient times, the Hawaiians removed the flesh from the bones of the dead Ali'i. They took the bones to the sea and surrendered them to the dark, blue waters. Once the bones entered the ocean, the water would change color

20 – Kalaupapa

to this brilliant turquoise blue. The meaning to the ancient Hawaiians was that the heavens had accepted their spirits."

I was so moved, I could not find words. However, I was aware that standing on the precipice looking down to Kalawao was a metaphor, a message on a larger screen showing me that no matter how dire the circumstances, in the end the spirits were received in love and grace. Again, life and my visions were to entwine.

I was in rapture with what I saw as I looked to the color in the bay. I stood fixed for what seemed a long time. Whenever anyone came near, I babbled about the bluest turquoise water. Perhaps they thought I was a bit crazy, but was it only me, or could the others see what I saw? Did they understand that so many disappeared or were devoured by sharks? Or that they would be carried to shore only to face more suffering and degradation. In this harsh place, the unfortunates could perish in the water, or eke out a meager survival followed by insanity and death.

Surely all the spirits who surrendered to the waves and the deep bay were accepted into heaven. The vision brought to me by my prayer had now been set before me. The sun moved through a cloud and a puka (opening) shone like a beacon on the wet shining black stones that tossed in the surf. I could not contain my emotions. I leaned heavily on the iron railing, donned my dark glasses, and wept silently. Mom had walked off to follow Dad, and I stood alone. Our guide came and stood next to me on the landing. While looking at the settlement he shared that he felt a sense of shame whenever he was at this spot. He knew that many of the crew who had pushed the victims overboard a hundred years before were Japanese and he was half-Japanese. The word he chose was ripe with the emotions he felt. "*Shibai*, shame that one," he spoke as he shook his head from side to side. He said his family in Honolulu could not understand why he'd chosen this life, but he understood this was his way of giving back, to make up for this injustice in some small way. He loved his people and his Japanese culture, but he felt a profound shame for this dark point in history.

As part of the arrangement for our special visit we had been asked to help, so when we reached the Kalawao side, we would do community work: some basic sweeping and cleaning of the old church that set silent, filled with history, and waiting for visitors. This was the church where Father Damien ministered. I felt okay with this, but for some reason I felt more comfortable outside cleaning the yard. The host grabbed a broom and mop, and my mother took an oilcloth in hand to attend to the old, worn wooden pews that had supported so many diseased hands with no fingers.

Our guides wife saw me searching for how I could help. Perhaps she sensed how much I was affected by the enormity of the experience. She said, "You go holoholo, take a walk. Me and your mama, we get em, okay. You go."

I did not argue. I stared from the old church window, looking past the large, sculpted lava Celtic cross erected by Father Damien, standing proudly inside the small graveyard surrounded by a bent picket fence. Beyond the graveyard was a wide-open field where tall golden grass bent to the ancient wind.

Philomena Church Built by Saint Damien.
Kalawao, Molokai.
Artwork by Philip Sabado

20 – Kalaupapa

My day and life are always more centered and focused when I have done my daily prayers. It took me years to develop a daily practice, morning and evening, the vow I made from a distant past for my enlightenment. The prayers are the gist of my marrow, the glue that holds me. Wandering into the field, I looked for a quiet spot to reflect and fulfill my daily routine.

I ambled along, looking for a good place to sit. I saw the perfect stone, a flat rock with a slope like the back of a chair. I wondered how many others had seen this place as a rest stop a hundred years ago. The high sun wrapped around my shoulders like a warm blanket. As I sat on this large stone the familiar cool breeze swept up from the shoreline, the makani. I smiled knowing this was the same wind that had greeted me as I took my first steps on Molokai soon to marry. The makani had come to surround and lovingly caress me yet again.

As I opened my small, tattered prayer book, the sun flooded the page and a lone bee landed in the center crease. The bee lifted off, made three perfect circles in the center of the page, hovered where we made eye contact, and then it flew away. Sitting on the solitary rock in the middle of a field, I was not alone. I was amid this carefully crafted life, uncertain as if I was to be stung or treated to a dance.

I completed my prayers and looked up to see my party preparing to move farther down the road. From the stone seat, I watched Philip cross the field toward me. I knew this place with its aptly shaped stone and the overwhelming feeling of peace and serenity would live in my memory forever, as would the dancing bee that had come to amuse and entice me.

I would learn this area held a mass grave of five thousand souls who had succumbed to the disease, the elements of nature, and abandonment. Debilitated sufferers unable to dig their own graves died where they fell. Tall swaying golden grasses and lava rocks were all that remained. In one way the silence was deafening, and yet if you listened closely, the rhythmic song of the wind in the nearby trees and the distant pounding surf seemed to synchronize in memory of the tragedy.

That night in bed, whispering as usual, Phil told me that as he walked through the field toward me, his feet felt heavy and harder to lift, as though something pulled at his entire being. With each step the pull and weight increased, and the feeling remained with him for three days. He remembered Mama and her lesson to always pray in a hushed tone, "Aloha aloha," stepping with thought, compassion, and respect as he passed through the grass.

Our day would soon be complete, and our guides were eager to avoid the tourists who came on a regular basis by way of the mules. We ventured up to the trail where the mule rides bring people down to the peninsula from the top of the cliffs. We traveled westward toward the settlement to explore. I felt sad that we would soon be departing from this place and our new friends.

The only access road to the settlement, where the mules arrive from the trail, was via the black sand beach. State workers used the trail to get to and from the settlement. They began their hike downhill in the early morning darkness. After work, they hiked back to the top. At the end of the trail, shimmering in the sun, the black sand of pulverized lava gleamed with specks of green olivine. Only fishermen frequented this spot.

Our guide shared a special story with me as we stood at the foot of the trail under the shade of the kiawe trees. With a warm, reflective smile he said, "The first time I was on this trail, I was a young man and I felt like a schoolboy on my way home. I knew every twist and turn of the trail."

I had the strangest feeling that if I walked the dirt path, I would know it as well. Years later when Father Damien became Saint Damien, the bishop walked this trail, returning a part of Damien in spirit to this place.

One of our last stops was the bookstore on the peninsula, the only store where you could buy information on the settlement. It was a little green plantation-style structure. Among the books written about Father Damien were others about Mother Marianne, whose mission assured Father Damien's work would continue. When Father Damien came close to death, his constant prayer was for the sisters to come. It was a blessing and an answer to his fervent prayers when Mother/Saint Marianne Cope and the sisters from upstate New York arrived to continue his work. Mother Marianne was born in Heppenheim, Germany in 1838. Her family immigrated to Utica, New York in 1840. In 1862 she entered the sisters of Saint Francis in Syracuse, New York. Later as a provincial mother, she received a letter from a priest in Hawai'i beseeching her help, at the behest of King Kalakaua and Queen Kapiolani of the Kingdom of Hawai'i. She had become a nurse. Of the fifty letters issued to other religious communities, by an emissary of the king, only Mother Marianne answered to come to Hawai'i to care for the people with Hansen's disease. She answered with the most beautiful words: "I am hungry for this work, and I wish with all my heart to be one of the chosen ones, whose privilege it will be to sacrifice themselves for the salvation of the souls of the poor islanders...I am not afraid of any disease; hence it would be my greatest delight even to minister to the abandoned lepers." Both Damien de Veuster and Mother Marianne Cope have been canonized as saints.

True miracles do happen, as shown in this second instance. A local Japanese woman in her prime, a friend of one of Phil's students, had been diagnosed with stage 4 cancer by her doctors in Honolulu. Her doctor, moved to take immediate action, made an appointment with the hospital to begin her chemo treatments. She agreed to begin after the weekend. She told him with utmost confidence, "I am going to go to Molokai and have a chat with Damien." Her doctor, perhaps not understanding said, "I do not care who you talk to, just make sure you are here at the hospital Monday morning." She agreed and was off. And yes, she returned cancer free. Stymied, the doctor suggested she walk up the street to that Catholic Church and let them know. That cinched it—the second miracle; and the rest as they say, is history.

History reveals King Kamehameha V signed into law the "Act to Prevent the Spread of Leprosy" on January 3, 1865. It remained in effect for 103 years. When leprosy came to Hawai'i is unknown, records as early as the 1830s make reference. It became known as Mai Pake (mai pa-kay), the disease the Chinese brought with them. Hawaiians, having no immunities to diseases, were vulnerable. By the mid-1800s, Hawaiians suffered death and disfigurement at alarming rates. Fearing future spread of the disease, the Kingdom of Hawai'i set aside land to confine leprosy patients.

Beginning in 1865, police and district justices were required to arrest people suspected of having the sickness. Kalihi Hospital and Detention Station in Honolulu evaluated them. Those with advanced cases were sent to Kalawao, located next to Kalaupapa.

Families were torn apart by the policy. People fled. Others hid family members from authorities out of fear they would be taken away and never seen again. Some families disowned sick relatives because of the biblical shame associated with the disease. Many sick people denied their own family members to protect them from being suspected as potential carriers.

Mother Marianne was sent to Maui where she founded Malulani Hospital, which is now St. Anthony's Church located in Wailuku. This was Maui's first general hospital for the ordinary sick on the island. Realizing the healthy children of leprous patients were at high risk of contracting the disease, yet had no place to live, she founded Kapiolani home on O'ahu for healthy children. Before leaving for Molokai, in 1888, she was on Maui for four years. Mother Marianne and her sisters spent months at the hospital at Iwilei, O'ahu. She commanded: "Roll up your sleeves, we are going to clean," and so they did.

Saint Marianne Cope of Kalaupapa, Molokai.
Artwork by Philip Sabado

20 – Kalaupapa

She led the first contingent of sisters/nurses to Kalaupapa, Molokai. Upon arrival, she opened the Charles R. Bishop Home for homeless women and girls with Hansen's disease. She improved the bleak conditions by creating a moral conscience among the residents and grew fruit, vegetables, and landscaped trees. While in Kalaupapa, she promised that none of her sisters would contract the disease. "Wash your hands, wash your hands" was repeated as a mantra. The sisters, being nurses understood, and stringently washed, as well as other sanitary protocol. Now over 140 years the sisters of Saint Francis continue due diligence and have never caught the disease.

I viewed a photograph of a man through a scratched glass case. His face was sallow with a long snowy white beard. His penetrating eyes spoke to me. This was Brother Dutton. I sensed that once sad, he had found joy in his mission in life by helping the boys of Kalaupapa. Brother Dutton built and opened the boys' home. In 1926, he built 144 beds to accommodate 1,376 boys and men, and made a home for them, whereas Mother Marianne cared for the girls. When Queen Kapiolani met him, she turned to an aid and said, "Make sure he has all he needs."

I found Brother Dutton fascinating. He was an American Civil War Veteran who felt he had killed and rampaged enough and dedicated his life to helping people. He chose Molokai. Joseph Dutton arrived in Kalaupapa in 1886, twenty-some years after those first afflicted were brought to Kalaupapa in 1865. He wrote volumes of letters to people in every corner of the world, seeking help for Kalaupapa. Because of his efforts, a ship docked every couple of months laden with goods from compassionate people from Germany, England, Japan and elsewhere. Some of these European vessels circumvented Honolulu and went straight to Molokai. Very few ships came from Honolulu, except those poor souls destined for Kalaupapa.

Photos abound of Brother Dutton and the boys' home. He posed modestly in the background, a tall thin man with his identifiable long white beard, surrounded by dark-skinned boys of all ages affected by the ravages of disease. In one of my favorite photos, he was seated in the center, bottom row, surrounded by boys with unsmiling faces, yet his face had a profound look of joy and sadness. As a tribute to Father Damien, Brother Dutton was quoted as saying, "One's Molokai can be anywhere they choose," meaning we all can find a place to give to each other.

In 2009, all of Hawaii prepared for the canonization of Father Damien to

The Essence of Time: PULE O'O

Saint Damien by attending many functions that celebrated this momentous event. One was hosted by the group Ka 'Ohana O Kalaupapa (The Families of Kalaupapa). Babies, now grown, or the children of those afflicted, taken at birth could reunite with their families because of the advent of DNA. The evening event, held in a conference room in the Pukalani Community Center was composed of two groups: Hawaiians and Haoles from Maui.

It was an up-country event hosted by those who lived in comfortable circumstances. As I entered the room, the mood felt polarized and heavy. After the perfunctory introductions, a dark-skinned Hawaiian man with hair the shade of the whitest snow, stepped forward from the back of the room, and spoke in an angry ominous tone. His gait and posture appeared constrained. Though agitated, he forced himself to speak his truth.

"You know this man, Damien, we have no problem with him. He was a good guy. What I would like to know is why were we there? I mean, why did we have to go to Molokai in the first place?"

Confusion rumbled through the room. As he continued to speak, I could see his controlled rage—this was personal, and the root of his pain was deep. The Hawaiians sat up straight, all eyes focused on this courageous man. The haoles glanced at their watches and shifted in their seats.

"You see, I am from Nahiko (past Hana). I came from a family of twelve children. One day, the bounty hunter came on our land and said to my mother, 'I will take that one and that one!' and he pointed his outstretched finger at my siblings who were attempting to hide in the folds of my mother's skirt. 'I gotta make my quota.' My mother protested, "Yah, but dey not sick!" The man was not fazed and only thought of his paltry bounty of five dollars each head.

He told how the man grabbed their small arms and pulled the children away. Hearing their mother's voice falter, the young ones sensed their doom. They screamed and rather than be pulled to an uncertain fate, clung to their mother. They had to be peeled from her like sea urchins that cling to the black rocks. Their forlorn screams resonated through the deep valleys for miles.

"He did take the keiki," he said. "That night, she packed us up and we fled to live in Honolulu, and we never saw them again. My mother thought he would return the next day for more children. I now return as a kupuna (elder) to see the chain across our land and a white man living there. How can this be?"

20 – Kalaupapa

His words hung low like a threatening storm cloud over the quiet room. He retraced his steps to the back corner where he took his former place.

His granddaughter walked forward next. "We will call this what this is—an attempt of genocide on the Hawaiian people!"

Many haoles looked to the floor embarrassed to see the faces of those telling truths hidden for so long. Again, some looked fleetingly at their watches. The Hawaiians in the room sat with folded arms, looking forward, seething in pain.

Tourist ads showed the pristine paradise of Hawai'i, yet as was the case with other Indigenous peoples, colonization had a sinister side. Many afflicted with Hansen's disease were sent to the Kalaupapa shores, but those who went and did not have the illness would eventually contract it while living there. Over and over, throughout the years we heard stories of family members having been taken away.

When I told this story to a good friend of Philip's, a Hawaiian man who served with him in the Army, he nodded as if he knew the story. Weeks later he returned to tell me that he had not believed my story and went home to ask his aged mother if this could be true. Her answer was absolute. Had he forgotten his uncle, the one with a skin rash, whom they had hidden in a cave for years in Keanae? The family had taken turns bringing him his meals.

Similar stories were common in Hawaiian families. Though the Hawaiians who lived it have always known, this part of their family history was hidden from the coming generations as if it had been their crime or somehow their fault. This was about land acquisition. There was a big puka (opening) in this history when Hawaiians stopped claiming to be Hawaiian. They would not pass down the language and went so far as to not have Hawaiian names. Disease and its aftermath so dearly devastated their population, the kupuna did not share this travesty to the coming generations. To this day, people wonder what happened.

Think about it this way: It is the nineteenth century, I am Kimo, and I have land from the mountains to the sea that has been in my family from before recorded time. You are my neighbor, and there is a spindly fence of kiawe between our lands. You are originally from the mainland and only know the Western world. One day you see a "rash" on my arm and report it, and the next day they come and take me. I am gone and then so is the fence. Now all the land is yours. I did not know enough to have palapala (papers) to secure my land. That was one of many ways the islands were taken. These stories were told by families of those taken to Kalaupapa.

The bounty hunters were given quotas to flush out those from outlying areas who were hiding the afflicted. The going rate at the time was five dollars per head, the quotas were usually three to five a day, and neighbors spied upon each other.

While we listened in this unforgettable up-country evening, we learned the youngest taken was four years old and the oldest was one hundred and four. How could a person at that age be taken? These numbers come from official records anyone can access. The numbers of those afflicted and affected were staggering, over eight thousand were recorded and countless others were unrecorded.

The agenda of these island families was to locate whatever might remain and begin the process of a memorial or perhaps a proper burial. This small sliver of land is maintained by the National Park Service, protected by law and never to be disturbed again. Current residents could live out their remaining days if they chose. Because of modern technology and DNA, the process to identify, rebury, and reunite families could begin.

Another Hawaiian man came that evening and stood to speak, full of rage and visibly shaking. "Where is my 'ohana?" I looked about the room and saw others with the same look of despair and anger. "I demand to know!" he said. "I expected to see them here." Tears were visible in the corners of his burning eyes and his face showed streaks of wetness. Many looked to the floor to avoid his pain. I held my gaze. I saw him and heard his message. Now I understood why the room felt polarized as I entered.

At the end of the evening many filed out silently still perplexed at how this could be true. I approached the granddaughter of the man who had spoken earlier. When she saw me coming toward her, with her hand outstretched, she began to apologize. "Oh, Auntie, I am so sorry, I did not mean you!"

I interrupted her by raising my hand. "Stop. You are not to ever apologize simply because I am haole. I am here to recognize you for your bravery and courage. Please continue to tell the truth, repeatedly. Someone will hear you. I have heard your voices tonight. This night has changed our lives! No matter how painful this is, you told the truth." Then I spoke words I did not completely understand until later. "Because I heard your courage tonight things will change." She only looked at me and did not speak.

Most everyone had emptied the room, and we were one of the last to leave. At the exit, I turned to see Philip as emotionally shaken as I was, and I let loose. "What the hell is going on? I thought this evening was about Damien. It's not. It's about them!" I gestured with an outstretched arm. "All those spirits are calling out and using us to tell the world their story with your art and my words. Shit! We are not even Hawaiian! Look at me, I am blonde. F***!"

He was silent. Why was I so angry? In a word, a Hawaiian word: kuleana (one's responsibility). Our life's destiny now included this mantel, perhaps it always had. I felt shaken to my core. I knew there was no escaping this.

When we celebrated St. Damien in 2009, we reveled in the understanding that the world would know what an amazing man walked this earth, and more so, on Molokai. That year was full and eventful. We had submitted artwork for the new Disney hotel and resort in Honolulu. It had been accepted, and then replaced. I was furious and was going to pursue legal measures. Phil was philosophical, and in his wisdom said, "It is just business; something better will come."

I countered, "You sure? Disney is pretty good!"

Well, he was right because the Damien project came later that year. At the time, I was the director for the Alzheimer's Association on Maui. I had volunteers on Molokai and would take the 6 a.m. flight to meet and motivate my team. As always, my pule came first, and I stopped at my favorite place in the world, Kapuaiwa, Coconut Grove. Kamehameha V planted the trees there in perfect rows a mile or so outside Kaunakakai. I pulled onto a dirt road on the edge of the grove to watch opalescent drops dance on the water and prepare for my day. I placed my beads between my palms and began my morning ritual. My flip phone jangled in my bag, and I checked my watch. Who would call me at that early hour? It was Eugene, my brother-in-law.

"I need to ask you a favor." This was a first; he had never asked me for anything. He sounded excited and I sensed urgency in his voice. "I need you to have my brother paint Damien for his canonization." I started to tell him that Philip was too busy, but he interrupted. "Yes, yes, I know, that is why I am asking you. He will listen to you, and I think somehow you will convince him."

I took a deep breath and said, "I will agree to be your messenger with no promise of an outcome. Agreed?"

Then he spoke faster. "It should have been done a couple of months ago, but now is good. Do not wait too long!"

I decided to seal the deal. "By the way, did you know that I am on Molokai?"

"Better yet! You will remember…kinolau, perfect timing!" Kinolau had a special meaning, that this moment would be imbedded in time connected to the scene, weather, and more so, the location, and the lesson learned. Every time you saw that place the mind returned the lesson and memory…kinolau.

Phil picked me up that evening at the small Kahului commuter airport. I felt tired, save for the important message I had to deliver, like a wave ready to crest. "Your brother called me very early today with a question and asked me to deliver it to you. He wants you to paint the portrait of Damien for the upcoming canonization. He feels you are the only one to do it."

Phil's curiosity gave way to a long exhale. "Babe, cannot, you know how busy I am."

I nodded in agreement. "Yep, told him that, so we are pau? I delivered the message. So, what's for dinner?" I never tried to convince him. I knew him well enough to not push.

The next morning, I was still in bed as the morning light filtered shards of creamy speckled light into our room. With my eyes closed, my hand searched the empty space beside me. Phil had gone to the living room to begin his pule. Feeling a presence in the room, I looked up. Phil stood holding the door frame. He looked ashen; the color of his dark complexion had drained from his face.

"I do not know how to tell you this," he said in a strained voice, "but as I was in prayer, Damien came to me three times. I saw him! I will begin this work today."

Astonished, I sat up with the blankets pulled around me. "Okay, I will not say that I told you so; 'das how.'"

He worked from early daylight into the dark night. I stayed with him, and only once did I walk into his studio to ask how it was going, thinking we should go home soon. He never looked up from his watercolor paper. Extending his hand like a traffic policeman as if to keep me back, he said, "We are talking story." His eyes never veered from the paper. I literally backed out of the room, speechless. I never entered the room again and waited for him to be pau. Damien would belong to the world. As a side note, Disney did call at the end of the year and our art was placed in all the suites– ah, fate!

Saint Damien de Veuster of
Kalaupapa, Molokai.
Artwork by Philip Sabado, 2009

During a three-month period when Philip and I had worked on a promotion of Damien artwork, not a single day passed when a person did not approach Philip to say, "You know, brother, I am buying this for my mom, or my sister, uncle, whomever. You know they were taken, and they were not sick!" I would overhear these discussions and file them into my memory, knowing this story must be told.

I had always maintained that the spiritual dimension and various interventions were about Phil. The gist for me was to promote is paintings. For him the world was slightly out of reach, the world of deities that beg to return via the artist's brush, is his kuleana. I was the one swept in on the tide, hanging on to a length of limu (seaweed) no doubt. In essence, I had joined the journey as a civilian, the big city girl from the mainland where even talking about a crystal was met with a glaring, "Have you lost your mind?"

One cloudless night, I had a restless sleep, tossing and turning, tucking my hand under the pillow seeking a cool spot. Kicking the blankets off and on made it worse. I was worried, probably about money, though we were comfortable enough. Our son and his family slept upstairs, and the downstairs was ours, providing a little privacy. We drove forty-five minutes from Haiku to town daily. We'd rented a studio for Phil in Wailuku to paint and work on commissions. He had completed the Saint Damien painting. Now the real work began: to promote, distribute, and make new products. I had to balance too many balls in the air, yet it all needed to be done.

To dispel my fears, I'd created a habit of chanting my Buddhist prayer to distract me in those moments when I was overwhelmed. I created a visual scenario in my mind where I would place fear in one cupped hand, and my fervent chant in the other. The chant would dispel the fear. One hand would cap and extinguish the other. It had always worked, and I soon fell asleep.

But not that night. I began a dialogue, or more precisely, a correction to what I usually recited. *No, no*, my mind spoke, *not Nam Myoho, say Kamiano*. I returned to my chant and the correction came to me stronger...*not Nam, it's Kam, Kamiano*. This debate continued for some time until I gave in and began repeating this slow chant to myself, *Ka Ka miano Kamiano*. Eventually, I felt calm and drifted off to sleep.

The next morning as the dawn crept into our bedroom with pinks and umber tones, I gently shook Phil and said, "I had the strangest night. I literally had an argument with my mind! My mind won. On that note, what or who is Kamiano?"

He bolted upright from his cushiony pillow and stared at me, propping up his torso, wide awake. "Where did you hear that?"

"That was what my mind corrected me about, over, and over, to say Kamiano. I think I spoke out loud, 'Okay, Kamiano, now let me sleep!'"

Phil spoke slowly with purpose. "That was what the Hawaiians called Damien; it was his Hawaiian name. Very few people know this."

I fell back into my pillow with a soft thud, speechless. I chose not to react. I believed I was to absorb the moment for the future.

The next night was similar, but visual. I saw myself walking in a cloud with the most stunningly beautiful colors I had ever seen. I was mesmerized. Soft pinks and opals revolved and splashed light onto azure-turquoise puffs of clouds tinted like spun cotton candy that floated around me. My voice said to me, *this is very nice, and you have enjoyed this cloud for quite a long time now, but it is time to step out. All is about to change for you. You will no longer be the same person you are now; you will change.* I resisted and shook my head. *Yes, but I love it here.* In my vision, I was suspended with half my body in the cloud and the rest of me stepping out to a lower precipice. I addressed the cloud. *Can I keep some? I will only need a small puff of cloud.* I reached into the cloud, grabbed a handful, and stuffed it into my back pocket where it overflowed. I became happier, somehow satisfied, and that was where the dream ended.

I lay with my eyes open, searching the room. I got up and went to the bathroom to look in the mirror. If I have changed…how? I stood there in the semi-darkness and said, "It is still me! What just happened?" I contemplated this often.

At a much later point, I realized in a strange way that because of Damien, the person I was before the vision had been very judgmental, high maka maka, as we say in Hawaiian, and opinionated on many levels. Afterward, I worked with hundreds of people on behalf of Saint Damien. The trick was to be me, yet compassionate about this amazing human that had done more than any other on the planet, a man who assisted and held and comforted over eight thousand people till they passed. I have had to find a balance, to chant, to be Buddhist; oddly perhaps, that was the small cloud in my back pocket. I kept that part, and also became a huge admirer of the man named Kamiano.

Philip met a patient during a visit to Kalaupapa, a woman who had a crooked finger from birth. When she attended a typing class as a girl, the teacher thought it was leprosy and the girl was sent to Kalaupapa. Another girl taken had a bad reaction to a flea bite. Over 90 percent of the people sent to Kalaupapa were of Hawaiian blood.

While standing in the small weather-beaten bookshop, I had to turn away when I saw photographs of the children. There were no smiles or happiness, no hope of a life without suffering. They had been torn from their families, from their mother's arms. A Hawaiian's life force was knitted in their family, and nothing could have been more dire than a life sentence of exile at Kalaupapa. As at any point in history, there were always shades of gray. The stories told here were shocking and difficult to accept.

Despite the tragic stories, there were others of hope and compassion, for example, Mother Marianne, who came with her fellow sisters to establish the girls' home at the settlement. They provided shelter and care. Before their arrival, women and girls lived a brutal life. There was no law in this place, and all would be subjected to leprosy. Roving diseased men constantly victimized women and girls. The endless threat and reality of rape and degradation would eventually drive many insane; the dedicated sisters provided a haven for them.

Before I left the small bookstore, I saw an old, tattered photo, probably donated from someone's album, of a Japanese priest in formal Shinto dress. A delegation of men had come from Japan to offer prayers and apologies. I think these were the only people to return to apologize.

Once I met a man who made a pilgrimage to Kalaupapa every year. He had a boyhood friend from Hilo who contracted the disease and had been taken from his family. The man never forgot his friend, and when the Health Department made it possible to visit and stay at the settlement, he returned to visit his friend every year. They are old men now, still friends.

On the peninsula it was easy to forget the tragic events of the past when viewing the pristine beauty. Philip once escorted the Maui Camera Club on an excursion to Kalaupapa. One of the women on the tour commented to their guide that he was fortunate to have grown up in such a beautiful place, momentarily forgetting the real reason. In no uncertain terms, the guide told her and the busload of visitors that he could have been a police officer or perhaps a doctor or lawyer or maybe a thief, but he had never been given a choice. He had been brought to this place against his will, never to return to the world he once knew. The woman bit down hard and cried openly. She apologized for her ignorant remark, realizing that living here was never a privilege.

Philip and I would take our leave the next day from Kalaupapa. My parents were up early to walk to Mass. The night before, our friends said there was no distinction here if you were Catholic or Protestant. With broad smiles they proclaimed, "Everybody can go to all da church, same, same dats why." And my parents did. They went to the Catholic Mass first, then the Protestant church, then the Mormon Chapel.

Too soon, the moment came for us to depart Kalaupapa. We encountered a little commotion at the airport—a horse on the field was running wild. Someone got on a scooter and chased him off so a circling plane could land. We were momentarily entertained. Our guide commented that everyone knew who owned the horse, but the owners did not like to tie anything up. Freedom was more important than anything else here.

Her words carried the weight from over a hundred years of suffering and pain. Volumes have been written about Kalaupapa, but none of it conveys the enormous feeling this small bit of land holds. As Philip aptly said, "Molokai was whole, then it was separate, divided without our knowing, much less our permission."

When our time came to leave, I found it hard to look at my new friends. In these short days, I had come to love them. I dreaded the moment when we would share a final hug and promised to return.

In 2019, we celebrated our fiftieth wedding anniversary. We had a large party and then traveled to Japan for a month. Upon returning, we had a Molokai class reunion at the end of August. I was exhausted and begged off to stay home and rest, knowing Philip wouldn't miss it, no matter what. As often happens, my mind spoke to me and advised me to go. I resisted, but the notion tugged at me, *Go, you will see, just go*. I mentally put up a defense, though in the end, Phil wanted me there. I surrendered, thinking I would read or maybe sleep in a lounge chair as I expected the classmates would all gather at the center tables laughing and reminiscing while the wives and families hung out on the sidelines. I made gifts of his artwork for all those attending.

The reunion was held at One Ali'i Park, a few miles past Kaunakakai. A bright summer sun baked everything it touched. Kaunakakai is hot almost all year long. Summer is a killer! We arrived late and dusk colored the park in warm pinks and burnished golds. The tents that some had erected were still warm from the heat of the day. A cool breeze welcomed us as hugs and alohas resounded. Phil was in his bliss and feeling in his prime. "Howzit, howzit?" he repeated with a wide smile fixed on his beaming face.

A Hawaiian woman approached and wrapped her arms around me with a tight squeeze. "You are here, you're here! You were not going to come, but you came, and I am so happy you did."

I looked at her a little confused. I smiled and said, "Yes, I am very happy to join you too!" My mind ticked away, wondering how I knew her. I thought it best to fake it until I could figure it out. After she returned to her table, I asked Phil if I knew the woman.

He shrugged, "Maybe. She is my classmate. She had cancer and we were raising money for her."

Everyone enjoyed dinner and a skit that followed. The gold hues of the sunset wrapped the performers on stage as they sang their favorite Molokai songs. I saw her on stage, singing and laughing and having a great time.

Phil shared that for the graduation ceremony from Molokai High School the class rehearsed the songs from Oklahoma *and that choice was right for the time. When the kids from the east end of Halawa stepped on stage, they sang "Molokai Nui Ahina." Phil said it was the first time he'd heard the song, and it brought tears to his eyes for his home and island.*

Philip delivered all the prints to his friends. I thought I'd made enough. I saw the woman who had greeted me sitting to the side with her husband and another girl, younger, maybe her daughter? She was waving me over to join them at their table. I smiled and moved in her direction. Her face was excited and mirrored all the warmth of the festivities. "I never got a print; I was on stage." I sat beside her. I apologized and said I would take her address and mail it to her. She then said the strangest thing. "You know, I never knew my mother. I never ever saw her! You see, I was born in Kalaupapa and was hanai (adopted) topside to a Molokai family after my birth."

I took her hand in consolation, did the quick math, and realized that my husband was already in his seventies, as was she. "Can I ask you some questions?" I asked, my hand squeezing hers. She agreed. "Can you tell me how your life was?"

Her answer came in a rapid beat. "My life was hell! Yes, they loved me, but I was always separated. I had my own dishes, towels, and went to the doctor all the time to be poked at. I always knew I was different, but never understood why."

I let her speak her truth and held space for her to reveal her emotions. After a brief pause, she added. "You know my daughter said that someone should write my story."

I squeezed her hand once more and held tight. "I am a writer, and it seems that is why you did not get a print, and why I needed to meet you again." What were the odds of my meeting someone from Kalaupapa? My story had felt incomplete, and her story helped to fill in gaps only she could provide. Our meeting became another reminder of how the 'uhane (spirits) worked on my behalf.

On a quiet afternoon in the studio, a local Japanese woman came in requesting a Saint Damien shirt. We made these along with the posters during the year of the celebration. She shared a story: that she had been cured of cancer after praying to Saint Damien in Kalaupapa, Molokai. I knew the story well. She was buying the shirt for her priest, a man from Africa who did not know of Hawai'i's esteemed saint. There was a comfortable chair across from my desk where she chose to sit. I found the correct size and saw a spot on the cuff. I offered another if she returned the next day.

"Do you know how Damien died?" she asked.

Everyone knew he had been afflicted with Hanson's disease. Sadly, Damien learned this when some scalding water scorched his leg and he never flinched. I answered in an unusual way that surprised me, "Yes, but something tells me that you know more, and you have come to tell me."

In the space between us, she made a circular motion with two fingers pointing down, then stopped in midair holding them pointing up.

"That's it!" I exclaimed. "It is that simple? Poi?" She smiled and nodded. "Poi! He, I mean, they all ate poi! And they spoke fluent Hawaiian at the table." I smiled in return with the understanding her mission was to tell me this story, one that perhaps no one knew.

The circular motion with their bare fingers is how Hawaiians traditionally eat poi. I understood in a heartbeat. Two fingers go into the poi, into the mouth, and back into the poi, saliva and all; one finger is for a thicker mix. A communal bowl of poi is always placed in the center of the table. Celebrating kalo (taro) and the creation story of Haloa, the first Hawaiian man, continues in Hawaiian homes to this day.

"I can tell this story." And more so, I had to tell this story.

She prepared to go by placing her purse in her lap. Before standing she said, "You see, my uncle was the postman there for some forty years. He was afflicted with leprosy, and taken, but he never told the family. *Shibai* (shame) is why." She sat up straight and inhaled deeply, feeling his despair and condemnation. "He told us he returned to Japan, but he never. He knew Damien in his later years." She stood. "We pau, I go now."

I was on my feet as well. "Mahalo auntie." She walked out and her figure dissolved into the bright Maui sunlight. She never returned for the shirt. I understood.

Carmel-by-the-Sea on the California coast is a sleepy little seaside village with iconic trees, sweeping cliffs, and a challenging surf. As we drove the shoreline, Philip saw the greens in this place as deeper, denser, and older than our island colors. We had just ordered a sunset dinner at a café, when my phone rang and I saw the Hawai'i number, a call I had to take. It was Cheryl. We'd met while campaigning for Brother Dutton's sainthood.

"I am going to ask you to step away from wherever you are," she said, "and give me a moment. I have something very important to tell you. They are going to come after you for what you have written, but I have your proof. I am in the vault; I am in the archives of the seminary in Kaneohe doing research."

I gulped and took a breath. "Please, go on."

I knew the place where Cheryl had gone, a seminary nestled against the pali, the ridge that separated the island. Within the seminary was a separate area known as the vault. Philip had done research there for the portrait of Mother Marianne, soon to be a saint as well. It held important records, timeless pieces in a temperature-controlled vault. In his portrait of Mother Marianne, there is a small thumbnail portrait of Damien in the corner. His arm, affected from Hanson's disease, is secured by a fabric sling adorned with a rose-colored fleur de lei. Mother Marianne made

20 – Kalaupapa

this for him. Though very small in the portrait, Philip wanted to research the color. Amazingly, a scrap of the cloth that had touched the saint was also held in this vault. Phil wanted to glimpse it to confirm the accuracy of the red color. The pastor graciously offered to send it to us via courier. We refused; a mere glimpse was all Phil needed.

"I have your proof! I am inside the vault." Cheryl's voice sounded as if the walls had swallowed the sound. "I am looking at the manifests. I have them in my hands, I have your proof; the manifests show they were not all sick!"

I gasped and let the magnitude of her message sink in. This was our kuleana, and our time, mine as well as yours, to embrace this uncomfortable history.

Into the open sea on a chilly November morning a lone canoe with a crew of eight piloted by Kimokeo set out from Maui. Their destination: Molokai, across the Pailolo Channel. The dark waves were illuminated by a cresting moon in the ocean's salty mist. The outline of the distant Molokai pali was in focus as their paddles dipped into the inky waters with sure steady strokes. The small inlet on the eastern side of the jutting peninsula of Kalaupapa was not an easy voyage on this day. The sea fought back with fury and force. Every frothing wave crested with white foam that rose to the paddlers' eye level. They pulled forward with Herculean force, slicing into the indigo channel to deliver an important gift once they reached this infamous place—Kalawao.

At a beach outing, Uncle Kimokeo approached me and asked if I knew that he'd gone to Kalaupapa. His eyes were clear and seemed to dance with the anticipation of telling me more.

He affirmed this. "Yah but cannot. The sea was rough. I took the kane (men)." To explain, he asked why the voyage was important and then answered his own question. "It is their way out. The uhane (spirits) are trapped here and now have a canoe to take them to all the places they dreamt of going or returning to!" He said there had never been a canoe in this place before.

Prior to the voyage a canoe was located that was deemed worthless, split in half, and not seaworthy. A team of twelve paddlers worked two months to mend the canoe, parts needed were donated. Extra care to clean, prep, and shine the hull was made to make sure this canoe was not only sound but was perfect. "We were bringing a gift that needed to be flawless."

I knew of this voyage beforehand. Jackie, my grown daughter, had been invited to paddle with them. I was confused at first and wondered what the remaining residents of the settlement would do with the vessel, since they were elderly. I then realized I was trying to understand this mission, this voyage, as a literal expression. This was spiritual. A fireman, looked up to the razor edged pali and heard the wailing winds. He, the fireman, had heard their cries as they clung to the pali. They needed to go home. How could they get home? The sea foam and salt rose to buffet the stones as his eyes burned and teared as he could not look away. He then shared this vision with uncle, and Kimokeo immediately knew that this gift of a canoe was what they needed.

As one of the paddlers explained the journey, he retold the voyager's moments at sea. They took two days to reach Kalawao. As they came to the sharp turn into the bay, the canoe was met by a gargantuan wave that engulfed the canoe. As the paddler explained, "The sea was churning and spinning like I'd never seen or experienced. We knew the gravity of the mission." They bucketed the flooding water from the canoe to be met with another wave that replaced and refilled the canoe yet again. As the paddler told his tale, his voice faltered to say; "This was the place where those poor afflicted souls met the cold waters from the ships." I was silent as he told me of the journey. "Uncle fashioned a rope and pulled the canoe forward till we were in calmer waters. Now we could paddle to shore, we were so weary, but the canoe must be anchored on the island and sand to fulfill the mission."

Once anchored on the rocky beach, the canoe would not return to Maui and would remain fixed on Molokai sands. Kimokeo, with his steely determination, understood why his gift of a canoe would be what was needed. As Uncle explained it, a haole boy had suggested the mission. Kimokeo answered the call and rose to the occasion.

My eyes stung as tears formed. This story resonated with me on so many levels. Imagine understanding your ancestors and the compassion of the ages to deliver a vehicle, a priceless canoe with a spiritual mission—to release and return those torn souls to their families and to their homes.

"Uncle," I said, "did you dock Kalaupapa side or—"

"Kalawao, of course, that was where—"

"Yes, the ships."

We passed a poignant moment looking down at the sand crusted at our feet now stuck between our toes.

"You know why? Even those who never made it to shore will have a way out. A way out," he repeated in a subdued tone, again and again.

Now I could understand Uncle Kimokeo with his mission to travel by canoe to release the trapped souls, to heal the amputation of life and spirit and families torn apart.

I felt privileged to understand the mission. I wondered what the remaining residents of the settlement would do with the vessel, since they were elderly.

I was mindful of the fact that this deed had nothing to do with religion, but from a pure heart. I was overwhelmed and brought again to understand my humble place in these islands. This was the first time we had ever spoken, and why he chose to tell me this story was more about his being Hawaiian and a treasure to all men. Whereas my mission was to pass along these stories to you, the reader. I understand the canoe is still where they placed it.

Acknowledgments

For years I have felt the grasp and embrace of all those who have reached out to ensure this task was completed. From those who have encouraged, typed the first draft, edited, and have had my back, I offer my most sincere gratitude. Mahalo Nui Loa.

For Philip, whose faith and encouragement never wavered, I say mahalo and my eternal umauma, the deepest aloha.

About the Author

Christine Sabado
Artwork by Philip Sabado

Christine Sabado has spent her adult life embracing the warmth and mixed cultures of the Hawaiian Islands with her husband, Philip, and their six children. After years of moving around, they settled on Maui where she represents Philip's artwork in their galleries. A true creative, Christine enjoys reading, writing, and time with her large family.

"In my career as a writer, I am honored and privileged to translate the Hawaiian mana'o of the paintings created by my talented husband, Philip Sabado."

Please visit: https://www.sabadobooks.com
sabadoarthawaii.com

Upcoming Books by the Author

The Essence of Time: PULE O'O – Book 2

Book 3 – *Gift of Fire*

Book 4 – *Shakabuku*

Preview of Book Two

Book Two begins with the Sabado family in Hilo where Christine struggles with the first of three more pregnancies. Her uneasiness changes to wonderment as her newest son, Ian, displays unusual abilities into a world not seen by others. Philip's career zigzags downward with scarce work on the Big Island and he becomes consumed with painting a mysterious figure, an enigma that creates conflict in light of the family's dwindling resources. Trusting on better opportunity and the advice of a seer, the family moves to Maui to improve their prospects.

In the dusty valley of central Maui, Christine grows close to a neighbor who introduces her to Buddhism. Chanting and manifesting prove crucial in the days ahead as her young friend fights cancer. Philip's paintings bear fruit with recognition and consignments. After a move to the upcountry, Christine experiences a life-shattering moment with a boy she has never met. In the subsequent months, her struggle to find peace amid tragedy forever shapes her view of life. Steady as the makani winds, and as strong and sure as the consistent tides, her belief in the power of loving prayer provides the relief she seeks, even as others try to hold her accountable for a crime she did not commit.

www.ingramcontent.com/pod-product-compliance
Lightning Source LLC
LaVergne TN
LVHW081537070526
838199LV00056B/3697